Walking with James Hogg

Walking with James Hogg

The Ettrick Shepherd's Journeys through Scotland

Bruce Gilkison

Edinburgh University Press is one of the leading university presses in the UK. We publish academic books and journals in our selected subject areas across the humanities and social sciences, combining cutting-edge scholarship with high editorial and production values to produce academic works of lasting importance. For more information visit our website: www.edinburghuniversitypress.com

© Bruce Gilkison, 2016

Edinburgh University Press Ltd
The Tun – Holyrood Road,
12(2f) Jackson's Entry,
Edinburgh EH8 8PJ

Typeset in 10/12 Adobe Sabon by
IDSUK (DataConnection) Ltd, and
printed and bound in Great Britain by
CPI Group (UK) Ltd, Croydon CR0 4YY

A CIP record for this book is available from the British Library

ISBN 978 1 4744 1537 8 (hardback)
ISBN 978 1 4744 1539 2 (webready PDF)
ISBN 978 1 4744 1538 5 (paperback)
ISBN 978 1 4744 1540 8 (epub)

The right of Bruce Gilkison to be identified as the author of this work has been asserted in accordance with the Copyright, Designs and Patents Act 1988, and the Copyright and Related Rights Regulations 2003 (SI No. 2498).

Published with the support of the Edinburgh University Scholarly Publishing Initiatives Fund.

Contents

Preface		vii
Acknowledgements		xiii
1	First Steps: A rough road	1
2	Hogg's Ettrick (1802): A state of nature	13
3	Central Highlands (1802): Their remarkable inhabitants	24
4	Western Highlands and Islands (1803): Strange and wonderful views	43
5	Western Highlands and Islands (1804): Misfits and misfortune	83
6	Arrivals and Departures: Life and other journeys	103
7	Life after Death: A never-ending journey	134
	Appendix A Walks with James Hogg: Some possibilities	158
	Appendix B Walking the Highlands: Gear carried	163
Select Bibliography		165
Glossary		170
Index		174

Preface

GROWING UP WITH JAMES HOGG

I knew from my early years, growing up in New Zealand, that my great-great-grandfather was a Scottish poet. And in my early years, nothing about that excited me.

An old painting of the Ettrick Shepherd hung in our cellar, mildew creeping in from the edges. He looked grim, and he frightened me. Some old brown books gathered dust on our shelves. If I had ever opened one I would have seen lots of words I didn't know and it would have gone straight back on the shelf. I was disappointed he wasn't a Highlander, too, which seemed more romantic. And later in a high school English class, when we had to read one of his poems, I didn't admit I was related to him.

A family publication in the 1970s said: 'Hogg's works are now 150 years old, and not attractive to modern readers.' Then it listed a few, mainly poems, which 'descendants could try'. But I'd heard enough, already.

Much later, from an inauspicious beginning, our relationship started to change.

I knew that he was a poet and a shepherd. But I discovered he was other things too, a novelist, songwriter, singer and sportsman. And a lover, a misfit, a battler, a voice for the disadvantaged. He seems to have been fun to be with. And eccentric, too; I loved eccentrics.

I started to meet people who impressed me, who were impressed by him. Some bright young scholars, not just older people, studied him and taught and wrote about him. They liked him and spoke about him in the present tense – he who died three decades before the penny-farthing was born. 'He loves the hills,' I heard, and, 'He has a wonderful sense of humour.'

Even famous people said they liked him: Ian Rankin, Irvine Welsh, James Robertson, Sir Sean Connery, Lord and Judy Steel. His contemporaries, too, such as Walter Scott, William Wordsworth, Lord Byron, S. T. Coleridge, Thomas Carlyle and John Galt. And those that came next, such as R. L. Stevenson and the Brontës. Apparently, people even knew about him in North America. And more recently, biographies were coming out that breathed new life into him. The titles that had been gathering dust were being republished and rediscovered. Clearly, for me, it was time for a reassessment.

ABOUT SCOTLAND AND NEW ZEALAND

I was born in Dunedin, in the south of New Zealand. Apart from somewhere out at sea, it is as far from Scotland as you can get. In some ways, at least.

My ancestors sailed from Scotland to Dunedin in the 1870s, with no stops along the way. The street names came from Edinburgh and Glasgow; they were tossed up and used wherever they landed. An impressive statue of Robert Burns marks the city centre, as it has since 1887. The climate is convincingly Scottish. I grew up to the sound of bagpipes. Our top rugby team is the Highlanders.

In 2004 Edinburgh became the world's first City of Literature, under the UNESCO programme. But ten years later it was joined by Dunedin, one of only two such cities in the Southern Hemisphere.

New Zealand/Aotearoa is my home. More specifically, the South Island/Te Waipounamu is my home, my *tūrangawaewae* – my place to stand. But Scotland has never been a foreign country to me. It's not just that I love the land and the culture. It's more that it feels like a part of me.

I love the character of the Scots: the *spirit*, for example, that led the people of Glasgow to change the address of the South African consulate to 'Nelson Mandela Place', when Mandela was still a prisoner in his own country; and the quirkiness and sense of *fun* that led women in the Borders (one of them aged 104) to 'yarn-bomb' Selkirk and Ettrickbridge under cover of night in 2015, wrapping public amenities like park benches and bridges in colourful hand-knitted fabric. Why not?

The countries share similarities and links. They value education, and breed inventors, explorers and humanitarians. A high proportion of New Zealand's immigrants came from Scotland, including all of my ancestors. Most people in both places speak English, and tend to call a spade a spade.

New Zealand has 4.5 million people; Scotland has 5.4 million. Each country is mountainous and has a long coastline. New Zealand is larger, about three times Scotland's size (it just looks small next to Australia on the map).

ABOUT ANCESTOR WORSHIP

From 2003 I spent two special years in the Solomon Islands, a nation of 900 islands to the east of Papua New Guinea. I was an adviser to the Province of Malaita in their post-conflict era. I was supported by Volunteer Service Abroad, New Zealand. In a region of strong oral tradition but no written language until recently, I was drawn to the local stories: of pig-theft and shell-money, sorcery and sharks. And I learnt about ancestor worship.

In our early days there, my partner and I visited a nearby beach; mid-morning, and already hot and humid. The dorsal fins of a dozen sharks cut through the surface of the otherwise-inviting water. 'Where do we swim?' we wondered. 'The sharks will not harm you,' we were told. 'They are our ancestors.' Some of the Islanders' forebears had been reincarnated as sharks, and they were here to protect them. When canoes had capsized at sea, there were stories of sharks helping people get safely back to shore.

We deliberated: the sharks were only about our size, but were better swimmers and had more teeth. Was this perhaps a joke that locals played on new arrivals? But the people were convincing. They spoke to the sharks often, they made sacrifices and never offended them. We slipped into the water and drifted with the tide. The sharks slid gracefully past us, happy to share their world.

Human ancestors are revered there too. The oldest son has a special role in learning about them, to teach the next generation. The deceased are consulted on major decisions. I was impressed by the knowledge that people had of them, often going back over hundreds of years. Their memories were even better before the missionaries had discouraged this.

In many other cultures, it seems, the ancestors are remembered. Some Māori can trace their ancestors back at least twenty-five generations, and perhaps as far back as the great Pacific migrations. Mohawk poet Pauline Johnson mentions Onondaga, Cree and Sioux families who can count back 900 years.

I was embarrassed that I knew so little about my ancestors. I could go back three or four generations only, and even that was patchy. I decided: I won't worship my ancestors, but at least I'll get to know them better.

There was a partial remedy on hand. I knew there would be no movies or TV and not much Internet access in Malaita, and surely there would be some quiet nights. So I brought music with me, and books from home I had never read, including my Hogg collection. In the second year, I read them. I was lucky, and happy, to have such a resource.

ABOUT JOURNEYS

I have long had a fascination with travel. I spent a couple of years trekking through Asia and Africa. I lived in Uganda and Canada and Europe, and explored from there. It was never about the destination. It was all about the journey, and what you do and what goes through your mind on the way.

I love to walk. You move at a human pace. You find destinations you hadn't even thought of. In literature, walking is often a prelude to change. For some writers and philosophers, walking is a key to the thought process. Rousseau said, 'I can only meditate when I am walking . . . my mind works only with my legs.' Nietzsche tells us, 'All truly great thoughts are conceived by walking.' And Charles M. Schulz, of *Peanuts* fame, said, 'No problem is so formidable that you can't walk away from it.'

I was fascinated by landscapes and the influence they had. The character of the Scots, of Kiwis, of African hill country people or the Nepalese, for example, would surely be different if their lands were flat.

An expert on Hogg suggested that I should do some of my ancestor's journeys, and write about them. The idea lodged in my brain. I was voluptuously tormented by it. That was a few years ago and the time wasn't right. And then it was.

HOGG'S HIGHLAND JOURNEYS, AND MINE

When Hogg began his Highland journeys in 1802, it was a pivotal time in his life. He was thirty-two and unmarried. He had been working on the land since he was seven. He had taught himself to read and write. He had written some poetry, and even had some published, but nothing that would have been remembered if he had stopped right then. His father and brothers and grandparents were farmers or shepherds. He assumed his future was in farming, and he was setting out to find a farm to lease. He wanted to be a great writer too, but had no idea how to do that.

He wouldn't have known it then, but he was exactly half the age he would ever reach. The journeys would change the next half of his life. Had their outcome been different, it's unlikely we'd know him now.

After his 1802 trip there were two more journeys in the next two years. All of them were aimed at securing a farm. But because he was keen to learn and to write about Scotland, they would take on a greater significance.

When I set out, I was double his age. I would follow his journeys, but not every step. The land has changed: large areas are built up, and in others the traffic is too heavy or noisy. But I would go to some places he missed, and I'd cycle in some parts, and hitch or take ferries or other public transport where nothing else worked. I would camp where possible – it's what I could afford, and luckily what I love. I'd get blisters and bruises and sometimes get into tricky situations.

More importantly, I'd meet people. Writers and artists and Hogg experts, some descendants of people he'd met. I'd climb hills he'd climbed or admired, I'd eat and drink and sleep in some of the same places, and compete in a sports event he started almost 200 years ago. I'd travel to Canada, too, for the 'James Hogg and His World' conference.

For various reasons, I couldn't always do his walks in the sequence that he did. In 2014, I travelled in the Borders, out west to Harris and Skye, then through the Central Highlands and the Cairngorms. In 2015, I started and finished in the Borders, went up through the Central and Western Highlands, out to Lewis then back through the Hebrides and Loch Lomond and The Trossachs.

This is a story of my ancestor's journeys, through the Highlands and Islands, and through life and literature and other strange places. It's about a journey that continued after he died, and hasn't finished yet. It's a story about my own journeys too. And I had no idea where any of these might lead.

ABOUT THE HIGHLAND JOURNEYS STORY

Hogg sent reports on his journeys as letters to Walter Scott, who had some of them published. For a while Hogg thought of publishing them in book form, but did not ever do this. Not all of his records survived. By 1808, *The Scots Magazine* had published some of his reports from his 1802 trip, all of them from 1804, but none from his 1803 travels. In 1888, over half a century after his death, his daughter Mary Garden published the first half of his 1803 journey from an original manuscript, now at the University of Stirling. Much later, in 2001, Gillian Hughes found a typescript of some of the second half of that journey, at Washington State University. These two parts were published in *Studies in Hogg and his World*, in 1995 and 2002. The reports on the journeys were now complete, apart from gaps in the middle of the 1802 travels, and the middle and the final part of his 1803 trip.

Then, in 2010, Hans de Groot brought all the available sections together in one volume, *Highland Journeys*. This was published as part of the Stirling/South Carolina Research Edition of the Collected Works of James Hogg. It was the first annotated version, it has good maps, and is highly recommended. Before and during my own Highland journeys, and in my work on these since, this was my bible.

A NOTE ON PUNCTUATION AND SPELLING

Where I quote Hogg directly, his spelling and grammar have been left intact; some of his usage would have been correct at the time but looks odd now. Ellipses show that I have abbreviated that section. And in direct quotes from Hogg's reports, the paragraph breaks are often my own; the typescripts of his 1803 journey, for example, are often unbroken over several pages and these breaks, I hope, will make them easier to read.

GREENHOUSE GAS EMISSIONS

These days I think we all try to cut our carbon emissions, but air travel is a challenge. For this project, these have been offset by contributions to an approved New Zealand native forest restoration project, paid for at higher-than-market rates. This is not a perfect solution, but it's a start.

Acknowledgements

Many people were extremely helpful to me in this project, and I mention some of them in the text. Perhaps this was because they are extremely helpful people anyway, but I detected something else as well. Sometimes, and especially with people I had never met before, this seemed to be driven by an affection for my long-dead ancestor that I hadn't expected. I do not recall writing to anyone, whether a duke or author or some other perfect stranger with every reason to ignore me, without receiving a reply and an offer of help.

Just a few people I'll mention here: Suzanne Gilbert, who suggested the project first. Hans de Groot, whose book and support made it possible. Gillian Hughes, who knows my ancestors better than I do, and whose book *James Hogg: A Life* was vital. Staff at Edinburgh University Press, who were instantly intrigued by the plan. Researchers and writers who were generous with their work, and some family members, living or dead, who had recorded information and sparked my interest.

Each of these helped but any errors are, of course, all my own work.

1 First Steps: A rough road

UNCOMMON ANCESTRY

For a future storyteller, shepherd, sportsman and eccentric, James Hogg's ancestry was impeccable.

There had been lots of shepherds before him. Robert, his father, would tell James later that the Hoggs had farmed or worked as shepherds in Ettrick Forest for generations, probably for hundreds of years. For much of this time they had leased land from the Scotts of Fauldshope.

There had been an unfortunate incident in the 1600s, though, when a Hogg ancestor led a Scott ancestor astray. Willie Scott had been captured as a result. And as punishment, he was forced to marry the captor's ugly daughter, 'Muckle-mou'd Meg' (she had a very big mouth). The Hogg ancestor, William, was known as 'The Great Boar of Fauldshope'. He was famed for his strength, ferocity and courage, though possibly not for his wisdom. Such incidents could take a few generations to get over.[1]

Further back, they may have been descended from one 'Haug of Norway', described in family records as 'a gallant reiver and destroyer' ('gallant' seems to mean courageous and honourable, so presumably whatever he destroyed, he did it well). There is no real evidence of this connection though.

Other ancestors were witches, including one Lucky Hogg.

---

[1] Poor Meg was known as the ugliest woman in the Scottish Borders. Her father, Sir Gideon Murray, caught Willie Scott stealing his cattle (William Hogg was not caught) and gave him two choices: marry Meg or be hanged at dawn. On reflection, Willie decided Meg looked better than the noose. It was a smart decision. James Hogg wrote much later 'they lived a most happy an' social life; / The langer he kend her, he lo'ed her the mair'. A statue of Meg and Willie on their wedding night was unveiled on the banks of the Tweed in 2011.

> **Who's Lucky?**
>
> Lucky Hogg was the wife of one of Michael Scott's tenants, and was 'the most notable witch of the age'. Michael was a famous wizard, and was becoming jealous of her powers and reputation. It was time for a chat.
>
> He set out with his dogs and found her at home, alone. He asked her to show him some of her tricks, but Lucky denied having supernatural skills. He continued to press her and she asked him to leave, or he would 'repent the day he troubled her'. Michael would not go.
>
> At this point, Lucky grabbed his wand and gave him three lashes with it. She changed him into a hare, and set his own dogs on him. He fled, had to swim the river, and took shelter in the sewer of his own castle to escape the fury of his pursuers. It was one–nil to the witch.
>
> Michael changed himself back into a human, and was itching for revenge. He sent a servant to Lucky's place and told him to ask her for bread. If she did not give him any, he was to put a spell on the house. Knowing the request had come from Michael, Lucky gave him none, and the spell was cast. She went into a trance, threw off her clothes, and started singing and dancing wildly around the fire. Others who came into the house came under the same spell and joined the dance. Her husband went to see Michael, who agreed to lift the spell, and the people returned to their senses. But alas, poor Lucky ... she was exhausted by now, and died overnight in shock.
>
> (Michael Scott was a thirteenth-century intellectual, who seems to have earned his name as a wizard from his knowledge of eastern languages, medicine and science, which were treated with suspicion in Christian countries then. He translated Aristotle, for example, from Arabic into Latin. He was said to have predicted his own death, from being hit on the head by a stone, so he wore a metal helmet but died when he removed it in church and was hit by a stone that fell from the ceiling. He is also remembered for alchemy, and for splitting the Eildon Hills into three peaks. Clearly, Lucky was pushing her luck too far with Michael.)[2]

Robert Hogg, James's father, was pragmatic but perhaps a little dull. Margaret Laidlaw, James's mother, was not. She was full of energy, ideas and lively conversation. She sang songs and told stories. One of her sons said later, 'her mind was stored with tales and songs of spectres, ghosts, fairies, brownies, voices, &c. These had been both seen and heard in her time.'

She was opinionated and took nonsense from no one. Some viewed her as a 'wise woman' who could predict the future. It is easy to think of her as

---

[2] Lucky's story is included in Hogg's notes to *The Queen's Wake*, pp. 183–4. Michael Scott appears again later in James Hogg's *The Three Perils of Man*, by which time he is occupying Aikwood Castle.

a feminist, but she predated the term and would have rejected it. Karl Miller said she could be seen with her 'pipe, her lore, her hereditary connections with the spirit world, as a little witch-like'.[3] When a man she was arguing with once had started to sing an anti-Jacobite song, she drowned him out with a Jacobite song of her own. She was entertaining and a powerful role model.

And many of these qualities would have been acquired from her father, William Laidlaw, the multi-talented Will o'Phaup.

Will o'Phaup

William Laidlaw, James Hogg's maternal grandfather, was a shepherd, storyteller, athlete and drinker. And he spoke with fairies, the last person in the district to do so.

Speaking with fairies sounds cosy, but wasn't. One time when he heard their conversation they were plotting against him. Hogg tells us later:

> He had seen them sitting in seven circles, in the bottom of a deep ravine, drinking nectar out of cups of silver and gold, no bigger than the dew-cup flower; and there did he behold their wild unearthly eyes, all of one bright sparkling blue, turned every one upon him at the same moment, and heard their mysterious whisperings.

It was still daylight, so he thought he was safe from them. Then he realised it was All Hallows Eve, a day on which the usual rules in fairyland could change. Suddenly terrified, he dashed for home. This time, and on some other occasions, he escaped unscathed, but there were some close calls.

And luckily, he was a fast runner. Hogg said that 'For feats of frolic, strength, and agility, he had no equal in his day ... many a race he ran, generally for wagers of so many pints of brandy, and in all his life he never was beat.' (Smuggled French brandy was an important part of his life, and was far more valued at the time than whisky.)

One time he was nearly beaten. He arrived in Moffat in his regular clothes, unaware that plans had been made for him to race a visiting champion. He started reluctantly and dropped behind 'till a very queer accident befel me': his trousers came undone and he was left naked below the waist. Cheered on by the 'wild gillies' he went on to win. But he turned down an invitation afterwards to have dinner with the ladies: 'in this state, I kenna how they might tak it'.

---

[3] Miller, *Electric Shepherd*, p. 15.

He was famous too for leaping the flooded Ettrick River while rushing to get medical help, at a place known later as 'Will o'Phaup's Leap'. (Elsewhere it is written that he jumped over the river here 'every year until he was 82' but it's hard to be sure.)

And with brandy or not, he was entertaining. Hogg said later, 'In the hall of the laird, at the farmer's ingle, and in the shepherd's cot, Will was alike a welcome guest, and in whatever company he was, he kept the whole in one roar of merriment.'

He died in 1778 when Hogg was just seven, 'the first human being whom I saw depart from this stage of existence'. In life and beyond, though, his influence seems to have been profound. Did young James inherit his grandfather's genes, or did he set out to emulate these sporting and social tendencies and his connections with other worlds?

Will had six children and lived at the head of the Ettrick Valley. Hogg wondered later how, in such a lonely, dismal place, he 'could live so long, and rear so numerous and respectable a family'. We know less about his wife, Bessie Scott, but one suspects she had a hand in this.[4]

EDUCATION AND INSPIRATION

James Hogg was born in Ettrick in late 1770 – the actual date is unknown – and was baptised in the nearby Ettrick Kirk on 9 December. He was the second in a family of four boys.

And already, there's a story. It seems that before he was born, a messenger was fetching a midwife on horseback, but was too scared to cross the flooded Ettrick River. A brownie – a helpful supernatural being – leapt onto the horse and carried the midwife home, and 'gave a wild shout when Hogg was shown to his parents'.[5]

He attended school for about six months in total before his formal education was ended, abruptly, by his father's bankruptcy and the family's consequent destitution. His father had been a tenant at Ettrickhall and Ettrickhouse farms, but got into trouble as a stock-farmer and sheep-dealer when prices dropped. Their possessions were sold by auction and 'my parents were turned out of doors without a farthing in the world'. But a compassionate neighbour took a lease of the farm of Ettrickhouse and put Robert Hogg there as his shepherd.

James was sent out to work on the land for the rest of his childhood, probably from the age of seven. (His teacher did not remember later that he had ever attended school.) In his first half year of work his wages were a ewe lamb and a pair of shoes. He started with cows, progressed to general farm work and eventually to shepherding. He received 'very hard usage' from some of his masters.

---

[4] Quotations are from Hogg, *Shepherd's Calendar*, pp. 103–12.
[5] Miller, *Electric Shepherd*, p. 18. Hogg also told a version of this story at a Burns dinner in London, 1832 (Hughes, *James Hogg*, p. 247).

FIRST STEPS 5

A

BIRTH-PLACE OF THE ETTRICK SHEPHERD.

B

Figure 1 Ettrickhall, James Hogg's birthplace. A: From a newspaper cutting about 1870, artist unknown. (In public domain.) B: By David Octavius Hill. (Source: Thomson, *Works of the Ettrick Shepherd*.)

He was often hungry, and on occasions he was witness to great violence. He learnt to read parts of the Bible, the only book he had access to, and listened to legends and ballads told by his mother, by visitors and by co-workers.

He wrote later of his love of women, from a young age: 'Indeed I have liked the women a great deal better than the men ever since I remember.' At the age of eight he was sent out herding for some days with Betty, 'a rosy-cheeked maiden', and would lie down on her lap after dinner and pretend to sleep. He cried when he heard her say, 'Poor little laddie! he's joost tired to death.' He relished the contact with her, and hoped she would stay there forever.[6]

Around the age of fourteen he bought an old fiddle, having saved five shillings out of his wages. He went out to his bed in the stables or cowshed after work and taught himself to play, often practising in the dark. He wrote that 'This occupied all my leisure hours, and has been my favourite amusement ever since.'

Then for the first time, from the age of seventeen, he had access to literature. On a farm in Willenslee, his master's wife lent him books and newspapers. He read *The Gentle Shepherd* and *The Life and Adventures of William Wallace* with great difficulty, while tending sheep.

And later, from the age of nineteen, he began work as a shepherd for James Laidlaw of Blackhouse, where he would stay for ten years. He later described his kindness as 'more like that of a father than a master'. Hogg read his books, as well as those of a local library, and began to compose songs for the local lasses to sing.

He formed close friendships with his master's eldest son, William Laidlaw, and with Alexander Laidlaw who lived nearby. With his elder brother and some cousins and friends, he formed a literary society of shepherds, viewed with suspicion by some of their neighbours. One night there was a violent storm while they met, and the group was blamed for this – they must have summoned up the devil. He was steadily learning to read and to write, and composed some plays and pastorals as well as songs.

It was his poem *The Mistakes of the Night* that appeared in print first, anonymously in *The Scots Magazine*, in October 1794. He was nearly twenty-four. In retrospect, it was classic Hogg. It was written in Scots, and is a story of love and ambiguity and confusion. Geordie goes to court his shy young Maggie in the dark of night, and accidentally sleeps with her widowed mother instead. The mother becomes pregnant and, sadly for young Geordie, he is obliged to marry her. Clearly, there were dangers in those long, dark nights in Ettrick Forest.

Then, when he was twenty-six, an epiphany. A 'half daft man' came to Hogg on a hillside and repeated a poem by Robert Burns, *Tam o' Shanter*. Burns had died the previous year, but until this moment Hogg had never heard of him. By the time the man left, Hogg had heard all about 'the sweetest poet that ever was born', and had committed the poem to memory.

---

[6] Hogg, 'Memoir', p. 13.

His mind was racing. And he wept. What was there to stop him from succeeding Burns? A shepherd had more time to write than a ploughman, which Burns had been. And – a sign from Heaven? – they shared the same birthday. Clearly, it was meant to be. 'But then I wept again because I could not write. However, I resolved to be a poet, and to follow in the steps of Burns.'

A nice story, but is it true? Hogg's memory of his own birthday was not; he discovered shortly before he died that he had this wrong. And while he says that he decided at this moment in 1797 to be a poet, he had been writing some verse for years, he'd had the one piece published, and was already known to his neighbours as 'Jamie the Poeter'. The 'half daft man' probably existed. Such people were sometimes seen as a direct link to Heaven. The story is probably mainly true. But it's also a very convenient beginning to his life as a poet.

Robert Burns

Burns is widely regarded as the national poet of Scotland and is known and celebrated around the world. He was born in 1759, about twelve years before Hogg, and died in 1796. He was just thirty-seven and died in poverty and debt.

There are similarities between them. Each was the son of a poor tenant farmer. They had limited education, though Burns had more. Both wrote in English and Scots. Both would have regular financial problems. Each fathered children out of wedlock and repented in the kirk for this. Each wrote from the heart, and would be known for their compassion and tenacity. Both could extend love beyond their friends, beyond humans even, to a mouse for example, or a dog. Each was considered a gifted child of Nature.

Hogg identified strongly with Burns and would not only adopt his birthday, 25 January, as his own – wrong but perhaps unintended – but also he 'expected to die at the same age and on the very same day of the month'. He did indeed get suitably ill around that age and time, and the illness did not subside until the date had safely passed.

Throughout his life, Hogg would strive to be seen as the successor to Burns and in some fields to surpass him – a high goal and a major challenge. In time he would move to prose as well as poetry, and would write and sing more songs, partly with this goal in mind.

Scottish writer John Wilson would discuss the two in a comparison of 'agricultural' and 'pastoral' poets in 1819. He referred to Burns, and to 'his only worthy successor, the Ettrick Shepherd', and said, 'There can be nothing more delightful than to see these two genuine children of Nature following the voice of her inspiration.' He said Hogg was 'more attuned to landscape, more enthusiastic, and better at the supernatural'. He spoke that year, too, of 'the high and holy connection' between them.

To Hogg, Burns would be forever a hero, but also a competitor.

In his time at Blackhouse, Hogg first ventured into the Highlands but left few records of this. There was a droving trip about 1792, as far as Glen Orchy, and another by horseback about 1799, to the north of the Grampians. This latter one had frightened him. He had been riding to Tomintoul by night when his horse refused to go on. He dismounted, stumbled through the darkness and found a man's body, not just dead but – on closer inspection – recently murdered. He galloped into town to tell others, but found them reluctant to get involved. He was shaken by this and headed speedily south, with 'a sort of lurking dread that I might be taken up for the murderer'.

Despite such inconveniences, the trips had given him a taste for the Highlands. They were wild and exciting, and he was starting to hear stories from a Highlander's perspective, rather than from fellow Lowlanders.

Somewhere around this time he composed 'Donald Macdonald', a patriotic song. Hogg said in his *Songs by the Ettrick Shepherd* that he wrote it 'when a barefooted lad herding lambs on the Blackhouse Heights, in utter indignation at the threatened invasion from France', and that the song 'had run through the Three Kingdoms like fire set to heather, for ten or twelve years'. But elsewhere he said he composed it in 1800 or later – when he was about thirty, and presumably no longer a barefooted lad.

Figure 2 Farmhouse at Blackhouse, where James Hogg worked from 1790 to 1800. (Source: Reproduced with permission of Andy Stephenson.)

He had the song printed in Edinburgh, then 'Edition followed edition', and soon 'the whole country rang with the patriotic strain'.[7] He described this later, with constrained modesty, as 'perhaps, the most popular song that ever was written'.[8] There were few who knew or cared who wrote it, but it would be a massive boost to his confidence.

Scotland in 1800: A Quick Guide

At the turn of the century the population of Scotland was 1.6 million (based on an 1801 census, up from about a million in 1700). Edinburgh and Glasgow each had more than 80,000 people, but Glasgow was growing faster and would soon surpass the capital. There had been a Union with England since 1707 and Scotland was sometimes called North Britain. (Ireland was added in 1801, to form the United Kingdom.) Only men with property over a certain value could vote (there were just a few thousand voters in Scotland). Britain and her allies had been at war with France since 1792, more or less, and would continue until 1815.

The population of the Highlands was growing rapidly, and in the fifty years to 1830 would rise by 50 per cent. Growth was helped by potatoes, which produced more food per acre than any other crop; by 1800 they provided about 80 per cent of the Highlanders' diet. The Jacobite rebellions, intended to restore a Catholic Stuart king to the British throne, had been crushed in 1746. Since then private armies and the bearing of arms had been banned, and tenants were being cleared from the Highlands to make room for more profitable sheep farming. A ban on wearing Highland garb had been lifted in 1782. Roman Catholics had suffered under oppressive rules since the sixteenth century, but the process of emancipation had begun. A network of military roads had been built in the eighteenth century.

Efficiencies in agriculture and the textile industries were under way and gathering pace. An efficient steam engine was patented by Scottish inventor James Watt in 1781. This was a catalyst for the Industrial Revolution and boosted demand for coal, mined in dismal conditions. Glasgow's growth was led by textiles, ironworks, trade with the Americas and later, by shipbuilding. The *Charlotte Dundas*, the world's first practical steamboat, would soon be tested on the Forth and Clyde Canal.

The Scottish Enlightenment had been under way since the mid-eighteenth century; Edinburgh was known as 'a hotbed of genius' and Scotland led the world in philosophy, economics, science, medicine and literature. But it would be decades before dinosaurs and evolution were discovered, and 128 years before all women aged over twenty-one could vote.

---

[7] Groves, *Growth of a Writer*, p. 7.
[8] Hughes, *James Hogg*, p. 59.

> Scottish Romanticism was an artistic, literary and intellectual movement that developed in the late eighteenth century, and was part of the wider European Romantic movement. The movement was started partly by *Fingal*, in the 1760s, apparently an ancient Gaelic poem by the blind bard Ossian, but there were some questions later about its authenticity. Robert Burns, the ploughman poet, had burst onto the scene in 1786 with *Poems, Chiefly in the Scottish Dialect*. He died before the century was out but his legacy lived on. His authenticity was never in doubt.

Apart from sheep, songs and writing, what else had Hogg been up to? He'd had a love of sports and running from a young age:

> I was wont to strip off my clothes, and run races against time, or rather against myself; and, in the course of these exploits, which I accomplished much to my own admiration, I first lost my plaid, then my bonnet, then my coat, and, finally, my hosen; for, as for shoes, I had none. In that naked state did I herd for several days.

Later he wrote:

> ... for speed had not my marrow
> Thro' Teviot, Ettrick, Tweed, and Yarrow
> Strang, straight, and swift like ony arrow.

He was remembered for being beaten in running only once, by a rival by 'half a heel'.

There must have been some romance. The best clues to this are to be found in 'Love Adventures of Mr George Cochrane' in *Winter Evening Tales*, a story he wrote much later but confessed was partly autobiographical. He tells us, through George, 'I declared my most violent affection for her. In the most respectful manner I was capable of ... During the space of three years we were seldom asunder, and enjoyed all the delights of the most pure and tender affection.' He (George) then says that he had been deeply in love several times since, 'sometimes for a fortnight, sometimes for a month, but never exceeding the space of half a year'. And: 'I was always a favourite with the girls, but never with their parents or guardian.' The young man's amorous adventures sound very real.

And undoubtedly, there were opportunities. Hogg's lifelong friend William Laidlaw describes him entering the kirk as a youth:

> rather above average height, of faultless symmetry of form ... light blue eyes that beamed with gaiety, glee, and good-humour, the effect of the most exuberant animal spirits ... a singular profusion of light-brown hair ... which rolled down his back, and fell below his loins. And every

female eye was upon him, as, with light step, he ascended the stair to the gallery where he sat.[9]

Hogg's athletic, poetic and musical abilities would also have been attractions. A biographer describes him in his early years as 'highly sexed and extremely attractive to women'.[10]

In 1800, he left Blackhouse and took over the lease of Ettrickhouse, and the care of his elderly parents, when his older brother married and moved out. The lease would run for three more years, until mid-1803. It was a small farm, which would allow more time for writing.

His poetry appeared in print again in 1801. Once more, there were elements of spontaneity and confusion. He had been in Edinburgh to sell sheep, with a day to spare before the next market, and decided to publish his poems in a pamphlet to pass the time. He had no notes, so had to write them from memory and to print the ones he remembered the best. He called the collection *Scottish Pastorals* and paid to have 1,000 copies printed; they duly arrived, with 'errors abounding on every page'.

Next we learn that he won three guineas from the Highland Society of Scotland, in February 1802, for his 'Communications on the diseases of sheep'. Even his pragmatic father, who had not encouraged his writing, would have been impressed. And sometime early in 1802, though dates and details vary, Hogg met and impressed a lawyer and sheriff and story collector, Walter Scott.

Scott was gathering traditional ballads for his *Minstrelsy of the Scottish Border*; the first two volumes had been published and he was collecting for the third. Scott had been advised to contact Hogg, and they may have met in Edinburgh first, then in Ettrick. For Hogg, seeing one of these volumes was 'the first book I ever perused which was written by a person I had seen and conversed with', and must have been inspirational. His first meeting with Scott in Ettrick was described by William Laidlaw later: 'The qualities of Hogg came out every instant & his unaffected simplicity and "fearless frankness" both surprised & charmed the Sheriff.' They told stories and laughed and talked into the small hours. Scott engaged Hogg as a ballad collector. It was the start of a long, significant and complex relationship.

Scott met with Hogg's mother too, for help with the collection and to hear her sing. He got more than he bargained for. Old Margaret Laidlaw lectured him on the authenticity of his work, and the effect of publishing old ballads: 'there was never ane o' my sangs prentit till ye prentit them yoursell, an' ye hae spoilt them a'thegither. They war made for singing, an' no for reading; and they're nouther right spelled nor right setten down.' Take that, Sheriff.

The Biographical Dictionary of Scottish Women: From the Earliest Times to 2004 describes Margaret as a 'tradition-bearer'. Women, apparently, were

---

[9] Thomson, *Works*, p. xiii.
[10] Hughes, *James Hogg*, p. 23.

especially important in the transmission of traditional ballads. Historian Alistair Moffat says that collectors of folk songs and stories 'depended heavily on the memories and musical skills of women who ensured the survival of much that would have been lost . . . the ballads may have had more resonance in the hearts and minds of women, and particularly women like Meg Laidlaw'.[11]

> ### Walter Scott
>
> Walter Scott was born in 1771, so was a close contemporary of Hogg. He survived a bout of polio at a young age which left him lame. He grew up in Edinburgh and the Scottish Borders, and had a good education, including studies in law, philosophy and German. He met Burns briefly, when Scott was fifteen. When he was at grammar school he met James and John Ballantyne, who later became his business partners and printed his books.
>
> After completing his studies he became a lawyer in Edinburgh. As a lawyer's clerk he made his first visit to the Scottish Highlands, directing an eviction.
>
> From childhood, Scott was fascinated by the oral traditions of the Scottish Borders. He was an obsessive collector of stories, and developed a way of recording them, using carvings on twigs to avoid offending the storyteller.
>
> He married Charlotte Charpentier in 1797. Two years later he was appointed Sheriff-Depute of the County of Selkirk (the principal law officer, a role he would have for life). They would have a good income, with his salary from this new job, his work as a lawyer, some revenue from writing, with Charlotte's own income, and with some from his father's estate.
>
> At this stage he set about collecting ballads for his books. And hence, the big night of merriment with Hogg, and some tear-jerking songs from Hogg's mother . . .

And then, in 1802, Hogg would take a significant Highland tour. Significant, especially, because he would write about it to Walter Scott. And Scott made sure that others would read it. For Hogg, this was the beginning of something entirely new.

---

[11] Moffat, *The Borders*, pp. 305–7.

2 Hogg's Ettrick (1802): A state of nature

MIRTH AND JOLLITY

Hogg's description of his 1802 journey starts with a visit to Ettrick Forest, his homeland. Ostensibly, he was writing this to Walter Scott who knew Ettrick well, so why did he want to describe this place?

He was probably aiming for a wider audience already, and hoping that Scott would help get this published. Before embarking on a journey, of course, it makes sense to know where you're coming from. Importantly, he tells us 'it will form a striking contrast' with the areas he was about to visit.

Here, then, is Hogg's view of his own stamping ground. Or at least it is the view that he wanted to have:[1]

> The hills are generally of a beautiful deep green, thick covered with sheep; high and steep, though nowise rugged or tremendous. The highest is Phaup-penn, which rises 2,370 feet above the level of the sea . . .
>
> The river Etterick taketh its rise five miles S.S.E. of the village of Moffat, and runs a course of 30 miles. About a mile and an half above Selkirk, it is augmented one half, by the tribute of its sister Yarrow; and as far below that ancient burgh, the Tweed is increased nearly one half by these united streams.
>
> His Grace [the Duke of Buccleuch] is the principal proprietor, both in Etterick and Yarrow, and is the father and benefactor of his country. His name is never mentioned but with respect: His health is the first toast at all convivial meetings . . .
>
> Since my remembrance, his Grace's tenants have only had leases from one year to another; but so assured are they of their welfare being consulted, and of their Chief's stability, that every man cultivates his farm with as much assurance as if he had a liferent tack. He hath now offered them leases for ten or eleven years . . .

---

[1] Here, and in the next three chapters, extracts from Hogg's reports are shown indented.

The two rivers, Etterick and Yarrow, form properly what is called Etterick Forest . . . In the upper parts of the country small indeed are the remains of the wood with which it was once wholly covered; but in the lower parts there is some, both natural and planted . . .

The lives of the principal shepherds . . . are very easy, and, to those who can relish such a life, elegant and agreeable. They are much employed during the Summer in arranging and marketing their flocks. Their chief rural diversions, in that season, are fowling, and fishing with the rod. In Winter, they assemble in mixed clubs to curl on the ice, and trace the fox or hare, when the evenings are spent in the highest mirth and jollity. Singing, dancing, and drinking, alternately ensue; and in very few families is the latter ever carried to excess.

They delight greatly in poetry and music, in which sundry are considerable proficients. Burns's are the favourite songs, and the Scotish strathspeys the favourite music. Their more quiet and retired diversions are, cards, the dam-board, and backgammon.

The manners of the common people are truly singular, from their simplicity: they have generally the musical ear; are passionately fond of songs; and, for variety, greatly excel their superiors . . .

The shepherds having much spare time on their hands, devote it to active pastimes. They assemble at certain places in the month of March, in great numbers, where sundry prizes are exhibited for the best runners; and it is extremely diverting to see with what eagerness the palm is contested. This should be by no means discouraged; as agility and swiftness in a shepherd is a principal qualification . . . the thoughts of contesting the victory with his opponent, who perhaps has vanquished him before, presides in the shepherd's heart above every consideration . . .

There is likewise one small prize for him who leaps farthest; one for him who puts the stone farthest; and two or three for the best wrestlers: all of which are well contested, but never with such avidity, as the races are.

And lastly, the remainder of the day is spent in playing at the ball. This is the most furious contest of all.

A Gloomier View

The Statistical Account of Scotland (1791–9, 'Parish of Etterick, County of Selkirk', contributed by its minister, and published a few years before Hogg's account) shows a rather less rosy picture:

> Upon the hills the soil is in many places mossy, and fit for nothing but fuel and pasturage. In other places, it is pretty deep and hard, but, on account of the immense height and steepness, it is susceptible of no cultivation. The air is in general moist. This is occasioned by the height of the hills which continually attract the clouds and the vapour that is constantly exhaled by the sun from the mossy grounds . . .

> [The population seems] to have been considerably greater in former times than at present. In one place, about 50 years ago, there were 32 houses; but at present there are only three. From this circumstance, it would appear, that the population hath decreased...
> This parish possesses no advantages. The nearest market town is 15 miles distant... The snow also at times is a great inconvenience; often for many months we can have no intercourse with mankind... There are ten proprietors of land in this parish: none of them reside in it.

FANTASTICAL SHAPES

Could anything be more innocent and positive than Hogg's view of Ettrick? But under the surface it is a little more complicated:

> In no part of the south of Scotland hath the ancient superstitions so long kept their ground. The fairies have but lately and reluctantly quitted its green holms and flowery glens.
> Some yet alive have had intercourse with them; and the stories of their pranks and gambols are listened to with more attention, and as much faith annexed, as the gospel according to Matthew. I have heard my own grandfather relate how he had spoken with them... We are persuaded that they have not power to stay where the Protestant religion is so firmly established; but that, in the Papist countries, they are as thick as ever.[2] The last brownie that left the south of Scotland, haunted Bodsbeck, in our vicinity; the tenor of whose lamentation for the extirpation of his tribe, on the night of his departure, is yet well known here-abouts.

Fairies and Brownies

Having grown up with Tinkerbell and the tooth fairy, I assumed that fairies were tiny and female, cute, aerobatic and entirely benign. This was not so in Hogg's time. 'Fairies were not blithe and captivating... They belonged to times of bad powers and evil confusion, and their intentions were oftener than not malicious, or even deadly.'[3] And:

> The world of faery... is also a world of darkness, ugliness, callous superficiality, terror and tragedy... their appearance varies from extreme beauty to grotesque ugliness... Fairies could be

---

[2] 'Papist countries' were Roman Catholic parts of Scotland, mainly Gaelic-speaking regions to the north and west.
[3] Munro, *View from Castle Rock*, p. 13.

mischievous or even cruel, capable of stealing human children . . . if anything angered them they could use their magical powers to inflict disease.[4]

Changelings might be left in place of stolen children, and adults might also be abducted. Someone who was 'away with the fairies' might be gone forever.

Fairies were thought to be deceased humans, demons or some entirely different species. They were sometimes referred to as 'the good people' to avoid giving offence. To mess with fairies was to play with fire. 'Leave well alone' was the safest stance.

Hogg's grandfather Will o'Phaup said they were the height of two-year-old children, far bigger than I'd imagined, and some descriptions have them even larger. Had I known this as a child I doubt if I would have let a tooth fairy into my room after dark, despite the potential financial gain.

Brownies were usually more constructive. A brownie was 'a personage of small stature, wrinkled visage, covered with short curly brown hair, and wearing a brown mantle and hood'.[5] They sometimes inhabited farms or empty parts of houses, possibly for centuries. They could bring good fortune and help with tasks, usually in exchange for small gifts of food. If given too much for their services, though, they might feel offended and leave.

Fairies are found in many parts of the world. New Zealand is better known for hobbits now, but has been home to the Patupaiarehe, small forest dwellers known to the Māori. Despite the distance from Scotland, the fairies have similarities: these southern fairies were nocturnal too, afraid of fire, and had the bad habit of abducting people. But they were often guardians of sacred places, and usually peace-loving.

Kakamora live in forests in parts of the Solomon Islands. They are usually 3–4 ft tall (about 1 m) with long black hair and long fingernails. I was told they are six times stronger than a human, can bound through forests with massive strides, and can make travellers immobile, invisible and mute, so searchers would never find them.

A nervous group of teenage boys in Temotu, a remote province, told me more. A man had recently had some body parts removed by small creatures in the forest; these grew back but he died later. 'I'll be careful,' I told them.

'But you don't have to worry,' the boys explained. 'They can't do anything to you because you don't believe in them.'

Hmmm . . . that was a relief of course, but I thought I'd found a solution for the boys. 'Why don't you decide not to believe in them too, like me? Then they couldn't do anything to you either.'

But somehow, I'd missed the point. One of them told me: 'You don't understand our culture.'

---

[4] Greenwood, *Illustrated History*, p. 75.
[5] Keightley, *Fairy Mythology*, p. 357.

There are further concerns in Ettrick Forest:

> Gaists and bogles are as plenty as ever . . . awful, terrible bogles, who assume the most fantastical shapes, and play the maddest-like actions, which the most whimsical spirits can invent. Scarcely is there a steading without a place near it that is not occasionally haunted . . . I could tell you fifty stories of the causes of these apparitions, of their laying, and how vilely they have fooled some of our parsons.[6]

And more: 'There are many of our old ill-looking women that are rank witches.' Hogg gives some examples of witchcraft: of a hunted hare which runs into a house and is changed back into 'the old wife . . . hanging out her tongue with the heat'; of emaciated cats, worn out from being ridden by witches in the night; of a grouse or partridge, shot and wounded, flying down a chimney then reappearing as an old woman, her skin peppered with gunshot; of a farmer he knew who had been ill and had recurring problems with his plough because (he later realised) he'd argued with an old woman a few days before, who must have bewitched him.

Witches and the Devil

Witchcraft had been known in Scotland for centuries. A witch was not necessarily good or bad, and the term applied both to males and females who worked with magic, potions and spells. These practices often provided real health benefits, though the reasons they worked might not be well understood.

But the image was damaged in the sixteenth century when links were made between witches and the Devil. This made them dangerous; they were now working in opposition to God. King James VI's book *Daemonologie* described the demonic pact: witches were committed to the triumph of evil. They should therefore be executed, and burning was the recommended method of completely erasing a witch's existence.

Laws were changed throughout Europe to support this. Guilt was established by confession (usually following torture), by pricking (piercing blemishes on the naked body to check for signs of the Devil), or by the testimony of others. Water tests – those who floated were guilty – were not used much in Scotland.

More than 4,500 people, about 80 per cent of them women, were burned at the stake in Scotland between 1590 and 1680, 'a hideous death . . . insisted on by a population who sincerely believed that they were bound to perpetrate scarcely imaginable barbarities in the best

---

[6] 'Gaist' and 'bogle' are Scottish variants of 'ghost'. ('Bogle' is linked to the term 'bogey-man', and 'gaist' to 'ghost' and 'ghastly'.) To 'lay a spirit' means to prevent a spirit from walking among the living.

interests of a godly commonwealth . . . carried out with sadistic enthusiasm in the Scottish Borders'.[7] Why were so many of them women? They were often elderly, living alone, with knowledge of traditional remedies, and they were least able to defend themselves. (Along with pointless deaths and suffering, knowledge of many of these remedies was an unfortunate loss in the period.)

The passion for witch-hunts waned in the eighteenth century and the laws prescribing the death penalty were repealed well before Hogg's birth, but prejudices lived on. Hogg made his fear of witches clear, but he must have had conflicting views on this, with several of his ancestors thought to have been witches. But surrounded by frequent unexplained misfortune, it must have been hard to live in that era and not believe in unnatural beings, in witches and in their master, the Devil.

Such beliefs were not restricted to those places and times. In parts of Africa, Asia and the Pacific, witchcraft is still widespread. A practitioner is often blamed for another's distress, something that might elsewhere be put down just to coincidence or bad luck. And as in Europe earlier, the witches killed are usually elderly women, single or from poor families.

In the Solomon Islands it is rare for someone to die of 'natural causes' and even a heart attack can be blamed on witchcraft. A spell might use anything that a person has touched to attack them: food scraps, banana skins, and even faeces. For this reason, such items are carefully disposed of.

A 'good news' story from Africa gives some clues as to why older women have been targeted, and a possible resolution. In South Africa's North Province, witch-killings almost stopped when a pension scheme was introduced in the 1990s. Elderly women were now better able to protect themselves and were no longer seen as a risk or a burden to those around them.

Witchcraft, commonly known as Wicca, is still active in the Western world too; apart from cults linked to Satanism, though, this is usually not seen as working with the Devil. Some modern-day practices, such as naturopathy and even weather forecasting, might have been seen as witchcraft in earlier times.

Hogg tells the story of a woman he meets at the start of his 1802 journey (below), a sad picture of prejudice. One can feel her trepidation and degradation. We might mock the reluctance of villagers to reach out to her. But we should respect the bravery of the young man who did, given the fear of the Devil and his cohorts. And we should consider present-day parallels: the fear of infectious disease, or of 'getting involved' that might stop someone from helping a victim in a similar situation today.

---

[7] Moffat, *The Borders*, p. 372.

Hogg concludes his view of Ettrick:

> You will think this no very favourable picture of a country which is beginning to emerge into notice, where indeed there are many very sensible people, and where the youth, as you know, have made great proficiency in the arts and sciences, as well as in trade and manufactures. The fact is, the forest being surrounded by high mountains, remained long excluded from any intercourse with the more fertile districts surrounding these: even to this day, the cross roads are in a state of nature. The consequence of all this was, a later and more sudden emergence from barbarity.

As he began his journey, Hogg tells us, he met a 'poor woman that halted much'. He found that he recognised her, and stopped to hear her story. Her life had been a 'chain of misfortunes', with one of the worst being in Ettrick, but she believed that since it was the will of Providence that she should suffer 'it could not have happened amongst so kind and benevolent a people'. He continued, 'this pleased me so well, that I made a stretch in charity, and gave her a shilling, which redoubled her blessings on the good people of Etterick'. The woman had been compelled to beg, following a series of accidents:

> She had for some time traversed the higher parts of Dumfriesshire, and finding, by experience, the superior hospitality of the mountaineers, she left Eskedalemuir, and went to cross the heights into the head of Etterick, when on the tops of the mountains a little to the east of Phauppenn, she fell and broke one of her legs . . . a thick mist or hoar frost floated on the hills; here she lay crying until her voice failed, but no help appeared; and finding that she must soon perish of cold, she took some few appendages, necessary to her occupation, and fastening them round her waist, tried her last effort to save a wretched life.
>
> Night was now coming on, and there was but one experiment left; namely, to crawl on her hands and trail her body and her legs. This she actually put in practice, and continued with a perseverance almost incredible; it was not an hour, nor a day; but all the long, dreary, winter night; all the next day, and all the following night, until about two o'clock, when she was descryed from Broadgarehill . . . She had a red napkin tied on her head, the implements of her profession trailing far behind her, and was as grotesque a figure as can well be imagined.
>
> The people seeing such a horrible phaenomenon approaching them, and knowing that no such monster inhabited their mountains, readily concluded it to be the devil, and began a dispute which of them he was come in quest of. Several times they attempted to go near her, but as often their courage failed them, and they turned their backs and fled.
>
> One lad at last had the boldness to approach her, but still involved in uncertainty to what class of beings she belonged, he stretched out his hand, and with one of his fingers made a trial if she might be felt, and finding her real flesh and blood, he alarmed his neighbour, who came

and helped him to carry her home, where they took all possible care of her, and the parish of Etterick taking her under their protection, by the care of the family, and the neighbours around, and the attendance of an able surgeon, she so far recovered, as to be able to walk a little: and then, poor creature! was again turned on the wide world to beg her bread from door to door!

Had this happened to a person of rank, it would have been recorded in all the news papers of Britain, yet what would the one have felt that the other did not feel.

These were challenging times. The Devil – Clootie, Auld Hornie, Satan, Nick, the Deil – was always there, inveigling, waiting for opportunities, round every corner and prominent in every mind; through his link with witches or in any other guise. In Ettrick Forest in 1802, it seems, there was plenty to worry about . . .

NOTES ON MY LATER VISIT – ETTRICK FOREST

I arrived at Tibbie Shiels Inn, on the southern shore of St Mary's Loch, late afternoon in patchy drizzle. The trip from Edinburgh had been an easy combination of bus, hitch-hiking and walking. I contemplated pitching my tent. But the drizzle might pass, I thought, and it'll be easier to put it up later.

I looked up at Hogg's monument, gazing back down at me from across the road. I needed support and some local knowledge from someone who'd been in these parts a long time. 'You'll be fine,' I think he said. I ducked into the bar and ordered a wee dram. In his portrait by the fireplace, Hogg confirmed my good sense. Encouraged, I ordered another. Still light drizzle, so I ordered a burger. And another dram.

Just on dark the heavens opened. I peered out from the bar. Big fat raindrops were bouncing up from new puddles. The wind had picked up. I'd run out of options – all the rooms were full. I'd just have to be quick with the tent. I dashed out into the storm, glancing up at the monument. 'You'll be fine,' he said . . .

The previous week I'd been packing up in New Zealand. My Scotland visit was to be a walking and camping trip. Walking is one of my special loves, but it's much more fun if you don't have much to carry. Everything I bring should have at least two uses, I decided. And then I had a Very Good Idea.

My poncho, I thought, could be my raincoat by day and my groundsheet at night. And my puffer jacket, I decided, looked so much like my sleeping bag – why carry both? The poncho would keep my jacket dry on rainy days. And I'd wear my jacket and all my clothes, my entire but modest wardrobe, in bed at night. Perfect! I smiled, I tossed out my raincoat and sleeping bag, and I shoved my gear into a smaller, lighter backpack. I was ready for Scotland.

But now, the realisation. Pitching the tent in a downpour, there would be an awkward transition. First, off comes the poncho, then down it goes as a groundsheet. It starts to gather rain, and quickly resembles a children's paddling pool – the perfect place to float my tent. Damn. But no time to rethink this now. I poke in pegs and poles and wrestle with soggy fabric until my tent resembles a tent, more or less. And while this is happening my puffer jacket, stripped of its protective poncho, is quickly resembling a sponge. This wouldn't be the cosy sleeping bag I'd imagined.

I dash back into the bar. I have a couple of hours before closing time to dry off and warm up. I order a whisky. From his frame beside the fireplace, Hogg is smiling. 'Welcome to Ettrick Forest,' he says.

The next morning is clear and cool. I'd crawled into bed around midnight, still damp. I warmed up a few hours later. And now, inspired by a big mug of coffee, I was looking for mountains to climb.

I headed for Berrybush, relishing the fresh air and big open spaces. This, I knew, was the area where the Justified Sinner met his tragic end; he'd died at Eldinhope and was buried at Cowans Croft or Fall Law (Hogg decides to keep this ambiguous). But nothing that morning could dampen my spirits. The land was moist and warm and alive. Black-faced sheep bellowed, challenging me, then decided they'd won and lost interest. Woolly clouds floated above.

I hadn't intended going to Ettrick. I'd planned to go there the following day when the James Hogg Exhibition would be open. But my boots kept pointing in that direction, and by early afternoon I'd reached the road a short distance to the west, and was approaching the kirk.

Shafts of sunlight slipped through gaps in towering trees, lighting the graveyard. Hogg's grave, bold and simple, was easy to find. I was respectful and suitably impressed.

But my eyes were drawn to the left, to the grave of William Laidlaw, 'the far-fam'd Will o'Phaup'. The larger-than-life being, the epitaph tells us, who 'had no equal in his day'. A grave with a mosaic of moss and lichen and stone, of shades of greens and greys, that grew more beautiful and harder to read with every decade.

He lived from 1691 to 1778. He is Hogg's grandfather. My own grandfather's grandfather's grandfather.

It was Will who conversed with the fairies. Until his mid-teens, Scotland was an independent country. I was visiting his grave in 2014, on the eve of the referendum on Independence. I wished he could have conversed with me now.

I carried on eastwards, past Hogg's birthplace. The house is long gone, but there is a chunky Victorian memorial to him here, erected in 1898. I arrived at the James Hogg Exhibition, which had opened in the moth-balled school in 2013. Unexpectedly, it was open today to coincide with the fifty-seventh annual Ettrick Flower Show, across the road at the Boston Memorial Hall (the hall was a modest memorial to Thomas Boston, the fire and brimstone preacher who used to attract 800 sinners here for a sermon, including some Hogg ancestors). It was my lucky day.

I strolled around the Exhibition. I saw Hogg's plaid and his spectacles, his curling stone and his handwriting. I took a photo of his 'death mask', eerily catching my own face reflected in the background, a ghost behind the mask. I introduced myself to a group of volunteers. And then I knew I'd arrived.

'You look so much at home here,' I was told. 'You have an Ettrick chin.' I had no idea what an Ettrick chin was. But right then, I was glad I had one.

I was swept away to the flower show for supper. 'You must be starving,' they said. I was, of course. They seemed to know me already.

My visit was later described in a local newspaper under a headline: 'James Hogg's Kiwi descendant becomes living exhibit'. Then: 'Ettrick folk got a surprise at the James Hogg Museum, when his great, great grandson walked in from New Zealand.' This might have given the impression I'd walked further than I had. But I was pleased to be called an exhibit, not a relic. And I was delighted to be living.

It was music night back at Tibbie Shiels Inn. The lead singer inserted his own lyrics: 'Hey you, over there, get yourself up off that chair!' We did. Young bodies swirled. Mine did too. At least, I thought it did until a badly placed wall mirror shattered my illusion. I was a few years older, it seems, than I recalled. And what had felt like fluid movements looked more like, on reflection, just bad posture. Damn the mirror, I decided, and carried on swirling.

Occasionally someone who knew the words would jump up on stage and share the microphone for a while. It was cold outside, but inside there was noise and sweat and colour. And I was part of it – I had just arrived in the Borders and was stomping and singing and laughing with my new mates. I just didn't know their names.

And here, maybe right here in this room, my ancestor had drunk and sung with Tibbie the innkeeper almost two centuries earlier. Hogg had courted her too, Tibbie said, 'but he never came to the point'. What was 'the point', I wondered. And where would I be now, if he had ever come to it?

I slipped into my tent around 1 a.m., feeling very, very happy. It was a clear, calm, cold night. I was warm and dry. I'd found an unexpected sense of belonging. I stroked my Ettrick chin and, just for a moment, I felt a poem coming on . . .

I headed north the next morning, on the Southern Upland Way and on to Innerleithen, then by cycle path to Peebles. In the next few days I met a farmer who told me, 'Hogg used to ride these hills naked on a bull' (he made it sound so normal and recent). A woman told me that other literary greats had lived in the district and moved away, but Hogg had never wanted to leave. I passed places he used to meet with Scott and De Quincey and Wordsworth. I visited the International Festival of Literature and Thought at Traquair, and the museum to the St Ronan's Border Games, an event that Hogg had founded in 1827. I had a night in a log cabin bothy. No bogles or brownies anywhere, but I could sense where they had been. I stumbled into great cafés and a lively Independence debate.

On music night back at the Inn, a young woman had given me a book of poetry she'd written. She said: 'I wasn't going to miss an opportunity to share this with a Hogg relative.' She'd been to visit his grave that morning. I took

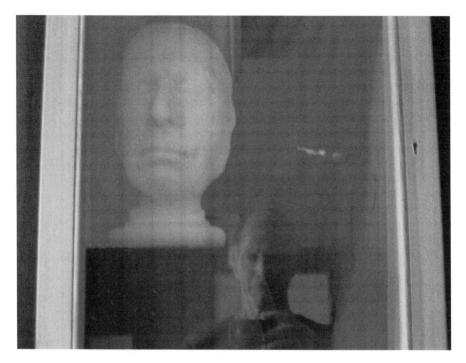

Figure 3 Death mask at the James Hogg Exhibition, Ettrick. But who's the ghost?

time out to read it along the trail, sitting amongst the heather. It was as fresh and unpredictable as the Ettrick Forest wind.

I had expected the Borders to be quaint, full of history, and dull. I found the area alive and well, with creative, welcoming, energetic people. And here at least, I thought, Hogg is not yet dead.

3 Central Highlands (1802): Their remarkable inhabitants

A QUEST

On 23 July 1802, Hogg set out from Ettrick on horseback. He was on a mission. He had been farming and caring for his elderly parents on the small farm at Ettrickhouse for two years. But the lease would expire the following year, to be taken over by a wealthy neighbour. He and his parents would have no source of income and nowhere to live. The hope was to find a suitable farm to lease in the Highlands:

> I had, alongst with my aged parents, been thrust from our little patrimonial farm, and though possessed of more partiality for my native soil than I am willing at all times to acknowledge, my heart exulted in the thought, of finding amongst the Grampian mountains a cheap and quiet retreat in the bosom of some sequestered glen, where unawed by the proud, or unenvied by any, I would nourish and increase my fleecy store, and awaken, with the pipe and violin, echoes which had slept for a thousand years.

The trip would take him north, through Perth and into the Grampians, and initially as far as Dalnacardoch to the north-west of Pitlochry. From that point some of his reports have been lost, but they start again a week or two later near Tomintoul, in the north of what is now the Cairngorms National Park. He then returned home via Braemar and Perth. The quest for a farm was earnest, but there were some big distractions on the way.

EDINBURGH: DECENCY AND THE CITY

Hogg's first stop was Candlemaker Row in the capital. The New Town was under construction then, and the well-off were migrating there. The Old Town was crowded and squalid, and the poor would remain. He had been to Edinburgh before, but one can imagine this would still be mind-boggling

CENTRAL HIGHLANDS (1802) 25

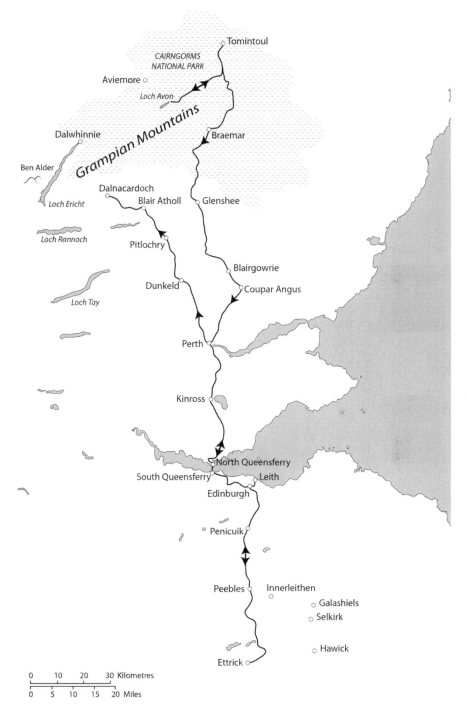

Figure 4 James Hogg's horseback journey, July to August 1802. (Source: Revised from originals in de Groot, *Highland Journeys*.)

for a wide-eyed shepherd from Ettrick Forest. Even now, it's easy to sense the excitement and the smells. He visited some contacts and theatres here. Along the way he shares his views on society, morality and piety. And there was a horse race in Leith, and his views on velocity:

> I pitied the poor animals that were strained at such a rate, and trembled for the riders, who were cleaving the atmosphere with a velocity I had never before witnessed, saving in the bolt that precedes the peal of thunder; even the Lochskene eagle, in all her pride, methought, could scarcely have kept above their heads.[1]
>
> ... other things that I noticed on my way to and from Leith were, two men with each a handful of printed papers, the contents of which they were crying nearly as follows, 'A true list of all the ladies, &c. &c' I was shocked at this open violation of decency, such an advertisement I had never heard before: but I hope they were not such ladies as I really took them for.[2]

He had 'sundry other gentlemen' to visit, but often had trouble finding an address, 'and if I find it, which is not always the case, my intellectual powers are commonly so much disordered by fatigue and heat, that I seldom relish their conversation so much as their drink'.

And he gives his reader some thoughts on poverty: 'the next poor ragged, emaciated wretch that begs your charity, try to put yourself in his place ... believe this for a little, and you will find how it will melt you'.

He left Edinburgh and crossed the Firth of Forth to North Queensferry on 25 July, a Sunday:

> We had a fine passage across the ferry: I was glad to see the rough sailors pay a respect to that holy day; they spoke little, and I did not hear an oath minced by one of them. One young gentleman, being newly come from such variety of entertainments, had forgot, I dare say, that it was the Sabbath, for he placed himself on the stern of the boat, and fell a whistling Greig's Pipes with great glee, the passengers looked at one another, and even the boisterous ferrymen laughed in their sleeve. When he understood himself, his looks were amusing ... he kept silent during the rest of the passage.

---

[1] The horses would have travelled at about 40 mph (64 kph) and the eagle at around 80 mph on a horizontal flight. Within 200 years of Hogg's comments on their velocity, humans had broken the speed of sound (over 760 mph) in the air and on land, and travelled at nearly 25,000 mph/40,000 kph in space. The bolts of lightning he saw would have travelled at about 224,000 mph; light itself is much faster still, at 186,000 miles per second.

[2] This list may have been similar to a book published in 1775, *Ranger's Impartial List of the Ladies of Pleasure in Edinburgh* (reprints of this are still available). The book provides details of some fifty ladies: names, addresses, ages and attributes ('good teeth ... sulky temper ... utmost satisfaction ...'). It even gives careers advice: The young woman who had an offer of marriage from a client recently should accept it urgently. Presumably, if Hogg is shocked by the papers, it is the commercial aspect and marketing strategies that he finds distasteful.

TO THE HIGHLANDS: STRANGERS AND STRIFE

From Queensferry, Hogg and his horse went north:

> it is certainly the greatest arrogance in a stranger pretending to describe a country from what he sees by the way side, or to give the character of the inhabitants, from those he accidentally meets or converses with. It is probable, I will err in this respect.

And as he predicted, he erred immediately:

> I met, and overtook great numbers of the inhabitants going to, and coming from church, and although they appeared to advantage, dressed in their Sunday's clothes, on a fine summer day, I found the peasantry, especially the fair sex, much inferior to our borderers, both in person and features . . .
>
> I now arrived at the town of Perth, the capital of that extensive county, and was astonished at its magnitude, but more at its elegance and clearness, considering its low situation. Although I have traversed its principal streets over and over again, I can make few remarks on it from my own observations, for indeed I had no other method of ascertaining its wealth and traffic than by reading the sign-boards, and examining the goods exhibited in the windows of the shops; nor of its population than by counting the inhabitants by scores like sheep, and even then, I would have been uncertain, as I might have reckoned some twice over . . .
>
> THE peasantry on the borders of the Tay and the Erne, through which I passed, are habited in the same manner as those south of the Forth, saving that the broad bonnet is universally worn; they are rather below than above the middle size, stout made, have ruddy healthful countenances, and are much more mild and frank in their disposition than the austere Lothianer. They generally enter into matrimony when young, and appear to enjoy as much happiness, both social and domestic, as their capacity or their situation can admit of . . .
>
> The Duke of Athol hath erected a farm-house, with all suitable conveniencies, in a fine holm, about two miles above Dunkeld, the land around which he manageth after the most liberal plan . . . I found that his Grace is beloved by his people in general; I conversed with one who told me, that he was one of nineteen farmers who were removed from the Duke's land to make way for one man, who now possessed the whole of what they, with their families, lived happily upon; on expressing my astonishment what could move his Grace to such a proceeding, he replied, 'ah! Cot pless him, hit pe nane of his doings.'[3] . . .

---

[3] 'God bless him, it be none of his doings.' It was common for Lowland Scots writers to show the English of native Gaelic speakers in this exaggerated and stereotyped form. It was also common for tenants not to blame the landowner for their eviction. Obviously the loyalty of the evicted farmer had not been reciprocated.

> NOT far from hence, [from Pitlochie] I went into a little public house, merely in order to obtain some intelligence about this interesting place ... I began my enquiries with avidity. My anxiety to gain intelligence of some particulars raised suspicions, and my writing of them confirmed these suspicions. In short, from less to more, a disagreeable fracas ensued ... I escaped without receiving any injury either in purse or person, for which I have to thank you. Remembering that I had an unsealed letter of recommendation from you to a respectable character, I produced it with a look of the utmost assurance, which entirely turned the scale of affairs in my favour ... [4]
>
> I would however recommend it to all travellers to avoid these whisky houses, unless in cases of necessity ... in general, they are certainly nuisances; hurtful to the morals and industry of the country people, and being often kept by the most lazy and tippling individuals, they are apt to take every advantage of a stranger.

LOOKING UP

There were loftier thoughts along the way:

> I WAS quite sick of travelling between two hedges, and wished to be amongst hills again wherever they were, having been bred amongst mountains, I am always unhappy when in a flat country; when ever the skirts of the horizon come on a level with myself, I feel myself quite uneasy, and have generally a headache. This was the reason why I flew over the lands of Fife and Kinross like a Hebridean eagle ... the objects that would have ravished others, were by me quite overlooked. There a large river winding between two romantic hills ... Here a compact, elegant city ...
>
> These scenes would have rivetted the eyes of most travellers, but like the old wooers, I looked too high for them, and fixed mine eyes on the lofty mountains which now arose to my view in the head of Angus and district of Glenshee, specked with the snows of the last century.

And, perhaps with eyes still raised to the hills:

> I'll tell you, my dear Sir, religion is a very good thing of itself, but it is dreadful, when abused as a mask; and here hath been more evil done under a pretence of religion than any thing else – love not excepted. We're oft to blame in this.[5]

---

[4] The person being thanked is Walter Scott, to whom these travel letters are addressed. Even though intended for publication, they were written and signed off to Scott (e.g. 'Sir your most obedient and affectionate servant, J. H.'). They were written as if at the end of each day, but in fact were completed later. The letter format was not uncommon in publications at the time.

[5] Hogg seemed to show no real religious prejudice, declaring that 'he would never esteem a man the less because he differed from himself in religion but on the contrary thought each should adhere to the religion in which he had been brought up' (Hughes, *James Hogg*, p. 51). He had been brought up in the Calvinist Presbyterian Church of Scotland.

INTO THE GRAMPIANS: SNOW AND SAVAGERY

The scenery is a mixture of the beautiful and the sublime, although less of the latter is intermixed than in most highland views; yet, as a contrast to the fine openings and beautiful villas on the west and north of the loch [Loch Rannoch, west of Pitlochry], over against us the skeleton of the black forest reminded us of what it once had been; above which the mountain of Schehallion rose to the height of 3,587 feet above the level of the sea. This mountain is famous for the experiments made on it by some of the most noted philosophers to ascertain the powers of attraction and gravity.[6]

Beauty and Sublimity

Descriptions of scenery in Hogg's time were subject to protocols. 'Beautiful' was usually smooth and associated with love, and could include pastoral and arable land; philosopher Edmund Burke said the soft gentle curves appealed to male sexual desire. 'Sublime' was rough and linked to fear, and might include mountains. 'Picturesque' was somewhere in between: it meant a landscape suitable for painting which might look rugged, but could be viewed with love as well.

To a modern reader, Hogg's descriptions of scenery could appear analytical and negative: 'horrid grandeur', 'gloomy sublimity', 'savage wildness' and 'an accumulation of the awful and the sublime'. Some of these words have changed meaning over time – 'awful' and 'awesome', for example, once had similar, positive meanings, both akin to 'awe-inspiring'.

Scotland's wonderful wilderness, in any case, had not always been seen as attractive. Writer H. G. Graham describes a common reaction of an eighteenth-century visitor: 'Not even in the wild scenery did the traveller see anything of beauty or sublimity, but rather forms of ugliness and gloom which deepened his dislike of the land.'[7]

In much of Christian Europe, nature had been seen as alien to man; to conquer it meant progress. A seventeenth-century theologian decided mountains were so horrible that they could not be the work of the Creator. They were hostile places with wild animals, wild people and wild weather. Rock and ice were cold and unwelcoming; mountains were hard to farm, and could kill. So why and when did they become beautiful?

---

[6] These experiments in 1774–6 used a plumb line to measure the attraction of the mountain, and so to estimate the mass and density of the earth and, extrapolating from there, the solar system. They proved the earth's core was much denser than its surface (some years earlier, many had thought the planet might be hollow, including comet-tracker Edmond Halley). The experiments also led to the development of contour lines on maps. Note that Hogg's use of the term 'philosophers' was appropriate at the time; such study was then referred to as 'natural philosophy' with the term 'physics' not in use until later in the nineteenth century.
[7] Graham, *Social Life of Scotland*, p. 3.

Views began to change when wild landscapes could be fenced and drained and tamed, and as wildlife became endangered. The Romantic movement both inspired and reflected a new way of seeing nature. Artists and writers began to show wilderness as dramatic and aesthetically pleasing, and the people who lived there as rugged and proud. English poet Thomas Gray wrote of the Scottish Highlands: 'The mountains are ecstatic . . . None but those monstrous creatures of God know how to join so much beauty with so much horror.' Walter Scott promoted the Highlands as a symbol of Britain, and his poem *The Lady of the Lake* brought a flood of tourists. Art critic John Ruskin (whom Hogg would meet in 1832, when Ruskin was a teenager) wrote later: 'Mountains are the beginning and end of all natural scenery.' Their inhabitants found that the areas they lived and worked in were suddenly seen as charming and romantic.

Love of the wilderness can grow as lives are detached from it. With most of us now living in urban areas, mountains are a source of physical challenge and spiritual renewal, an escape from the pressures and ugliness of the city. Wildlife, once feared and eradicated, is now more likely to be photographed. And we are valuing wild places for their 'environmental services': in controlling climates, cleansing air and water, stabilising soil, and as havens for biodiversity.

I once spent a week in the Rwenzori Mountains in western Uganda, a range on the equator higher than the European Alps. We sweated our way through bamboo forests. An ancient swamp sucked my boots off my feet. We shivered in snow and climbed on old ice. We engaged two young men from the foothills as guides. They were convinced that we must have been paid to go to such a hostile place. We were there because it was wild . . . and sublime.

We now shaped our course northward, traversing a large tract of country, and at length landed on the confines of Loch Erocht [Loch Ericht] . . . This country must have made very rapid advances in civilization; it is not yet 60 years since it was noted as a nest of robbers and free-booters . . . prior to the year 1746, a regiment of soldiers was scarcely sufficient to have brought a thief from Ranoch, but the natives are now as docile and intelligent as any of their neighbours . . .

About three o'clock afternoon, we reached the top of a high hill on the south-east side of Loch-Erocht where we sat down to contemplate an extensive scene of the most savage wildness that the fancy can conceive; a scene which hardly one out of a hundred Scotsmen could even have imagined he should have seen in his own country, on the last week of July; indeed it looked much more like the last of January.

I had hitherto been able to count the wreaths of snow that were in my view, but as the upper stories of Ben-Arlenich came in sight, one half of its surface was yet adorned with the massy badges of winter that eternally load its shoulders; each gap was crammed brim full of it, 'by its own weight made stedfast and immoveable,' and nearly as hard as the rocks which here and there peeped from its surface . . .[8]

This is one of the most stupendous of those huge masses of deformity that stud the Grampian desert, and rises about 4,000 feet above the sea . . . the others which we saw around Loch Laggan [to the north-west] were in the same state and form. Westward, saving a deep chasm or two that led into the valley of Glencoe, the country was one waste uninhabitable moor . . . [The view to the south and east] was lost and bewildered amongst the vast range of hoary headed Alps . . . These, every time the fatigued eye wanders through them, remind one exactly of the billows of the ocean; such a prodigious extent of country is crouded with them, rising and swelling behind one another, and that which the eye fixeth on always appears the largest . . .

I never in my life partook of a dinner with more heart-felt satisfaction than on the bare turf on the summit of this hill . . . [We reached Dalnacardoch] at a late hour, weary and fatigued. We had, for the sake of the view, placed ourselves at dinner quite out of reach of any means of allaying our thirst, save what the whisky flask afforded, the frequency of our visits to which entirely disarranged the remarks, both sentimental and philosophical . . .[9]

Snow and Ice

Hogg mentions large quantities of snow on 'Ben-Arlenich', in July 1802. I thought there would be less snow in recent years, and wanted to check. The Cairngorms National Park Authority confirmed: 'It's pretty rare these days to see large expanses of late snow as he describes lying in July.' A 2001 Scottish Executive Central Research Unit report notes that the number of days with snow lying had decreased since the late 1970s by about twelve days per decade.[10]

A study published in 2010 concludes: 'snow, and also ice on hill lochs, prevailed more frequently and for longer duration on the Cairngorms in the 1700s, 1800s and early 1900s than since 1930'.[11] The study had analysed written reports from those times. The authors advised later:

---

[8] 'Ben-Arlenich' seems to have been Ben Alder, due to its location and prominence (it is the highest mountain between Loch Ericht and Glen Spean) though the name that Hogg uses does not match its Gaelic name, Beinn Eallair. Its height is 3,766 ft (1,148 m).
[9] Despite various references to alcohol on his travels, Hogg does not seem to have been a big drinker at this stage. He tells us, 'as long as I remained at my pastoral employment, I could not calculate on more than a bottle in the year at an average', and that shepherds would be found in the public houses perhaps just once or twice a year, when they 'tak a rouse wi' ane anither, an' wi' the lasses' (Hughes, *James Hogg*, p. 21).
[10] Harrison et al., *Climate Change*.
[11] Watson and Cameron, *Cool Britannia*, p. 28.

'The description by Mr Gilkison's great-great-grandfather would have been used by us for the book had we known of it, because it does fit well with descriptions by others in the hills.'

Hogg did not mention snow in the Loch A'an/Loch Avon area in his visit in August 1802 (perhaps because it was less impressive than he'd already seen at Ben Alder) but the above study includes a description by a visitor there in August 1836: 'every part of the mountains that did not exist of perpendicular rock appeared to be covered by snow', and he referred to 'fields of eternal snow'.[12] On my visit in August 2014, I saw just a few remnant patches of snow on some north- and east-facing slopes of Ben Macdui.

It is difficult to project future snow cover trends, these being affected by both temperature and precipitation, but ongoing losses are likely. Winter precipitation might be higher in Scotland in future decades, but less of it will fall as snow. By the 2080s there could be 40–60 per cent less winter snowfall in the Cairngorms and up to 80 per cent less in parts of the east. With warmer temperatures this would melt faster and would change the pattern of river flows.[13]

NORTH: MOUNTAINS AND MONSTERS

We now left our foot-path, and turning to the North-west, entered Glenaven by a pass, like all the other highland glens. At the mouth of it there is a linn, over which the water falls from a height of eighteen feet yet over which a number of salmon ascend into the glen; and a great many more are taken at the fall. It is by much the clearest and purest river, that I saw in all the highlands of Scotland.[14]

After entering the glen, we saw part of wood which disappeared as we advanced: we went a good way past the head of Loch-Aven, and consequently got a [goo]d general view of the whole glen; and, though I can scarcely tell why, I never saw a scene that I took more pleasure in contemplating.

Though destitute of the elegance of the scenery in Athol and Bredalbin; and even of the horrid grandeur of Glen-Nevis and Glen-Coe; it hath a gloomy sublimity peculiar to itself, the viewing of which fills the mind with still solemnity: and the stories with which my guide was constantly entertaining me, certainly helped to deepen these impressions on my mind: all of which went to confirm, that it was the continual haunt of different species of the genii, and other phaenomena; there the

---

[12] Watson and Cameron, *Cool Britannia*, p. 24.
[13] Projections from Land Use Consultants, *Assessment of the Impacts of Climate Change*.
[14] 'Glenaven' (or 'Glen-Aven') is now known as Glen A'an or Glen Avon; 'Loch-Aven' is Loch A'an or Loch Avon.

fairies revel undisturbed; and there the water horse is frequently seen by the solitary wanderer.

Although the belief in the existence of this being is firmly established in sundry places in the highlands and islands, yet they seem not at all agreed in their opinions to what class of beings he belongs: they all however agree, that he is [am]phibous; and that he hath the rare priviledge of turning himself into whatever shape he pleaseth with the greatest ease and dispatch: and that his intents toward the whole human race are evil and dangerous.

He told me likewise of a little deformed monster, whose head was larger than its whole body, which was sometimes seen on the tops of these mountains very early in the morning, of so banefull a nature, that it was certain death to come near it, or even to touch the ground where it had passed, unless the sun had first shone upon it.[15]

Figure 5 Loch A'an/Loch Avon; 'sublime solitude' and a haunt of the supernatural.

---

[15] Hogg describes this creature further in *The Queen's Wake*, Note IV, p. 378: 'a little ugly monster . . . appears to be no native of this world, but an occasional visitant, whose intentions are evil and dangerous . . . His head is twice as large as his whole body beside; and if any living creature cross the track over which he has passed before the sun shine upon it, certain death is the consequence. The head of that person or animal instantly begins to swell, grows to an immense size, and finally bursts.'

The Water Horse, the Taniwha and Other Beings

Hogg was not patronising his guide in his description of the water horse; fear of this creature was genuine and widespread. The uncertainty about its classification is hardly surprising, given its ability to change shape. The term 'kelpie' is sometimes used as a synonym, but some consider that the water horse is more likely to inhabit inland lochs while the kelpie lives in rivers or other turbulent waters. (The water horse is not to be confused with the seahorse, those enchanting little creatures that are so gentle and supportive of each other that, unique in the animal kingdom, it is the male that gets pregnant and gives birth to their young.)

The creature is usually described as appearing like a horse, but is able to adopt a human form (sometimes the hooves remain unchanged, though, providing a handy clue to its real identity). It can be seductive, tempting the traveller to disaster. Almost every large body of water in Scotland has a kelpie or similar story. (The water bull or cow, such as the one said to inhabit St Mary's Loch, had similar metamorphic abilities but tended to be less hostile.)

Writer and linguist John Leyden told of a visit to Loch Venachar, Stirling District in 1800. In the spring of that year 'the people of the vale had been a good deal alarmed by the appearance of that unaccountable being the water horse'.[16] On a previous appearance it had carried off fifteen children into the loch.

In the mid-1800s, tenants living near Loch na Beiste in the North-West Highlands were so concerned about the 'Beast' that inhabited it (and after which the loch was named) that they pressured the proprietor, Mr Bankes, to exterminate it. The pressure mounted after some prominent citizens had also seen the creature. An attempt was made to drain the lake, with a crew of men and a horse-driven pump, but this hit a technical hitch: 'it was forgotten that the burn which came into the loch brought a great deal more water into it than the pump and the pipes carried out' and after two years the loch level had not dropped.

As thwarted leaders have often done since, Bankes's next step was chemical warfare. Fourteen barrels of 'hot lime', imported from Skye, were poured into the deepest parts of the loch. But still there was no sign of the Beast.

Bankes's final assault was on an even more defenceless target: 'So angry was the laird at his failure to capture the kelpie that he was determined to avenge himself on something or someone' so he fined the tenants a pound a head. 'Unlike the kelpie they, poor wretches, could not escape him.'[17]

---

[16] Leyden, *Journal of a Tour*, p. 35.
[17] Story and quotations from MacKenzie, *Hundred Years*.

> Such water-dwelling creatures are not unique to Scotland. The bäckahäst in Scandinavia, the wihwin of Central America and the Australian bunyip all had similar aquatic and antisocial tendencies.
>
> In New Zealand, the taniwha were believed to have lived in rivers, deep water and caves. They were usually thought to look like huge reptiles but could change into other shapes and animals. According to Māori traditions, they could be terrifying creatures that would capture and eat people. But they were not always so bad, and were sometimes protectors of local iwi or tribes, saving people from drowning, or warning of the approach of enemies.
>
> Out of fear or gratitude, taniwha have often been greatly respected. In 2002 there were objections to the construction of part of a major road because this would destroy the lair of a local taniwha. Eventually the government transport authority Transit New Zealand agreed to re-route this section of highway.

After contemplating the rude scenery of Glen-Aven for some time, we returned by the way that we entered. It is a large track of country, appearing to be, at least, ten miles in length, and entirely unoccuppied . . .

It is certainly the most elevated Glen of the same extent in Scotland: the water of Loch-Aven lying at the amazing height of 1,700 feet above the level of the sea, yet the hills are high around it. The famous mountain of Cairngorm forms part of its northern boundary, and rises to the height of 2,370 feet above the level of Loch-Aven, so that it is second in height to very few of the mountains in Britain.[18]

GLENSHEE: DEPARTURES AND REMAINS

Mr Makintosh, the proprietor of these lands, is certainly one of the most whimsical charactars in existence, and the occurrences of his life are well worthy the attention of biographers, as they would altogether form a history, more diversified by incidents and reverses of fortune, than ever fell to be related in the life of one person. Besides, the deep concern that he took in the affairs of both church and state, law and gospel; would form a compleat memorial of the times during his long life. Coming home to Scotland from a long absence in foreign countries, and finding his land overstocked with people; he tore down their houses

---

[18] Loch A'an is at 2,377 ft (725 m) quite a lot higher than Hogg realised. Cairn Gorm, to the north-west of the loch, is 4,085 ft (1,245 m) above sea level, the sixth highest mountain in Britain. Ben Macdui, to the south-west, is the second highest at 4,295 ft (1,309 m). All of the fifty-six highest mountains in Britain are in Scotland.

and chased them all away: but their curses had fallen heavy on him, for he never hath had the power to let it since.[19]

[In Kirkmichael in the district of Glenshee] . . . there is a chapel of ease here, where the parson is obliged to preach once every three weeks or so.[20] On entering this church, as they called it, I was struck with the barbarous appearance that it exhibited . . . as many of the inhabitants claimed the particular priviledge of being buried in the church, and the soil being of a loose gravel, the floor was become literally paved with human bones. Sculls, chaps, rumples, and shanks that had once pertained to gigantic highlanders were lying thick and threefold; and the ends of many of them were gnawed off by the shepherds's dog's for want of better employment while their masters were hearing sermon.

Clearances and Emigration

Hogg was seeing some signs of the Highland Clearances on this trip, a dreadful period of Scottish history which had been under way since the mid-1700s and would intensify in the early 1800s. But clearances had 'started earlier in the south of the country, lasted for longer and displaced more people . . . by being gradual in comparison to what happened further north the Lowland Clearances are recalled with far less emotion'.[21]

The process involved increasing sheep numbers, but with fewer farmers. Tenants in the south often had short leases which were easy to terminate, and landowners might seek to combine a number of these into a larger farm. Hogg and his parents would soon be victims of this, and he seems to have accepted it. But occupancy in the Highlands had often existed for generations and would not be surrendered so easily.

It is impossible to know how many were cleared. Thousands were moved to coastal settlements first, and often they emigrated when these became untenable. Emigration from the Highlands and Islands has been

---

[19] There is a record of thirty-five families being evicted from this area around 1790. Robert Mackintosh, the proprietor referred to, had a bumpy career in business, law and politics. Known as Mackintosh of Ashintully, his strange temperament ('whimsical' apparently means eccentric and unpredictable here) seems to have contributed to his fluctuating fortunes. As his fortunes varied, his family's land here was lost, regained, then lost again soon after his death in 1805. His nephew later wrote a biography of sorts, being a 'memorial of a Relative remarkable for his superior talents and his unfruitful application of them'.

[20] A chapel of ease was built for the convenience of parishioners living a long way from the parish church, and was not used every Sunday. In a later description, Hogg says the floor was paved with bones and 'hundreds of human teeth'.

[21] Oliver, *History of Scotland*, p. 363.

estimated at 70,000 up to 1800, with a similar number again up to 1860.[22] And while emigration from the Lowlands was usually in pursuit of better living standards, in the Highlands it was driven by desperation or compulsion.

Hogg was hoping to find farmland in the Highlands that he could lease cheaply. But he must have known that unoccupied areas did not exist then, and if he arranged to lease occupied land, some residents might have to be shifted. Habitually, he would side with the underdog: the powerless and the dispossessed. But he seems to have seen farm improvement and human resettlement as inevitable.

He opposed emigration as a solution though. He saw that 'in every district already stocked with sheep . . . the people have been by degrees expelled, and America hath been the resort and grave of too too many of them'. He referred to 'tribes and families annually vomited out by their own native inhospitable shores, and forced to seek for a more certain means of subsistence in the western world'. Instead, he saw a thriving Scottish wool industry as the best hope of livelihood for those displaced.

Hogg returned to Ettrick on 17 August 1802, just under a month after he had left. His farming future was still uncertain, but he would be delighted to see some of his letters in *The Scots Magazine* later that year.

NOTES ON MY JOURNEY – CENTRAL HIGHLANDS AND CAIRNGORMS NATIONAL PARK

The start of my Highland travel was inauspicious. I had flown from Auckland to Hong Kong, to London, to Edinburgh, in little more than a day. I'd hurtled through the lower stratosphere at over 500 mph, through a dozen time zones. And my contribution to the success of this incredible feat was to sit and do nothing; to eat, drink, sleep and to stay strapped into an unforgiving seat.

My lower back hated me for this. I stumbled into my Edinburgh backpackers' hostel at midnight, grimacing and barely able to walk. I was despairing about the effect this might have on my journeys, before they had even started. Would I have to abandon the walks and go home early?

---

[22] Undiscovered Scotland, < http://www.undiscoveredscotland.co.uk/> (last accessed 31 January 2016). The BBC gives a much higher figure for total departures: 'During the period of the Highland Clearances more than half a million people left the Highlands in search of a life elsewhere' ('The Highland Clearances', <http://www.bbc.co.uk/scotland/education/as/clearances/textonly_eng/1821.shtml>, last accessed 15 September 2015). Eric Richards is more constrained: the number of Highlanders directly cleared off the land 'is not known but must have entailed several tens of thousands' (Richards, *Highland Clearances*, p. 323).

I fell out of bed mid-morning, got dressed, but couldn't reach down to pull on my socks. A shop window across the road offered massage, physiotherapy and acupuncture. I shuffled across. The physiotherapist, it seems, had practised on the Scottish rugby team. I should be easy after them, I thought. I lay down, and she found a number of ways to increase my agony. Then, quite suddenly, it faded.

She asked: 'Are you really thinking of carrying heavy loads on your back, and sleeping on rocks? And running a half marathon?'

'Yes. I hope so.'

'Are you going to mention me in your book?' she asked.

I said: 'Maybe. If you could give me a massage each night.'

She told me: 'Your back's fine now. But you're mad.'

I headed north.

MOUNTAINS AND GENES

Early in his journey, Hogg wrote of his love of the hills, and his unhappiness, and even headaches, when he was away from them. And later, in the mountains at Loch A'an – even with their evil inhabitants and danger behind every corner – he wrote of his love for this area. And here was a revelation for me.

Many of his descendants share his love of the hills. Bob, his grandson, was still climbing mountains in his seventies. My uncle started a mountain-guiding business in his sixties. He and my father made numerous first ascents. My father was President of the New Zealand Alpine Club, just before Sir Edmund Hillary.

My own efforts are modest, but the love has been there from the start. I have been lucky to climb the Matterhorn and some other wonderful peaks, and my favourite in New Zealand: Mount Aspiring/Tititea. I have only once lived in a flat place, in Ontario for a few years, and escaped to the Rockies, and sometimes into a snow cave, when I could. My cousins are similarly smitten. Is this nurture or is it in the blood?

A friend grew up with a passion for long-distance running. As an adult, she discovered she'd been adopted at birth, and went to a gathering of her extended birth family. And as she looked around the hall, she found it was full of long-distance runners. She had always thought that the love of running had been her own choice. But perhaps, she realised now, the decision was made before she was born.

Hogg describes his delight when he ate on the summit. It's a simple pleasure I know well. The climb, the final push to the top, then a rest. With only the sky above. The view and the break have been earned. Everything you see is yours. For a while, you are invincible. A simple sandwich is a banquet, a drink of water is as sweet as wine . . . If such joy is partly inherited from him then I and his other descendants must give thanks for this.

LOST IN LOCH A'AN

I was looking forward to visiting Loch A'an; clearly it had impressed Hogg. A decade after his visit, he wrote:

> Glen-Avin exceeds them all in what may be termed stern and solemn grandeur. It is indeed a sublime solitude, in which the principal feature is deformity ... such a scene as man has rarely looked upon. I spent a summer day in visiting it ... My mind, during the whole day, experienced the same sort of sensation as if I had been in a dream ... I did not wonder at the superstition of the neighbouring inhabitants, who believe it to be the summer haunt of innumerable tribes of fairies, and many other spirits, some of whom seem to be the most fantastic, and to behave in the most eccentric manner, of any I ever before heard of.[23]

The trip I'd looked forward to would not go smoothly, however. The plan was to walk in to the loch from Tomintoul and back again – Hogg had done this on horseback – which I assumed was an easy overnight trip. I thought about buying a map. Then I saw a leaflet in a shop that included one, though it said 'Not suitable for Route Finding'. But the leaflet also said 'FREE'. I smiled, I thanked anyone who was listening, and tucked it into my pocket. There, I'd saved £3. I left in the early evening with my tent and some snacks, and camped by the river.

On my way up Glen A'an next morning I had a Very Good Idea. A friend I'd hoped to see would be travelling by car through Aviemore in a couple of days. Perhaps I could continue west, beyond the loch – though my map gave no clues as to a route – and meet her there. I'd camp an extra night along the way, and ration my food. I'll be fine, I decided, I'll just eat more when I finish the trip to catch up. Unusually for me, I had told no one where I was going or when I was coming out, so no one would notice a change of plans.

I reached the loch as light was fading. It had been a longer trip than I'd expected. Some final sunbeams slipped through big lumpy clouds. I watched them flicker and die. The greens and mauves on the hills around me grew dull. The loch glistened and greyed and matched the sky. Not a sound. Anywhere. The area was beautiful and sublime beyond words. I wanted to sit and watch it change until the last light was gone.

But there were things I needed to worry about. The map was hopeless – even large streams that I thought would be landmarks were not shown. (I'd resorted to using my Scotland road map now. The loch was about the size of a question mark.) No one knew where I was or where I was going, and I wasn't

---

[23] Hogg, *The Queen's Wake*, Note V, pp. 377–8.

so sure myself. It had been hot, my water was gone, and I'd been drinking from sources I didn't know were safe (if they weren't, I might know soon). I'd almost finished my food (I ate my sole bread roll that night, leaving half a macaroon and three cherry tomatoes for tomorrow). I'd broken a pole in my beloved tent, and it might not withstand a stiff breeze. I'd nearly stood on an adder (*Vipera berus*, I decided) and, coming from snake-free New Zealand, I know little about them. They are venomous, I knew, but do they bite to kill, and do they like exploring tents at night? And then there was the water horse, and other unknown beings.

I watched the night from the door of my tent. The moon had been full a few nights before; a little deflated, it struggled over the tops and shone through some patchy mist. The hills across the loch were softly lit, almost incandescent; they seemed to beckon. The water sparkled and lapped sporadically onto the beach, a couple of footsteps away. And I knew that if ever I was to believe in a kelpie, it'd be here. Certainly, in 1802, I would have . . .

The next morning was soft and gentle. I had slept well. The mist remained but would soon break up. Loch A'an was quiet and calm. I had to get into it.

Hogg had said of this area:

> there is no human habitation upon it; but the whole of that extensive glen lying waste for three quarters of the year. Let any man combine all these idea's at once, [he was including the area's supernatural and evil inhabitants here] and look round him at the wild, black, dismal-looking scenery and laugh if he can.

I was alone, and it would've seemed strange to try laughing. But as I prepared for my early morning swim, I stood on the beach and peeled off the clothes I had slept in. As was my custom on cold nights now, without a sleeping bag, I had worn my whole wardrobe. My puffer jacket came off first, number 1. Then a light sweater, number 2. Then a series of T-shirts: a long-sleeved blue one, number 3; a black one that I had won in a fun run, 4: a grey one I'd found, number 5; a once-white one with a logo was 6; and then number 7, an almost-new green one (I'd been gathering T-shirts in the interests of warmer slumbers).

The pile of my cast-offs grew. A cloud of female midges sensed an opportunity. Next, my khaki over-trousers came off, then my black shorts, and my beloved green polyprop long johns. And last, the pièce de résistance: my legs had been cold for several nights and I'd finally found a solution – one more T-shirt, red-and-grey striped, pulled on upside down with my feet through the armholes. Now, could anyone watch me get ready to swim – removing layers like a Russian doll, slapping in vain at invisible carnivores, leaping clumsily into the water to escape from them and confront who knows what – and not be just slightly amused?

I floated awhile. Naked, alone, loving where I was, delaying the midges, wondering why I was wherever I was, surveying the pile of my crumpled belongings on the beach, and I laughed. Even alone, I had to. And James, I think you would too.

I got brave enough to put my head under. Furtive glances to either side, and behind me. The water was cool and impossibly clear. But nothing else moved, above or below the surface. Out again, and I dried myself on my mountain towel, the size of a little handkerchief. Cleaner, pinker and dressed again, though minus some of my layers, I sat on the beach to relax.

And then I saw footprints. Round, five-toed ones, in the sand at the edge of the loch. Each was about 2½ in. (over 6 cm) wide. I was sure they hadn't been there last night. Too small and too many toes for a water horse, I thought . . . but could that creature change its size as well as its shape? The tracks showed that their owner had travelled 5 or 6 yards (about 5 m) beside the loch. Then they turned right, and disappeared into the water. There was no sign of a reappearance. That would rule out, I decided, a dog or wild cat. I was baffled, and could think of nothing that matched. I wondered if its head was bigger than its body.

I took photos of the prints and started walking west, in the general direction of Aviemore. I climbed a few minutes and found a rock to sit on, now warmed by the sun. The beaches, coarse pink granite and silica I think, were pure gold from this height. The greens and mauves were back. The silence was stunning. I ate my half macaroon. And right then, on that slope, there was nowhere else in the world I would rather have been.

I walked on. Hogg never mentioned midges on his journeys. I wondered why. Bonny Prince Charlie battled with them on his escape from Culloden, so they've been here a long time. Maybe shepherds just got over them. After a while, maybe I would too.

I found an easy saddle and crossed into the head of Strath Nethy. I met a young German man, the first person I'd seen in a day or so. He was going west too. It was mid-morning and he offered me whisky from a hip flask. I liked him already. But he was struggling: with route-finding, a big backpack, with blisters and a lack of food. It was clear we should travel together.

And so we did and nine hours later, at the end of a hot and hungry but happy day, we were enjoying cold beer and the biggest pizzas we could find in Aviemore. It had been a great walk from Tomintoul. I recommend it. But remember to take food and a map.

TWO POSTSCRIPTS

1. I wrote to the Cairngorms National Park Authority about the strange footprints. The answer came back:

   Thank you for passing on your photograph. After studying this and your description of the tracks (the way they moved parallel to the water and then disappeared into the loch) we are certain that these are

Figure 6 Loch A'an/Loch Avon. Dodging monsters and midges.

prints of an otter. There are records for otter at Loch Avon and they are known to occur at high altitudes.

And the Scottish Wildlife Trust website told me the otter (*Lutra lutra*) is classified as near-threatened, is one of Scotland's top predators, and has droppings with a pleasant scent, reminiscent of jasmine tea. I wished I'd stayed awake to meet it.

2. And a message from Germany, the nicest reference I ever had:

Hi Bruce!
   Billions of people live in this beautiful world, and millions of them travel around the globe . . . when I was in trouble of my motivation and energy, I found the best partner that I could wish for a situation like that = you Bruce!!!
   Your art of managing things and your inspiring stories about 1802 pushed me up to finish my own dream and will at this journey . . . I was a real lucky man that day . . . Cheers A

4 Western Highlands and Islands (1803): Strange and wonderful views

NORTH BY NORTH-WEST

On the 27th of May, I again dressed myself in black; put one shirt and two neck-cloths in my pocket; took a staff in my hand, and a shepherds plaid about me; and left Ettrick on foot, with a view of traversing the West highlands, at least as far as the Isle of Sky.

Hogg's mission, to find a sheep farm to lease, was the same as the previous year but more urgent. The Ettrickhouse lease had expired now, and he and his elderly parents would soon be homeless. He was also keen to 'investigate the different modes of farming and rural oeconomy existing in some of the most remote Highland countries'; perhaps this goal would make his venture sound more attractive to a reader, and less desperate. His journey would take him through Stirling, Inveraray and Fort William to Loch Broom, then by sea and land through the Hebrides.[1] In any case, he seems happy to be on the road and travelling light.

The Trossachs (May 1803):

The air was unusually still and dark; not a breath moved the leaves that hung floating over the impending precipieces of the trossacks, nor caused one dark furl on the smoothe glassy surface of the winding Loch-Katrine. Every species of the winged creation, that frequent the woods and mountains of Caledonia, were here joined ... every one sung his own song, from the small whistle of the wren, to the solemn notes of the cuckoo, sounded on E. and C. a double octave lower: and from the sprightly pipe of the thrush and blackbird, to the rough harp of the pye and raven. And that the anthem might be compleat, the imperial eagle hovered like a black mote in the skirts of the mist, at whose triumphant yell all the woodland choristers were for some seconds mute; and

---

[1] He barely mentions Stirling in his reports. He might have been more interested if he had known that, two centuries later, the James Hogg Society and much research into his life and works would be based here.

like menials in the presence of their lord, begun one after another with seeming fear and caution . . .

I fell into a sound sleep, out of which I was at length awaked by a heidous, yelling noise. I listened for some time before I ventured to look up; and on throwing the plaid off my face, what was it but four huge eagles, hovering over me, in a circle, at a short distance . . . I desired them to keep at a due distance . . . I was not yet dead, which if I had been, I saw they were resolved that I should not long remain a nuissance amongst the rocks of Glenfallach.[2]

Countries and Prejudice

Hogg talks often of 'countries' on his journeys, which were just parts of Scotland. He says in the Highlands 'the boundaries of a country are invariably marked out by the skirts of the visible horizon, as viewed from the bottom of the valley; all beyond that, is denominated another country'. The differences between adjoining countries at the time, in terms of culture and identity, could be as great as those between countries in Europe today. The distrust of those living over the boundary was often profound.

For travellers in the Highlands from the south, the sense of foreignness could be greater still. H. G. Graham describes the infrequent English visitor, even after the mid-eighteenth century, who found:

> regions where the inhabitants spoke an uncouth dialect, were dressed in rags, lived in hovels, and fed on grain, with which he fed his horses . . . [he then] wrote down his adventures as a modern [1901] explorer pens his experiences in Darkest Africa.[3]

Highland tours had been made by some significant writers before Hogg, including Daniel Defoe in the early eighteenth century, Thomas Pennant in 1769 and 1772, and Samuel Johnson and James Boswell in 1773.

Defoe came as an English spy in 1706, to assess the mood for a union; in time he would say that commitments to Scotland, 'lustily promis'd' before the Union, were not kept. A book that he wrote on a later trip sought to 'normalise' Scotland and break down the prejudices of English readers.[4] Pennant was famed for his knowledge and detailed

---

[2] These would be either golden eagles (*Aquila chrysaetos*), with wingspans up to 7 ft 8 in. (2.34 m) or white-tailed sea eagles (*Haliaeetus albicilla*), with wingspans up to 8 ft (2.45 m). Neither is considered overly raucous today; the golden eagle's call is described as 'weak, high and shrill' while the white-tailed species is a bit more vocal, 'a mixture of a bark and a yelp'.

[3] Graham, *Social Life of Scotland*, p. 2.

[4] Daniel Defoe, *A tour thro' the whole island of Great Britain, divided into circuits or journies* (1724–7). Defoe wrote more than 500 books or other publications, including *Robinson Crusoe*.

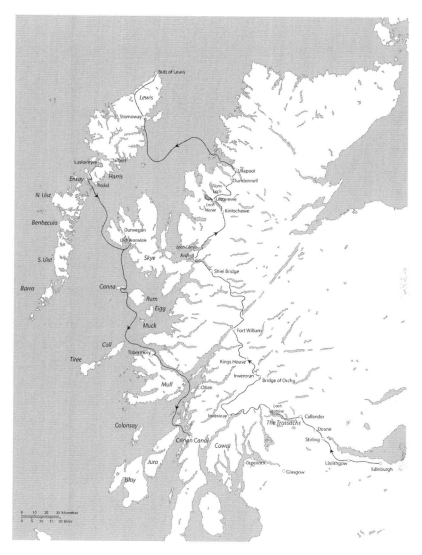

Figure 7 James Hogg's solo journey, May to (probably) August 1803. (Source: Revised from originals in de Groot, *Highland Journeys*.)

observations – on the economy, natural history and customs. Johnson had come to study 'primitive life' but felt he'd arrived too late; the bearing of arms and wearing of plaid had been banned, and customs he'd hoped to see were disintegrating. Boswell had come to study Scotland and Johnson. (William and Dorothy Wordsworth also made a tour, along with S. T. Coleridge for a while, in 1803; in their writing later, they would aim to romanticise Scotland.)

> Johnson saw that land which was 'intersected by many ridges of mountains, naturally divides its inhabitants into petty nations, which are made by a thousand causes enemies to each other', and that every Highlander could 'talk of his ancestors, and recount the outrages which they suffered from the wicked inhabitants of the next valley'. And while we most often read about southerners' fear of the north, the most savage clans, he was told in the Islands, were 'those that live next the Lowlands'. Prejudice flowed freely in every direction.
> Historian David Allan said that books written by Pennant, Johnson and Boswell were:
>
>> deliberate attempts ... to educate their English readers about Scotland. The intention was usually to instil a genuine curiosity and a profound sympathy for their fellow Britons, in marked contrast to the prevailing English ignorance and hostility to the people of Scotland.[5]
>
> Hogg was aware of these travellers' books but claimed not to wish to emulate them: 'I hate to write about that which everybody else writes about.' He had to travel very frugally; while other travellers might have interpreters and horses, Hogg was usually on foot, alone, and often frustrated by his lack of Gaelic. Some of his views on the cultures he saw might seem judgemental and even quite bizarre, but we all see the world through our own lenses. He wrote about what he saw, and not what he came to see.

In this journey, Hogg gives us glimpses of social situations he is far from comfortable in.

Ben Vorlich, his cousin's residence (May 1803):

The family consisted of eleven in whole that night, and indeed we were curiously lodged. They were but lately come to that place, and had got no furniture to it ... We slept on the same floor with four or five cows, and as many dogs: the hens being preferred to the joists above us.

During the night, the cattle broke loose ... which terrified me exceedingly, there being no rampart nor partition to guard us from their inroads. At length, I heard by the growling of the dogs, that they too were growing jealous of them ...they immediately attacked their

---

[5] Allan, *Making British Culture*, p. 231. The key books referred to were by Thomas Pennant, *A Tour in Scotland 1769* and *A Tour in Scotland and Voyage to the Hebrides 1772*; by Samuel Johnson, *A Journey to the Western Islands of Scotland*; and by James Boswell, *A Journal of a Tour to the Hebrides*.

horned adversaries with great spirit and vociferation, obliging them to make a sudden retreat to their stalls: and so proud were the staunch currs of this victory, gained in defence of their masters, that they kept them at bay during the rest of the night: had it not been for this experiment, they could scarcely have missed tramping the guts out of some of the children, who were lying scattered on the floor.

Add to all this confusion, that there was an old woman taken very ill before day: we were afraid of immediate death ... the other shepherd, manifested great concern, as not knowing how it was possible to get her to a christian burial-place ... mark my company here, in this hovel. I was in the midst of dying wives; crying children; pushing cows, and fighting dogs: and the very next day, at the same hour, in the same robes, same body, same spirit, I was in the splendid dining room in the Castle of Inveraray, surrounded by dukes! lords! ladies! silver, silk, gold, pictures, powdered lacquies, and the devil knows what! O! lord lord Mr Scott! thou wilt put me stark mad some day.

Inveraray Castle (June 1803):[6]

[Col. Campbell] led me through a number of the gayest apartments, and at length told me he was going to introduce me to Lady Charlotte. 'By no means' said I 'for Heaven's sake. I would be extremely glad could I see her at a little distance, but you need never think that I will go in amongst them' ... the idea of being introduced to a lady, of whom I had heard so much, as a paragon of beauty, elegance, and refined taste; and who had been the grace and envy of courts, raised in my breast such a flutter ...

I saw that, by her assumed vivacity, she was endeavouring to make me quite easy; but it was impossible. I was struck with a sense of my inferiority, and was quite bambouzled. I would never have known that I was so ill, had there not unluckily been a mirror placed up by my lug. Not knowing very well where to look, I looked into it. Had you seen the figure that I made, you would have behaved just as I did. My upper lip was curled up; my jaws were fallen down; my cheeks were all drawn up about my eyes, which made the latter appear very little; my face was extraordinarily red, and my nose seemed a weight on it. On being catched in this dilemma, I really could not contain myself but burst out a laughing ...

Now you will be expecting that I would still be in a worse condition when first introduced to his Grace the duke, and indeed I was within a

---

[6] A castle had stood here by Loch Fyne since the 1400s, but this one was built in the 1700s and completed, after forty-three years, in 1789. 'His Grace the Duke' refers to John Campbell, fifth Duke of Argyll and chief of Clan Campbell. He had fought against the Jacobites (including in the Battle of Culloden), had been an MP and was promoted to Field Marshall a few years before Hogg's visit; he was now almost eighty. Lady Charlotte was his daughter, Colonel Campbell his son-in-law and Mr Henderson his Superintendent of 'rural affairs'.

little of being very ill, but got better off than could have been expected: this plaguy bluntness! will I never get rid of it? . . .

He at length desired me to amuse myself with these books and charts, for that he must go and dress. I had not sat long until Col. Campbell entered, who in a little time left me also on the same pretence, that of dressing for dinner. I said he was well enough dressed; it was a silly thing that they could not put on cloathes in the morning that would serve them during the day. He swore that would never do and went his way laughing.

It was not long until the duke rejoined me all clad in black, as indeed all the gentlemen were who sat at table. I was always in the utmost perplexity as not knowing servants from masters; there were such numbers of them, and so superbly dressed, that I daresay I made my best bow to several of them. I remember in particular, of having newly taken my seat at dinner, and observing one behind me, I thought he was a gentleman wanting a seat and offered him mine . . .

On our return, his grace asked me several things, and amongst others, what I thought of Mr. Henderson? I said I did not rightly understand him; he was surely the worse of drink. That was impossible, he said, at this time of the day: 'and besides' said he, 'I conversed with him since your return; he is perfectly sober. You *surely* must be mistaken of Mr Henderson.' 'I certainly am mistaken my lord' said I; 'for I look on him as the worst specimen of your Grace's taste that I have seen about all Inveraray.' Perhaps I said too much; but I could not help telling my mind.

On Class and Confidence

Hogg made clear his awkwardness in genteel society at the time, and at Inveraray Castle he was far from his comfort zone. He describes his 'principal blunders and embarrassments; for every hour during the time that I remained there was marked by one or other' and 'I was truly ashamed of the attention paid to me.' There is a touch of faux naïf in his description, but one suspects he was happier in the hills, or even on the floor with the animals in Ben Vorlich.

His lack of confidence in such situations perhaps seems surprising. This is the young man who had heard of Robert Burns just six years earlier and, though he could hardly write, resolved straight away to follow in those big footsteps. His confidence shows in his love of debating and his refusal to change his poetry, even when others thought he should. He was positive and resilient, with a healthy ego.

His appearance was surely not as bad as he thought. He was described as:

> an attractive figure at the age of thirty-one, an athlete . . . with a well-proportioned figure and of neat appearance. His long auburn

hair was tied neatly behind with a black ribbon . . . notably clean
and well-dressed for his rank in life . . . In all there was a 'bright-
ness of . . . personal appearance' about Hogg that was extremely
attractive and engaging.[7]

But class distinctions ran deep in Scotland in 1803. Land owners were the
upper class, based more on ancestry than achievement. The middle classes
were mainly self-made men who lived in towns; they did not usually see
themselves as a group but took opportunities where they found them. And
below them 'little was seen of men from the humblest walks of life, the
landless agricultural worker, the unskilled labourer'.[8] Hogg was landless,
and would soon be losing his home and livelihood.

Yet often he seems to fit into places he felt he didn't belong, due to his
humour, stories and intellect. He must have known that few people then,
in that stratified society, would ever have been invited to sleep in a hovel
one night and a castle the next.

It is likely that his hosts in the castle felt more comfortable with Hogg
than he did with them. There is no suggestion that he was scorned or
made unwelcome here. Quite the opposite: when he described his simple
dining preferences, some of the gentlemen decided to follow his example.
Any sense of inadequacy seems to have been in his own mind. But even
here, among those he considered his superiors, he could not rein in his
fearless frankness: 'I could not help telling my mind.'

West Highlands (June 1803):

It is upwards of twenty miles from the Kings house to Fort-William
across the hills, and the road being extremely rough my feet were
very much bruised. The track is wild and mountainous . . .[9] I went to
the house of Mr Thomas Gillespie, who left our south country about
20 years ago . . . he being the first who introduced the improved breed
of Scottish sheep into that district, his advantages were numerous . . .

[Inverlochy Castle] is a large square building, with four propor-
tionally large turrets, one at each corner, but that looking toward the
North-West is much the largest;[10] but Mr. Stuart the tenant at Inverlo-
chy, with whom I dined one day and breakfasted another, had four most

---

[7] Hughes, *James Hogg*, p. 46.
[8] Smout, *History of the Scottish People*, p. 364.
[9] This distance is about 25 miles, over 38 km. But Hogg had already walked from Inveroran that morning, so his total distance that day was 35 miles, about 56 km. The track is still quite rough and steep today, and the bruising is understandable.
[10] Old Inverlochy Castle was built in the late thirteenth century. It is now in ruins, much as it was when Hogg visited, but is unusual in that it was never significantly altered since it was built.

Figure 8 Devil's Staircase, on Hogg's route from Kings House to Fort William. But not as bad as it sounds.

elegant daughters, whom I confess I admired much more than the four turrets of the castle . . .

The famous mountain of Ben-Nevis, the king of the Grampians, rises 4,380 feet above the level of the sea and hugs, in its uncouth bosom, huge masses of everlasting snow, and all that range, both to the east and west, is wild and savage beyond measure . . .[11]

Some of Lochiel's glens are beautifull sheep pastures, but the bulk of the hills are rough and ugly. There are a great many of the sheep not yet of a proper breed, and consequently not excellent . . .

While traversing the scenes, where the patient sufferings of the one party, and the cruelties of the other were so affectingly displayed, I could

---

[11] Ben Nevis (Beinn Nibheis) is now considered to be 4,409 ft (1,344 m) high. It was only in 1794 that this was confirmed as the highest summit in Scotland, pushing Ben Macdui into second place. The 'huge masses of everlasting snow' seem to have diminished, if indeed they were then everlasting. Snow patch expert Adam Watson notes in correspondence with the author: '[This] was certainly a period with greater cold and more snow than since 1930. You are right that all snow has gone from Ben Nevis and other hills in Scotland in several years, starting in 1933.' Hogg was 'uncommonly intent' on climbing this mountain but was thwarted by unsettled weather; I was likewise on my current visit, but had been luckier some years earlier.

not help being a bit of a Jacobite in my heart, and blessing myself that in those days I did not exist, or I had certainly been hanged.[12]

Shiel Bridge (June 1803):

I was greatly refreshed, and proceeding on my way, before it was quite dark I reached the inn. It is a large slated house, but quite out of repair, and the accommodations are intolerably bad ... I got the best bed, but it was extremely hard, and the clothes had not the smell of roses. It was also inhabited by a number of little insects common enough in such places, and no sooner had I made a lodgement in their heriditary domains than I was attacked by a thousand strong.

But what disturbed me much worse than all, I was awaked, during the night, by a whole band of highlanders, both male and female; who entered my room, and fell to drinking Whisky with great freedom. They had much the appearance of a parcel of vagabonds which they certainly were ... I had by good fortune used more precaution that night than usual, having put my watch, and all my money into my waistcoat, and hid it below my head: I also took my thorn-staff into the bed with me, thereby manifesting a suspicion that I had never shewed before.

I bore all this uproar with patience for nearly two hours in the middle of the night, until, either by accident or design, the candle was extinguished, when every one getting up a great stir commenced, and I heard one distinctly ransacking my coat, which was hanging upon a chair at a little distance from the bed. I cared not much for that, thinking that he could get nothing there, but not knowing where this might end, I sprung to my feet in the bed, laid hold of my thorn staff, and bellowed aloud for light. It was a good while ere this could be procured, and when it came, the company were all gone but three men, who were making ready to lye down in another bed in the same room ...

They were all gone before I got up next morning, and it was not until next night that I percieved I had lost a packet of six letters which I carried to as many gentlemen in Sutherland, and which prevented me effectually from making the tour of that large and little frequented county ... some one of the gang had certainly carried [the packet] off in expectation that it was something of more value.[13]

---

[12] The Jacobite rebellions effectively ended in 1746 after the Battle of Culloden, about twenty-four years before Hogg was born. They were supported by many in the Highlands. It was safe, and not uncommon, for Lowlanders to express support for the rebellions after they had ended. Hogg seems to develop even stronger Jacobite sentiments in later years, expressed in works such as *The Three Perils of Woman* and 'The Frazers in the Correi'.

[13] Iain Finlayson comments in *The Scots* (p. 34) that at that time 'Highlanders were, to Lowland eyes, light-handed with property not their own.' Likewise, Samuel Johnson had commented, 'Mountaineers [Highlanders] are thievish, because they are poor' (Johnson and Boswell, *Journey*, p. 64). This view perhaps explains Hogg's caution in sleeping with his valuables, which in this case was totally justified.

Ardhill to Loch Maree (June 1803):

> Among such a number of literary men, I could not miss getting a good deal of intelligence respecting the state of the countries in their respective parishes . . . I committed it wholly to my memory, where, setting it so effectually afloat on rum-punch, when I went to collect it, I could only fish out some insignificant particles . . .
>
> We met a most kind welcome from Barrisdale, whom we found in the midst of a great room-full of ladies . . . the drinking was renewed on our entering, which had before been going to fall into disuse, and we soon became remarkably merry; screwed up the fiddles and raised a considerable dance. It was here that I first ventured to sing my song of Donald Macdonald, which hath since become so popular; and although afraid to venture it, I could not forbear, it was so appropriate . . . It was so highly applauded here, that I sung it very often during the rest of my journey.[14]

With no sign of the ferry to cross Loch Carron he tried for a ride on another boat. He offered its crew triple freight but, not wishing to offend the regular ferryman, they rowed off and 'left me standing on the rocks, where I was obliged to bellow and wave my hat'. The ferryman finally came to collect him, and 'charged sixpence and *a dram of whisky*'.

Hogg was often frustrated by his lack of Gaelic for getting directions or buying food, even to the point of violence on one occasion. But it quickly passed.

Around Letterewe, on Loch Maree:

> It was this young lady [Miss Downie] who first inspired me with the resolution of visiting the remote country of the Lewis, by describing it to me, as the scene of the most original and hereditary modes and customs, that was any where to be met with in the British Isles; and I repented an hundred times that I ever parted company with her.[15]

The young lady's suggestion, along with the loss of the letters of introduction for Sutherland, led to his decision to travel to Lewis and Harris. He does not mention farming opportunities in the Outer Hebrides here, just an interest in modes and customs. But these must have been on his mind, as an affordable farm on the mainland was proving elusive.

From Letterewe they were persuaded to travel by boat on Loch Maree to Ardlair, rowing into a head wind without success, before abandoning the boat to continue by land.

---

[14] After a year of peace, war had just broken out again (in May 1803) between Britain and France under Napoleon, which would help to boost the song's popularity.

[15] Miss Downie, Hogg tells us, had 'a genteel education' and 'an extensive knowledge of the world, of which she had seen a considerable part for one of her age and sex'.

We were now much worse than if we had set off on foot from Letterewe: however, taking two men with us as guides, *we set a stout heart to a strait brae*, and explored a crooked way among'st the rocks; continuing for a long space to climb the hill in quite a contrary direction to the place where we were bound. Our guides then led us over rocks and precipieces, which on looking at I thought a goat could not have kept its feet . . .

I was in the greatest distress on account of the lady: the wind which was grown extremely rough, took such impression on her cloathes that I was really apprehensive . . . It was however a scene worthy of these regions to see a lady of most delicate form, elegantly dressed in such a situation, climbing over the dizzy precipieces in a retrograde direction . . . What would most of your Edin[burgh] ladies have done here my dear sir?

Loch Maree to Fionn Loch and Little Loch Broom:

To enumerate particularly the different appearances of each precipice that interlards this truly terrific scene is impossible . . . every feature of a most awful deformity, conveying to the attentive spectator ideas of horror which could scarcely be excelled by a glimpse of hell itself . . .

At a great distance he [a guide] showed me a large perpendicular rock, with the entrance to a cavern near the bottom. In this dismal hole, in the midst of this huge wilderness, wonderful to relate, a widow and her family hath resided many years![16] When she first took possession of this dreary abode her youngest son was a sucking infant. Yet she was obliged to cross the mountains once a week to seek milk and other articles of food; while owing to their being so inaccessible she was unable to carry her child along with her, and was obliged to put out the fire and leave him to shift for himself. He had by such lodging and treatment acquired a weakness in his back, and it was feared he would never overcome it, as he still could not walk, but only creep, though I think they said he was six or seven years of age.

[The guide] told me that he was once passing that way with an English gentleman, on business in that country, and observing no smoke, he suspected the woman to be from home, so without mentioning anything of the matter to his companion he led him to take a view of the cavern. The gentleman was almost out of his wits when he saw a creature bearing such a resemblance to the human form, come crawling towards him from the interior of the cavern. Alas! my dear Sir, one half of the world knows little how the other half lives.

Hogg then related his guide's story of a woman who had died in childbirth in this remote area recently for lack of help, and added: 'Nor how they die. . . .'

---

[16] 'Wonderful' could have a more negative meaning then, closer to 'startling'.

Figure 9 Fionn Loch and cliffs, between Loch Maree and Little Loch Broom; the Great Wilderness.

Poverty and Justice

It was a common view at the time that the poor were poor due to their failings or follies; those needing charity were sinners in need of punishment. Economic prosperity, apparently, was the mark of the Lord's approval. And the poor were a threat to the better off.

Vagrancy was discouraged. 'Strong beggars and their bairns' – effectively, all the able-bodied poor between the ages of fourteen and seventy who were not mentally disabled – should be employed in 'common work'. Heritors (feudal landholders, with particular privileges and obligations) could take the children of beggars into unpaid service. Scotland had poorhouses, rather than workhouses, providing shelter just for the destitute and disabled.

Hogg describes poverty here as something that happens to other people. He had known hardship from a young age, though, and would again at various times in his life. His family had been 'turned out of doors without a farthing'. He'd worked since he was seven. He wrote of his childhood in his 'Memoir': 'I was often nearly exhausted with hunger and fatigue.' But being poor was acceptable then, so long as one endured it gracefully.

Responsibility for the 'worthy poor' varied, but generally was shared between kirk sessions and heritors. Later, from 1845, responsibility for poor relief was transferred to parish boards, which were allowed to raise a compulsory rate to fund this.

> Demand for assistance, before and after this change, always exceeded supply and especially when compounded by crop failures. In the absence of poor relief, the option of emigration or even living in a cave must often have seemed attractive.

The truth is, there are several low-country gentlemen getting into excellent bargains by their buying lands in that country . . . and I cannot help having a desperate ill-will at them on that score. I cannot endure to hear of a Highland chieftain selling his patrimonial property, the cause of which misfortune I always attribute to the goodness of his heart, and the liberality of his sentiments; unwilling to drive off the people who, have so long looked to him as their protector, yet whose system of farming cannot furnish them with the means of paying him one fourth, and in some situations not more than a tenth of the value of his land . . .

I anticipate with joy the approaching period when the stigmas of poverty and pride so liberally bestowed on the highlanders by our southern gentry will be as inapplicable to the inhabitants of that country as of any in the island.

Highland and Island Clearances

The Highland Clearances, the forced evictions of people and families from their traditional homes, were gathering momentum in 1803 but worse was to come. They had started after the Battle of Culloden in 1746, and continued until at least the mid-1800s. The motive was to change from mixed farming to more profitable sheep farming. Mixed farming had supported large tenant populations, which were growing rapidly. The 'improvements' required mass evictions. The commitment of many landlords to these showed their confidence in their right to rule.

Tenants left in various ways: some because there were better prospects overseas or elsewhere, some because rents were raised to impossible levels, and others were evicted violently. The changes led to the loss of a distinctive society, and left Scotland with some of the most sparsely populated land in Europe. One historian says that within a generation of Culloden they 'had begun to convert the Highlands from a working landscape into mere scenery'.[17]

Because the Clearances targeted mainly Gaelic and Roman Catholic populations (their name in Gaelic, *Fuadach nan Gàidheal*, means expulsion of the Gael), some have seen them as a form of 'ethnic cleansing' – a similarly cynical euphemism. For some Scots, this might have been true. An article in *The Scotsman* (26 July 1851) referred to the 'removal of a

---
[17] Moffat, *Sea Kingdoms*, p. 8.

diseased and damaged part of our population'. Surgeon Robert Knox said 'the race must be forced from the soil'. The driving force was always economic, but such attitudes might explain some of the brutal methods used.

Occupants relied on traditional rights, and hoped for the support of their chiefs and landlords as in the past. But the loyalty was not reciprocated; with private armies banned, the chiefs wanted money more than men. Tenants had few legal defences, and often no time to organise resistance. Landlords or their agents would sometimes give notice of eviction and, to speed the process and prevent resettlement, would burn their tenants' homes. In parts of the Hebrides, tenants demolished their own homes before this could be done, leaving with just a few possessions and the roof timbers; stone walls and thatch roofs could be replaced, but with so few trees left it was vital to save the timbers.

The situation they were leaving was often far from idyllic, but those evicted were unprepared for change. In many cases they were moved to coastal settlements which were totally unsuitable. In Badbea, in the northeast, conditions were said to be so harsh that while women worked they had to tether their children to prevent them being blown off clifftops.

Other occupants moved south, or to North America or Australasia. Most that emigrated were outstanding settlers; some went on to expel native people from these new homelands as harshly as they themselves had been removed.

Some of the worst evictions were on the huge estate of the Countess of Sutherland, where her husband and their factor, Patrick Sellar, removed between 6,000 and 10,000 tenants between 1807 and 1821. Homes were burnt as the occupants, some of them elderly or ill, struggled to leave. An advocate for these clearances said the habits and ideas of the tenants were 'quite incompatible with the customs of regular society and civilised life'. Years later, the mention of Sellar's name was said to cause women to panic and 'lose their reason'. Where protests occurred in the Highlands, though, these were often led by women.[18]

In the Outer Hebrides, Colonel John Gordon of Cluny evicted thousands of tenants and cleared some islands completely. At one stage his tenants were hunted down and forced onto ships to be taken to Canada, with no real provision made for them there. When he died he was thought to be the richest commoner in Scotland (with a fortune that included compensation for more than 1,300 slaves in Tobago when slavery was outlawed).

Not all landlords were so uncaring. Until 1815, most clearances were intended to relocate people, not to remove them entirely, as their labour was still needed. But the evil done by some will live long after them.

---

[18] Richards (*Highland Clearances*, p. 316) writes: 'women were especially prominent in the sporadic resistance to the Clearances, often leading the affray and confronting the law officers and the police ... the involvement of women was striking and recurrent'. Similar leadership is often seen in Pacific Island protests against logging of rainforests; because this affects families and food sources, women may feel the threats most powerfully.

As a southerner seeking a Highland farm, Hogg would be seen as part of the problem. He thought movement of people in Scotland was needed, 'whether the country were stocked with sheep or not, owing to the glens and islands being already overstocked, and the people being so prolific'. His hope was for improvement of the land and livestock, together with higher rents. He believed that 'men, sheep and fish are the great staple commodities', to be supported by the development of 'woollen manufactories'. These would deliver the Highlanders from poverty. Later, though, he was more scathing about the effects of Clearances.[19]

Vitally, he said disruption to the Highland way of life should be gentle:

> the scheme must certainly be prosecuted with leisure, caution, and tenderness, nor must we drive the people from their poor, but native huts and glens, until some other source of industry is opened to them, which, by persevering in, they may become more useful members of the commonwealth.

NOTES ON MY JOURNEYS – CENTRAL AND WESTERN HIGHLANDS

Ben Alder

Before heading north on the 1803 trail, I had some unfinished business. In 1802, Hogg had looked at Ben Alder from the top of a hill to the south of Loch Ericht, and had been impressed. This was his 'most savage wildness' and 'one of the most stupendous of those huge masses of deformity', topped by eternal snows. The Walk Highlands website says: 'Ben Alder is one of the great remote mountains of Scotland, set in the very heart of the Central Highlands.' In his 1988 guidebook, *Wainwright in Scotland*, the author said this 'must be considered out of bounds to all but supermen'.[20] No doubt the power of flight would be handy. But sitting at home on the other side of the world, I decided this was one to climb.

It's a long walk in from the train at Dalwhinnie. People who plan better could save time by taking a mountain bike, or even a canoe for the Loch Ericht section. I slept in a soggy tent, part way in to the mountain.

---

[19] He wrote in his 1823 novel, *The Three Perils of Woman*, for example: 'Is there human sorrow on record like this that winded up the devastation of the Highlands?' These are the words of a shepherd in his story, in the aftermath of the Battle of Culloden, who finds a mother and child 'stretched together in the arms of death, pale as the snow that surrounded them'. It is likely they are also the views of the Ettrick Shepherd on the Clearances.

[20] Ben Alder (Beinn Eallair) is 3,766 ft, or 1,148 m. Hogg probably viewed it from about 1,000 ft lower on the top of Beinn Mholach. (Walk Highlands, <http://www.walkhighlands.co.uk/cairngorms/ben-alder.shtml>, last accessed 19 February 2016; Wainwright, *Wainwright in Scotland*, p. 179.)

Figure 10 Beinn Eallair/Ben Alder, exactly 213 years after Hogg saw it; the eternal snows have shrunk.

The weather was clear the next morning. I set out, not too early, and reached the top at midday. It was the last week in July, precisely 213 years after Hogg had looked in awe at this peak. Its huge eternal snows had gone. This was expected, but it was still surprising. Some patches were big enough to slide on and play on, but that's all.

The Culra Bothy was in a perfect location for a night on my way out, but a sign said 'Closed – Asbestos'. I'd have to keep walking, and camp on the way. But ten minutes later, a deluge. It's no fun pitching a tent in heavy rain, so I plodded on. And on.

James, I know you had a long walk out to your lodgings, and were left with nothing but whisky to quench your thirst that night. Tough. But spare me a thought. I got to Dalwhinnie just before dark, cold and wet. The town was closed. It was still raining hard. I slept on a sturdy wooden bench at the railway station. For company through the night, there were occasional recorded messages on a public address system. I would've loved to share a whisky with someone.

Scotland's mountains: a view from down under

I was thinking about mountains. And about what was different in Scotland, compared with the ones I knew back home.

New Zealand's mountains are bigger. I just needed to say that. Our highest, Aoraki/Mount Cook, is 12,218 ft (3,724 m). It is much higher than Ben Nevis at 4,409 ft (1,344 m), and we have nineteen others over 10,000 ft. New Zealand, a little closer to the equator, has 3,000 glaciers while Scotland has none.

But does size matter? The southern mountains are high because the Indo-Australian tectonic plate hits the Pacific plate, forcing it up. They grow and erode fast. Even our highest mountain got shorter a few years ago, when the top fell off. Scotland is older and more stable, with ancient rocks. (Much of Scotland itself started off near the South Pole, in the Cambrian period.)

I should feel comfortable at Scotland's lower altitudes. Often, though, these mountains scare me. I try to compare them with alpine areas I know, and they don't fit. I need different skills. I get lost when I shouldn't.

The weather moves fast in the Highlands. I don't always see it coming. Landscapes change their shape. Tops and landmarks vanish magically in the mist. Valleys can go from green and gold to dark and cold in a minute. I have to stay on my toes, and make new plans when everything around me changes. Then, just as quickly, the sun comes out again.

There's another factor too. People have lived in Scotland for maybe 10,000 years. There is so much history here. Over the years, the hills have been soaked in blood. There have been wars and raids. Romance and murder. Settlements and evictions, farms and failures, deaths and new beginnings. Fairies played and plotted. Close your eyes and all of these can come back. I am excited and humbled by their presence.

Human settlement of New Zealand began much later, perhaps just 900 years ago. The mountains hold fewer secrets, or fewer human ones at least. People passed through them, but not many stayed. They came to search for jade/pounamu or gold, to explore, to climb or to hunt. If they died, it was usually by accident, falling off cliffs or swept away by rivers. But their ghosts were taken away too – the bodies were usually found and taken home.

The Scottish mountains feel bigger than the numbers suggest. Along with New Zealand's, they've bred some of the world's greatest climbers. They can be dangerous: a browse through Scottish mountain accident reports are a reminder that they are not to be taken lightly. And they are beautiful: there are few views as mouth-watering as an old trail through heathland, fading from pink to purple, to the distant tops; or rocky cliffs dropping straight to the Atlantic, with the thunder of waves and sounds of seabirds and the smell of the ocean; or the dazzling scene from a snow-plastered top in the Grampians on a clear winter's day.

I love the mountains in both countries. In both, they can frighten and kill. But more often they protect and nourish. We visit them and they change us. They teach us and feed us and help to protect species that arrived before we did. They inspire and help to define us.

Inveraray Castle

I was feeling a little underdressed when I set out to meet the thirteenth Duke of Argyll at Inveraray Castle. I'd been three weeks on the road. My only trousers

Figure 11 Inveraray Castle, hospitable and delightfully normal.

were mud-stained in obvious places, and I had ripped them when I fell on a rock (I'd been patching them from the inside with blister tape). My only clean shirt was a polyprop T-shirt. It was fine, but technically it was underwear. I knew I shouldn't meet a duke with my underwear showing. It was time for a makeover.

I ducked into a charity shop and picked up a clean white shirt and a nice pair of trousers for £4 (I would donate them back in a few hours). The trousers were a bit tight and the cuffs didn't quite reach my boots, but they would be OK. Feeling newly clean and confident, I strode out for the castle.

Clearly, the duke had a sense of humour. I had written: 'My ancestor visited in 1803. I'd love an opportunity to meet.' I was surprised to hear back from his Secretary: 'His Grace will be delighted to meet you.'

And so we met. I told him Hogg's story, of the embarrassments and blunt questions. Then I asked, 'He was just four generations before me and he met the fifth duke. But you're the thirteenth already. What happened?' I thought I'd found a family flaw – did they breed fast or die young? He told me: 'Sometimes the title moves sideways on a death, to a brother.' It was a good point.

I liked this place. Despite its size it felt more comfortable and real than other castles I'd been in. Here, only a little changed, were the rooms where Hogg had told the gentlemen how to dress and how to eat. Dear Lady Charlotte, whom he admired and was so shy of, is preserved in oils here forever.

But I'd feel uncomfortable with so many portraits of ancestors. Hundreds of years of dukes and earls would haunt me. Some had been beheaded, most had just died, but all would remind me of my mortality. And more important than that: I think I would feel I was being judged on a daily basis. Some of the ancestors achieved a lot, some had come to nothing. How would history judge me? Had I done enough today? Their eyes would be on me always. Could I ever relax?

None of which seemed to trouble the thirteenth duke, who was hospitable and interested in my project. He has interesting involvements of his own. He twice led Scotland to victory in the World Elephant Polo championships. He is the worldwide Chief of Clan Campbell. He is Master of the Household of Scotland. He has a young family and a big castle.

It was late afternoon now, and time to be going. I strolled back down to Loch Fyne. Some of the trees in the castle grounds were growing when Hogg was here. The duke was off to help with dinner, to play with the kids, and to entertain the in-laws who had come for a visit. It was all delightfully normal.

Figure 12 Inveraray Castle dining area, a site of major blunders and embarrassments. (Image used courtesy of Inveraray Castle.)

Overnight robbery

The Highlanders' reputation for violence and theft has faded since Hogg's time. I found nothing but courtesy and honesty. But his overnight robbery in the inn at Shiel Bridge would have been unsettling.

I was robbed in Tunisia once, in slightly similar circumstances. I had hitched in from Algeria, arriving in a seedy part of Tunis around midnight. I was lucky, I assumed, to find a room in a flimsy building by the market and was told I could pay in the morning. I slept in my sleeping bag with my money belt around my waist.

A couple of hours later I woke with a start. A light is on, but glowing dimly. Two men, one of them the owner, are crouched by my bed. I look round, blinking. Something strange is happening here.

My sleeping bag has been unzipped – this might surprise those who don't know my sleeping skills – and my money belt is open and empty. My passport, money and traveller's cheques are gone, as well as my camera and some things from my bag. *My passport!* (For the record, I don't sleep with my money belt on at home. Clearly I'd been feeling a tad insecure.)

I check the room quickly. No sign of these. 'Give me my things back!' I suggest as boldly as I can in French (we'd spoken in French earlier but they seem to have lost the ability now). I repeat this a dozen times, at increasing volume.

Then, as threateningly as someone with no cards to play can manage: 'If you do not give them back I will get the police.' Repeat a dozen times. Nothing.

I'm in a quandary, and they know it. I don't know what police look like here, let alone how to find them. I'd probably be gone an hour – long enough for them to take my things somewhere, then deny I'd ever been there. But I'm getting nowhere here. I've run out of credible threats. I step out into a dark, empty street.

In the distance I see two men. I blurt out, 'I've been robbed, please get the police.' They look confused. 'Mais nous sommes les policiers,' they tell me. They are off-duty and have been drinking. They draw their pistols and are keen to help. We surround the house.

Here is The Plan, as I understand it: they'll enter through the front. I – the one without guns – should block the rear door and move in from there. Presumably if the occupants come my way I should look menacing and chase them back towards the police with pistols.

We've arrived in time. The police pin them down. My passport and camera are still in the room. Cash and traveller's cheques are gone. I am happy to have my passport back. And delighted not to have been the focus of any friendly fire . . .

There was a sequel of course. Culprits and victim were marched awkwardly to the Commissariat de Police. The former were locked up and sworn at, and I worried about their treatment. 'I don't need them to go to jail,' I told the police.

'It's not your choice,' they said. 'And we need you to be in court on Tuesday. To tell the story.'

Damn. Four days. 'I'll need help,' I said. 'I'll need food and money until then.'

'We can't help,' I was told. 'But you must stay in Tunis.'

I waited for daylight, then walked to the port, keeping to the back streets. I felt like a convict. A cargo boat was leaving for France that day. I poured out my story and the dregs of my funds for the captain, a few remnant coins in half a dozen currencies. It was nowhere near the amount they needed. I gathered up my coins, with quivering lower lip, and prepared to leave. 'OK,' the captain said. 'Student discount, OK.' And early next morning I stepped off the boat in Marseille. From here, I'd be fine.

Tracking Hogg to Kinlochewe

Hogg set out from Ardhill, on the north side of Loch Alsh, climbed over the hills, took the ferry across a narrow part of Loch Carron, and continued north on the west side of the loch. I set out a little to the east of Ardhill, climbed over the hills, then walked north on the A890.

On my way past the south of the loch, my peripheral vision caught a familiar but unexpected shape. I was drawn to an interpretive sign by the roadside. It said: 'The tiny village of Stromeferry has been ferrying people across Loch Carron for over a thousand years.' The ferry had stopped when the road was improved in the 1970s. The sign continued, in Gaelic and English: 'James Hogg, Scottish poet and writer, was delighted to catch the ferry in June 1803.' It included a snippet from his handwritten journal, and there was his portrait which had caught my eye. And it even showed the price he was charged – sixpence and a dram.

'It's my ancestor!' I told a perfect stranger who looked impressed. But then he left quickly.

Figure 13 Stromeferry sign. James Hogg's 'sixpence and a dram' ride is still remembered.

I continued past the loch and up Glen Carron. Then, late afternoon, another sign that I hadn't expected. 'Coulin Pass, Old Pony Track' it said, and informed passers-by that the route was 'used by James Hogg, the Ettrick Shepherd, during his tour of the Highlands . . . in June, 1803.' He'd been totally lost at the time, but at least this track seemed to be heading north.

Figure 14 South end of the Old Pony Trail over Coulin Pass, and part of a long day for Hogg.

I stayed in Craig that night, then walked over the pony track the next day. And at the Kinlochewe Hotel that night, over a pint of Guinness, I noticed a framed sign on the wall: Hogg's description of his arrival in the area and his happy consumption, after a long, hungry day, of 'whisky, oat-meal cakes, tea, and sugar, with some eggs, and stinking fish'.

Hogg had walked from Ardhill to Kinlochewe in one day, on 12 June 1803. On my trip, 212 years later, I'd found three signs of his walk. Over the years, thousands of people would've taken that ferry or walked those trails, but now no one knows; Hogg is remembered here because he wrote about them.[21]

---

[21] Similar references to Hogg's visit were found on the Walk Highlands and the Heritage Paths websites, at <http://www.walkhighlands.co.uk/> and <http://www.heritagepaths.co.uk/> (both last accessed 19 February 2016).

I calculate the distance he travelled that day: 38 miles (61 km). An average walking speed (from a quick scan of the Web) would be about 3 mph (5 kph), or 2.5 mph (4 kph) on rough or steep terrain. The section by Loch Carron was probably OK, but the other tracks would be rough or steep. So if we use an average of 2.75 mph (4.5 kph), his trip would take about fourteen hours. Plus he lost time waiting for the ferry, looking for food and crossing a flooded river. It would've been a big day.

And perhaps the biggest problem was that he didn't really know where he was going. 'None of us do, mate,' said the warden at the hostel at Craig. He must've heard me thinking.

Loch Maree to Little Loch Broom

Loch Maree must have been remote in Hogg's time; he said his host had been 'seldom visited by any from so distant a country'. Scottish geologist John Macculloch wrote in 1824 that 'This noble lake lies so completely out of the road, and so far beyond the courage of ordinary travellers, that, apart from Pennant, [in 1769 and 1772] I believe it has never been visited.'[22] This is obviously wrong – and amazingly, there was an ironworks here in the early 1600s – but at least gives an impression of its remoteness when Hogg passed through. With the A832 passing by now, though, it is no longer remote.

The area north of here, and around Fionn Loch, still is. It is known and sometimes shown on maps as the 'Great Wilderness'. It contains the remotest point in mainland Britain (the furthest point from a metalled road, at Ordnance Survey point NH 02550 77010), a short distance east of Fionn Loch, and the longest inland cliff, at Beinn Lair, north-east of Letterewe. On my 1:50,000 map, some contour lines are touching their neighbours, maybe even overlapping, suggesting the vertical drops that Hogg had peered over.

He could never have imagined that one day some people would climb these cliffs, which terrified him, for fun. The Mountaineering Council of Scotland website has a guide to climbing routes here.[23] It says 'in the Letterewe area is the impressive Lewisian gneiss cliff of Carnmore. This contains routes up to 300m [almost 1,000 ft] ranging from Severe to E6.' And just to be clear about the rating, the 'E' stands for 'Extremely Severe'. So this is a category that starts with E1 (perhaps only moderately extremely severe) and progressively gets severely worse from there.

There were strong, unpredictable wind gusts when I came through and I decided to avoid the clifftops. I wasn't keen on an E6 fall, spectacular though that might have been. I came in from Poolewe in the west instead, an easier route, and arrived at Carnmore Bothy, at the south-east of Fionn Loch, just before dark. Through the night, wild winds wrenched at the roofing iron. In this remote place, it sounded like a train passing straight overhead.

---

[22] MacCulloch, *Highlands and Western Isles*, vol. II, p. 297.
[23] Mountaineering Council of Scotland, <http://www.mcofs.org.uk/> (last accessed 30 August 2015).

There are some ominous-looking precipices around here. Rocks the size of buses have been tossed untidily into the valley floor. The area is frightening and beautiful. Hogg said it conveyed 'ideas of horror which could scarcely be excelled by a glimpse of hell itself'. This wasn't hell, in my view. But if one were going there anyway, a wrong step would speed up the journey. Landscapes like this take me somewhere quite different, though, somewhere spiritual, at the other end of the spectrum.

I was out of my league in these cliffs, with no guide or equipment, and I wouldn't attempt them. But I once abseiled 600 ft (180 m) into Harwood's Hole, the deepest vertical shaft in New Zealand, and the Southern Hemisphere's deepest sinkhole. (Its total depth is 1,170 ft, 357 m, but the abseil was our first drop.) One looks in from the top and loses perspective. Drop downwards slowly though, through ancient marble and limestone, from light to darkness and down through the millennia, and the feelings are profound. If I were to fear hell, this would be the time to do it. But it is silent and sacred, and all fear is gone.

I set out next morning with some chocolate and an orange. I followed waterways and rainbows, past Shenavall Bothy, and arrived at Little Loch Broom in the late afternoon. I loved this wild and wonderful area. Hogg stayed nearby, with George Mackenzie of Dundonnell. They 'always remained at the punch-bowl until the blackbird sung at the window', following the rules of the host. I went to bed much earlier, with a smile on my face.

Figure 15 At Shenavall Bothy, south of Little Loch Broom, and officially remote.

HOGG IN THE HEBRIDES

To Lewis (June 1803): Hogg sailed from Loch Broom, just to the east of Little Loch Broom, to Stornoway. This was his first sea voyage, a journey which took sixty hours.[24] They were becalmed 'for anything that I knew, condemned to hobble on that unstable element for a week, or perhaps much longer ... the vessel floating with her stern towards Stornaway' and, for a morning, accompanied by a whale 'exactly the length of the vessel, which is a sloop, if I mistake not, about 70 or 80 tons'.

After settling his squeamishness and nerves with a dram, Hogg came to appreciate:

> an ocean of heaving chrystal, of different colours in different directions, presenting alternately, spots of the deepest green, topaz and purple; for which I could not in the least account from any appearance in the sky which was all of one colour. Such a scene, so entirely new to me, could not fail of attracting my attention, which it did to such a degree that I remained on deck all night.

Isle of Lewis (June 1803):

> I produced my letter of introduction, which the minister read, but declared it perfectly superfluous, for that my appearance was a sufficient introduction. I knew that this was to let me know how welcome a stranger was in that country, for alas! I knew that my appearance commanded no great respect. I was only dressed as a shepherd when I left Ettrick, and my dress was now become very shabby, and I often wondered at the attention shown to me ...
>
> Their ploughs, numbers of which I saw, are very slender and shabby pieces of workmanship. They consist of crooked trees selected for the purpose. Through each of these a square hole is cut at the most crooked end, and here the stick that serves for the plough-head is fixed ... Then almost straight above the heel a small stilt is fixed, and this is the plough ... The ploughman's post being such a troublesome one he is mostly in bad humour.

There is a gap, perhaps of several weeks, in Hogg's correspondence here. From here on, reports of his 1803 journey were recorded from an early transcript of a long-lost manuscript and are undated. His next entry is set in the Isle of Harris, and opens with 'As I tarried so long in this country ...'. (Harris, of course, is not really an isle, it's a land of two halves. North Harris is firmly attached to the Isle of Lewis. South Harris is only just connected to North Harris by an isthmus at Tarbert.)

---

[24] Caledonian MacBrayne ferry timetables (2015) allow two and a half hours for this journey.

But meanwhile, there was a momentous decision: Hogg had found a large area of farm land in Seilebost, near Luskentyre at the north end of South Harris; he had met with an agent and on 13 July he signed an agreement to sub-let this, from May the following year, for seven years.

Harris (probably late July/early August 1803):

> they have always a part of their flocks domesticated which they herd and milk but the far greatest Number run quite wild on the hills; from the latter the Tables are generally supplied, and the victim being hunted down with the dogs they have no choice of the fatest, but put up with such as the dogs fix on which are most apt to be the leanest as the best of the flock always run foremost ... our dogs grew impatient & attacked the sheep which they worried and tore most shockingly. Being impatient to see sheep abused in this manner I stripped off part of my cloaths & pursued threatning them most desperately; but I might have saved the trouble for they had no English.

Farming

These were times of rapid change. Scotland was industrialising, and market forces were creating new farming challenges and opportunities. The percentage of the population living in towns nearly doubled between 1750 and 1800, and would nearly double again in the next fifty years.[25] These people were losing their connection with the land. They needed to be fed.

Demand in the towns led to changes in the country. The supremacy of the lairds and chiefs continued unchallenged, but the ties they had with those farming the land were weakening. Increasingly they were focused on financial returns from the land.

In the Lowlands, leases were often not renewed, in the interests of efficiency. This left fewer farmers with larger holdings, and often single-tenant farms. Demand for the services of servants and cottars, who rented small blocks of land from farmers in exchange for their labour, was reduced as a result. Specialists such as ploughmen were now providing services earlier provided by cottars. In many Lowland areas, cottars and their cottages had almost disappeared by 1800.

In the Highlands and Islands, where populations were increasing in the early 1800s, the tacksmen (principal tenants) were required to extract

---

[25] Percentage of total population living in towns of over 10,000: 1750 = 9.2 per cent; 1800 = 17.3 per cent; 1850 = 32 per cent (Devine, *Scottish Nation*, p. 152).

ever-higher rents from sub-tenants. Often they achieved this by reducing the size of holdings and by 'pinching' croft holders to ensure that they had to provide labour to survive.

Sheep varieties were changing too. The 'primitive' Highland sheep were hardy but produced little wool. They were replaced by Lowland sheep, initially the Blackface (or 'short sheep') from the 1760s, and then Cheviots (or 'long sheep'). At this stage, much of the Highlands and Inner Hebrides had been converted for sheep, but there would still be opportunities in the outer islands.

Hogg cared greatly about sheep farming; he wrote (in an essay, 'On the utility of encouraging the system of Sheep-Farming in some districts of the Highlands, and Population in others', in 1807) that this was 'a subject in which I feel my mind so deeply interested that I could write on it for ever'.

His approach to farming was quite scientific (from a young age he dissected dead sheep to learn about diseases). He was critical of some of the farming methods he saw on his travels, but his knowledge from the Borders did not always fit here. He disliked the fact that island sheep were not smeared (a laborious process of rubbing butter and tar into the wool to deter insect pests) but there are doubts as to whether this was needed here, and some Highlanders found this Lowland practice disgusting.

He derided the ploughs in Lewis, but wooden ploughs had been widespread in Scotland until recently. James Small, an inventor from the Borders, designed all-iron ploughs that dug deeper, turned furrows better, and used smaller teams of people and animals (for his efforts, he died broke and exhausted in 1793). These were just reaching the Hebrides in 1803, and their use would be limited in rocky ground. A plough called a rustle was also used in Lewis; this had an iron hook and was pulled by one horse to cut the furrow, before using the plough that Hogg saw.

It should be noted, in his comments, that it was common then for writers to criticise old farming methods, and for southerners to disparage the Highlanders' reluctance to change.

> The peoples attention is almost wholly turned to the Manufacturing of kelp and the rearing of cattle; which are both managed somewhat more Systematically ... the kelp is an Article of great importance both to the poor and rich and hath brought more money into many of these western isles than anyone Article; or rather than all other Articles put together.

Figure 16 Sheep in Seilebost. James Hogg's dream in 1803.

Kelp

Kelp was a major industry on the west coast and islands for about forty years, from the late eighteenth to the early nineteenth centuries. Kelp, a type of seaweed, was burnt to make soda ash, a highly alkaline substance used in the manufacture of soap, linen and glass (the ash itself was also referred to just as 'kelp'). A similar product was available from Spain but imports had been disrupted by the Napoleonic wars and high import duties.

Highlanders cleared from farm land were often resettled on the coast to provide cheap labour, and to harvest and process kelp. At its peak, up to 50,000 people were dependent on the industry. Hogg said the trade favoured the wealthy; processed kelp sold for eight or nine guineas a ton, while those that gathered and manufactured it received about two guineas a ton.

If he had returned to the Hebrides a couple of decades later, he would have seen that again the poor suffered most. The wars had ended and duties were removed; imports became cheaper and the local industry collapsed. These workers were then redundant, and the clearances and emigration accelerated.

More on Harris:

> The people are poor Ignorant and passive to their superiors in the highest degree; They are remarkably abstemious both in eating and drinking, which whether it proceeds from choice or necessity hath the good effect of preventing all riots or brawls . . . They are all of the present established Religion, a certain seign among the vulgar that they take little head about religion for the greater the Enthusiasm that prevails with respect to it in any Society the greater Number of Sectaries will make their Appearance.[26]
>
> They may be said to Labour under the feudal system in its most degenerate State having been for a long Time nothing benifited by the protection of their chief but rendered wholly dependant on a few tacksmen more intent on their own aggrandisement than of contributing to the wellfare & happiness of their retainers . . .
>
> The common people are generally rather low of stature but many of them have florid & animated features[.] some of the men wear bonnets but otherwise they dress like the people South of the Forth or rather like sailors. the Philibeg & tartan are there unknown; and they are jealous of such as appear in their country dressed in that garb:[27]
>
> The everyday dress of the women is very homely & unbecoming[;] it consists of a long waisted Jerkin & a plaiden petticoat, with a mutch or old Fashioned cap on the head . . . to a stranger [they] appear as grotesque a figure as can well be supposed; Ten or Twelve of these in all [their] native charms engaged in fulling Cloath (a Scene which I often witnessed) surpasseth all Description and can be compared only to so many Infernals or witches engaged in some horrible spell; While contemplat[ing] their dresses, features, gestures and the wild howling noise of their Choruses, I could scarcely perswade myself that they were rational Creatures; they perform this work sitting on the floor . . . constantly keeping Time to some of their Country Songs, one or more of them sing the Song and all of them join in the Chorus and as the wild air swells they all ply with increased vigor nor will they make a breach in the Song although the King were entering in the middle of it . . .[28]

---

[26] The predominant religions in the Outer Hebrides were Presbyterian in the northern islands of Lewis, Harris and North Uist, and Roman Catholic in the southern islands of Benbecula, South Uist and Barra, a result of differing allegiances of the clans in the past. Here, Hogg is suggesting a proliferation of sects ('sectaries') as an indicator of religious passion.

[27] A 'philibeg' is a walking kilt (*filleadh bheag*). Highland dress had been banned after the Jacobite Rebellions, but was legal again from 1782. ('Jealous' here means suspicious.)

[28] Highland cloth was made tough and weather-proof by 'waulking' or 'fulling': woven cloth was soaked in hot, stale urine then shrunk by kneading it vigorously, work usually done by teams of women using their hands or feet. Waulking songs were sung to pass the time and synchronise movements. Some earlier travellers had been similarly unnerved; Thomas Pennant thought these were a manifestation of madness. There were other views, though. Rev. John Lane Buchanan wrote, 'the sweet melody of their music seldom fails to collect a number of hearers, who join in the song' (*Travels in the Western Hebrides*, p. 84). In any case, singing and behaviour of the type described are found in many cultures where teams are doing harsh, repetitive work.

It must be owned that in a Group of them dressed in their Sundays Cloths, you may see many faces not disagreeable but as they are not all personable their only beauty consists of a Childish Innocence depicted in their Countenances.[29]

There are no ancient Castles in the Country that I saw[.] There are some relics of Druidism & a number of old religeous edefices which seem to have been erected about the Time of the Introduction of Christianity into the Scottish and Pictish nations; but the most remarkable is the monastry of St Clements at Rowdill [Rodel] which notwithstanding its intire state at present is supposed to have been errected in the thirteenth Century[.][30]

Figure 17 Church at Rodel. Old when James Hogg saw it in 1803.

---

[29] Hogg's descriptions of the people here might be somewhat unreliable. He says, for example, the people are 'low of stature'. A report in the *Toronto Star* (16 April 1923) on immigrants arriving in Canada proclaimed 'Race of Giants are Hebridean', and that the men from this area were 'all five feet nine and over'. Admittedly that report was much later, but it seems unlikely they had grown so much in that time. Note that Hogg's harsh descriptions were from an early manuscript, and he might have intended to modify them prior to public release. And while he seems critical of the people here, in his *Essay on Sheep-Farming* he describes them as the most indefatigable he ever saw in his life, and greatly superior in 'temperance and patience under labour' to those of the inland glens. It was not uncommon for visitors to make such blunt observations on appearances. John Leyden described women on another island as 'more squalid and dirty than the men, and their features more disagreeable' (*Journal of a Tour*).

[30] This church is at Rodel. A church had been built here in the thirteenth century but was rebuilt about 1528. It was often referred to as a monastery but there is no evidence it ever was one. It is still in existence and open to the public today.

Having, it seemed, achieved his goal of arranging to lease farmland, Hogg continued south through the islands on a range of vessels, landing on Ensay, Skye, Sanday, Canna, Rum and Mull, then back to the mainland.

Isle of Ensay:

> As the house of Ensay was crouded with friends and men of business the Ladies never came into our company excepting at meals, we however contrived to pass the Time not disagreeably[:] we sailed, fished, ate skate[,] drank grog[,] leaned forward upon the table & farted as loud as we were able.[31]

Isle of Skye:

> old Canny [a friend and local guide] and I went on board the sloop Grace of Greenock and set sail for the isle of sky. The breeze was fair and the day was fine ... proceeding along closs on the coast got a fine view of these bold precipitate shores which in many places overhang the ocean from an amazing height ... In one of the bays we also [saw] four whales one of which the sailors declared to be the largest they ever saw in those seas[.][32]
>
> I Remained ten days in sky most of which time I spent in McLeods Country and was Introduced by Canny to all the Genteel families Thereabouts ... here we had plenty of Music & Dancing[.] The Tacksmens houses are numerous Substantial and Commodious being mostly two stories high & covered with slates. The kitchens are never under the same roof with the rooms. The people are elegant & polished in their manners, have Tastes for Poetry music & dancing, and are Courteous and Social in the highest degree[.] on being Introduced to any family every one of them Saluted me with a Welcome to Sky[.]
>
> The Gentlemen have been Mostly in the army and the principal families are all related or connected with one another and there is so much kindness & unanimity amongst them, that I could not help pronouncing the people happy in my own mind And viewing Sky as a little Paradise ... I give the preferance to Sky of all the Countries in the Highlands of Scotland for Beauty & convenience. It is so deversified by lofty Mountains[,] Moderate rising hills covered or Mixed with the richest verdure, & intersected by extensive valleys so fertile ... the Inhabitants enjoy health and longevity in an eminent degree.

---

[31] A possible answer to the question: 'What *did* we do before television?'

[32] The species seen here is unknown. In recent years, the Hebridean Whale and Dolphin Trust has reported sightings of small numbers of minke, humpback, orca, pilot and sperm whales in these waters. Commercial whaling started early in Scotland and by the mid-eighteenth century many ports were involved (especially Dundee and Peterhead), mainly hunting in the Arctic and later in the South Atlantic. A whaling station opened in Harris in 1903. The industry ceased to operate in Scotland around the mid-twentieth century.

They are brave Generous & hospitable; of warm ardent passions and impatient of Controul . . . They enter commonly into the matramonial state in early life and have large families who are remarkable in an Eminent degree for their affectionate beheavour to one another & for a fraternal concern about every thing connected with their Wellfare.

Figure 18 Loch Bracadale, Isle of Skye: a place of 'music and dancing . . . kindness and unanimity'.

Isles of Sanday and Canna:

Sandy is only a mile in length, fertile & stocked with good short sheep, the two Islands may contain about 300 Inhabitants many of whom are Roman Catholics[.] there is an old chapel on Canny, and near it a tall oblisk whereon a great many heroglyphical figures are coarsely engraved[.] during our stay here we were much engaged in fishing and catched sceath and lyth in the greatest abundance[.]

Isle of Rum:

on one of these Excursions we made a descent on Rum an Island of considerable extent being about 35 Miles in Circumference in form of an irregular circle[.] it belongs to the Laird of Coll and is a Mountainous rugged isle fitted only for pasturing sheep or goats. Yet several Hundreds of the people contrive to live upon it; Its Western shore is prodigiously bold and high[.] the Mountains abruptly rise to a Considerable elevation the highest being 2,300 feet above the level of the Sea[.]

Isle of Mull:

in a short time we doubled the famous Rin of Ardnamurchan the farthest west point on the Mainland of Britain and struck unto the Sound of Mull. Here we had another instance of the uncommon instability of the wind amongst these Isles, after it had wavered for a few minutes we had the Mortification to find it again streight a head of us and to add to our Misfortunes a Ship going full sail to the North warned us by the help of a Trumpet to be upon the alert for that a Kings cutter was come into Tobermurray that was stripping the homeward bound vessels of all their hands[.]

The Sailors immediately betook themselves to the boat and fled to the mountains of Mull, and by some unaccountable neglect proceeding from pride, I refused to accompany them, but had reason to repent of my temerity[.] The boat was scarcely returned when the cutter appeared and came streight upon us and to such particulars which can do no honour to me nor any concerned. Suffice it to say that I got an ugly fright, and shall never be as near hauled a board a man of War untill I go altogether. Indeed I have often wondered since that they suffered me to escape considering the limited Time that [they] had for making up their quota[;] however escape I did & my heart in a few hours gradually recceded from the rapidity of motion to which the presence of a press gang had raised it.

The Press Gangs

Hogg seems to have narrowly evaded 'impressment', the unpopular and often forceful – but legal – taking of men into the Royal Navy. Prime targets were 'eligible men of seafaring habits between the ages of 18 and 55 years' but at that time, early in the Napoleonic Wars, the press gangs would have been less choosy. Sailing ships required a lot of manpower in a sea battle.

At the time of the Battle of Trafalgar, in 1805, over half the Navy's 120,000 sailors were said to be pressed men.[33] It is hard to be sure of the numbers, though, because many who were being pressed then decided

---

[33] There are references to these numbers in the World Public Library (Royal Navy) and Wikipedia (Impressment) (<http://www.worldlibrary.org/articles/royal_navy> and <https://en.wikipedia.org/wiki/Impressment>, both last accessed 19 February 2016).

> to 'volunteer', for the financial benefits this would bring. (A disadvantage of volunteering was that pressed men who deserted would just be re-impressed, while enlisted men or volunteers who deserted could be hanged.) Britain stopped impressment after Napoleon's defeat in 1814, but the laws that permitted it remained.
>
> Had Hogg been captured, this would have had a big impact on his career. And sometime soon, back in Ettrickhouse, his elderly parents would have been wondering where on earth he had got to. It would be several decades before a law was passed to limit pressed men's service to just five years.

At sea, Mull to Loch Crinan:

> I can never describe to you the pleasure that I felt during this part of our voyage, the day was fine the Atmosphere clear ... every five minutes new objects were bursting in on the view.

From Loch Crinan, Argyll, Hogg would set out on foot, hampered by a recent leg injury, but records of this part of his journey are missing. Significantly, he passed through Greenock and was surprised to be hailed as a poet and invited to dine with a large group of gentlemen, including future novelist John Galt and his friend James Park. Hogg later described the conversation of 'that enchanting night' as 'much above what I had ever been accustomed to hear'.[34]

He arrived home, to Ettrickhouse, in August 1803. He had done everything he had set out to do. He had studied modes of farming in some remote areas. Vitally, he had signed an agreement to lease a farm in Harris. And unexpectedly, he'd been recognised as a writer outside the Borders, in a town he'd barely heard of. It must have been a happy homecoming. But there were some complications to come.

NOTES ON MY JOURNEYS – THE HEBRIDES

Isle of Lewis

I spent just a short time in Lewis. There's a gap in Hogg's records and no mention of how long he spent there. He wandered through 'trackless wastes ... through swamps and deep morasses'. I found that a couple of hours of morasses were enough to learn all I needed to about them. Hogg hired a young guide at

---

[34] Galt has been called the 'first political novelist in the English language', due to his treatment of issues relating to the Industrial Revolution. Hogg, Galt and Park would develop a friendship and mutual respect. After this first meeting, Hogg described Galt's appearance, in a frock-coat and new top-boots, as 'dandyish'. How Galt might have viewed Hogg, after weeks on the road in the same clothes and hobbling on a lame leg, is anyone's guess.

eighteen pence a day, the only time he mentions actually hiring someone. And he took a long detour, required by his guide, to avoid the haunts of a water horse (Hogg describes this as 'an imaginary being' in the notes to his poem 'Mess John' in *The Mountain Bard* in 1807, but it was one which caused terror in parts of the Highlands). The creature had recently decoyed a man to his death, and nearly took his guide's father as well.

Impressively, Hogg carried letters of introduction for residents of Stornoway, and 'letters for the principal men of each district' – impressive because he had not planned to come here and had only recently heard of the town, so he must have been given them on the way.

There is no mention, in the surviving manuscripts, of a visit to the Callanish Standing Stones. It must have happened, though, because they appear in 'Basil Lee' in *Winter Evening Tales*. His protagonist witnesses a troop of unearthly visitors, who march to the stones, then disappear.[35] These stones, it is thought, were raised about the same time as the Egyptian pyramids, some 5,000 years ago. The central stones would seem taller now than in Hogg's time, a result of the excavation of peat in the mid-nineteenth century.

Figure 19 Callanish Standing Stones, Isle of Lewis. Still standing and still haunting today.

---

[35] 'Basil Lee', in *Winter Evening Tales*, pp. 49–52.

In Lewis, as in other islands and parts of the Highlands, I lamented the lack of trees. Hogg said that 'no tree was ever seen in the memory of man' here. It seems likely that much of the woodland was torched about 8,000 years ago to make way for grassland, but the damage would have continued after that. In 1900, only 5 per cent of Scotland was still forested. (New Zealand, lucky to be discovered so late, has about 31 per cent cover.) I am delighted to hear that Forestry Commission Scotland has plans to increase forest cover from 17 per cent in 2007 to about 25 per cent by the second half of the twenty-first century. For so many reasons – shelter, soil conservation, recreation, tourism, timber and firewood, climate change – forests must be a top priority. It's a commendable target.

Isle of Harris

I visited Harris twice. Recently I went to Lewis and North Harris. Earlier I went to the south, starting with the early morning ferry from Uig.

I was uncharacteristically grumpy on that ferry. The previous day was my birthday (I had turned sixty-five, the age that Hogg never quite reached). I'd had a lovely time on Skye.

But that night in Uig, I wanted to sleep indoors. I wanted that because I'd been camping for a while and was starting to miss clean sheets; because I had to catch the ferry at 5.30 the next morning, a time that seemed not just early but cynical; because horizontal rain was being blown in from the south; and mainly because I wanted to celebrate my birthday with a hint of luxury: with an electric light and a roof over my head.

But everything in town was full (there was one room left but the proprietor told me, 'I think it's a bit expensive for you' – she was right, but how did she *know?*). So I pitched my tent in a drenching gale, toasted my sixty-fifth alone at the pub with a pie and a Baileys, and set my alarm for 5 a.m.

And I cursed my alarm and ran through the rain in the morning, jumping puddles and holding my hat on my way to the wharf, with my bundle of tent flapping and dripping under my arm. I was the last to board, and a man in a uniform who disliked his job told me to get there earlier next time. I had a very strong wish to bump into the person who decided that ferries should sail at such an hour.

Once in a while I feel sulky for no good reason. This time I felt totally justified. I spoke to no one on the ferry and relished my well-earned grumpiness.

Tarbert charmed and cheered me though. It was compact and clean and seemed slightly too small for the ferry. I savoured a coffee with a view while the town woke up. The clouds cleared. Helpful people popped up everywhere. The Bunkhouse was locked but I checked in by phone and I was told how to let myself in: 'Make yourself at home, sleep upstairs, help yourself to anything and if you don't see anyone tonight, just leave £20 in the jar in the morning.' Shop windows, I noticed, were left ajar overnight ('If anything went missing, we'd just tell the ferries').

And great hitch-hiking round Harris, I discovered the next morning. Occasionally I love to hitch-hike. Buses don't always come when I want them, and rental cars are a nuisance – you need to park them, to find them again, and take them back later. Mainly, though, it's the conversations I like. Drivers who pick up riders are usually interesting people. For them, it's a chance to tell secrets, to test theories and share dreams with people they'll never see again, with people who won't judge them and will enjoy the ride. And I can conduct my random surveys: their views on the weather and Scottish Independence. (I have no wisdom to offer on the latter, but I can tell them that New Zealand, miles from anywhere, has thrived as an independent country and would not consider a union with a larger, more powerful neighbour.)

There's a better mode of travel of course. Most of the time, walking is best. If I need inspiration, or if I really want to know where I am, I walk. In *A Philosophy of Walking*, Frédéric Gros says, 'Walking is the best way to go more slowly than any other method.'[36] Harris is great for walking and hitching. You can walk till you're ready to drop, then try for a ride.

And cycling of course, the other best way to see the country. It depends. But now I was walking and hitching, and loving it.

I had to travel in at least three directions in Harris.

I had to visit the south, to Rodel, to the church that was old when Hogg saw it in 1803. It has seen changes of faith, damage by fire and lightning, abandonment and repair, and the burial of countless MacLeods. But it stands proudly today as a building of beauty and character. I passed through Leverburgh, an unfulfilled dream of Lord Leverhulme, the creator of Sunlight soap and one-time owner of the Isles of Harris and Lewis. (He bought Lewis as 'a delightful home' in 1918, but decided the locals were inefficient so he thought he should industrialise them, then had to buy Harris to complete the package. His soap, helped for a while by forced labour in the Congo, outlived his Hebridean dreams.) I saw the harbour where Hogg nearly met with disaster in his final visit here. And I was drawn to Seallam! Visitor Centre and genealogical research service, managed with passion by Bill and Chris Lawson. Bill remembers Hogg's visits to the area as if they happened a decade ago.

I had to travel to the east of Harris. I already knew what to expect. Hogg said there was no more barren and inhospitable scene in the Highlands. Stanley Kubrick used tinted shots of the area as the surface of Jupiter in the filming of *2001: A Space Odyssey*. The rock here is anorthosite, just like the light-coloured rocks in the highland parts of the moon, visible with the naked eye from Earth. There is so little soil here in the east that funeral parties had to carry their dead to be buried in the west (on the 'Coffin Route'). But it has a certain charm: tough and uncompromising, and dotted with the odd sheep and cottage, fishing boat and incongruous bright red phone box.

---

[36] Gros, *Philosophy of Walking*, p. 2.

And I had to go west. My main interest was Luskentyre and Seilebost, the area Hogg planned to farm, and would visit again in 1804 to pursue this. I could see the attraction – this was a huge area, covering perhaps a quarter of South Harris right across to the east coast. Even as a non-farmer, though, I could see some challenges. The west is more fertile than the east, a result of seashell fragments blown continually onto the land, but it is still rocky, treeless and windswept – Hogg refers to its 'wet boisterous climate' – and its thin sandy soil does not hold nutrients well. Now, long after the Clearances, the west is still sparsely populated by humans and sheep.

Figure 20 Seilebost, looking north to Luskentyre. Paradise in a cool climate. (Source: Image used courtesy of VisitScotland.)

Here, though Hogg hardly mentions them, I was gobsmacked by the beaches. Lonely Planet's *Scotland* guide says: 'The blinding white sands and turquoise waters of Luskentyre and Scarasta would be major holiday resorts if they were transported to somewhere with a warm climate.' I walked, I ran, I slid on dunes, I took photos and sat in the sun, but could not convince myself to swim. The beach was deserted and cool. Footprint Handbooks' *Focus Skye and Outer Hebrides* says, with a dash of hyperbole, 'This is paradise refrigerated.'

I walked, and I thought about walking. I was energised by the landscape and the sky and the breeze. Walking is something one can do alone or with others, and feel equally comfortable. You can chat easily with friends as you walk. Or you can walk in silence with them, and not feel awkward about it. You can walk alone, and the thoughts keep on coming. You think about others who have made the same journey for different reasons. People walked before me here, carrying peat and kelp. Or roof timbers and coffins.

I thought about Hogg's journey, in 1803. He covered some big distances quickly. I wanted to compare his walks with mine. It was strange I would want to compete with someone born 180 years before I was. But to really appreciate his journeys and challenges I needed to be objective.

On Day One of this trip, he walked from Ettrick to Edinburgh, about 45 miles, or 72 km. There was little traffic to worry about, but some of the tracks or roads would have been rough. A good walking speed in these conditions would be about 3 mph (5 kph). At this speed he would be walking 15 hours that day. If he was tired by this, he didn't mention it.

I could time myself there, but I'd be dodging traffic on the A701. The route might be flatter now, but I prefer hills to traffic. I'd need to find some other place for my competition. It's not a race though, not really, and I don't have to win. But I don't want to be beaten either. I walked, my mind wandered.

There's a problem of course – he didn't often record how long a part of his journey took. My thoughts went back to the Solomon Islands, asking locals how long a trip would take, by foot or canoe. One day someone told me: 'White men ask how long it takes to go somewhere. We don't know how long it takes. We just go until we get there. Then we stop.' Probably Hogg would've told me something similar.

A car pulled up, two women inside. It was late afternoon. 'Would you like a ride? The midges are coming.'

'Thanks,' I said, 'that's great.'

'Wait, we should check. Are you a serial killer or anything?' Laughing.

'No, I'm not. Are you?'

'Yes, we are,' they admitted.

'Good,' I said. 'Because I know you wouldn't say that if you really were.'

'OK, but maybe that means that you are . . . Oh, hop in, let's go . . .'

We were on our way back north to Tarbert. It was great to be on the road.

Isle of Skye

I wandered round the west of Skye and camped a few nights on the coast. I had a pleasant scramble up Healabhal Mhor one day. It's one of two hills with flat tops in the west, both called Macleod's Table. Hogg climbed one of them. I think it was this one – he'd injured his leg and this hill has easier access, and great views to the north, as he described.

I travelled through Loch Bracadale, which Hogg had loved. I was keen to make a connection with Ose, where he'd stayed, but how? The café was closed. I spotted a house on a headland just to the north, and knocked on the

Figure 21 Macleod's Tables, Healabhal Bheag (left) and Healabhal Mhor, in the west of Skye. Hogg climbed one of these, probably the latter, for the view.

door. The house, the owners told me, was built about 1760. They got out some old notes. A tacksman called McLeod had lived there in 1803. Was this the house where Hogg stayed? We couldn't be sure, but he would have visited here at least. Good, I thought.

But more: there was a rugby game starting now, they told me, on the other side of the world. New Zealand were playing Australia – would I like to come in for a coffee and to watch the game? This was more than I could have dreamed of when I crawled out of my tent an hour or so earlier. Completing my perfect morning, New Zealand won. Beating Australia in any sport is something for Kiwis to celebrate. Like Scotland beating England.

Hogg said the people here were 'brave, generous & hospitable'. The kindness today is alive and well. And in Scotland, I'd never doubt the bravery.

5 Western Highlands and Islands (1804): Misfits and misfortune

GREAT EXPECTATIONS

On 21 May 1804, Hogg set out from Ettrick on his third journey in three years, with two friends and high spirits. He had one major goal.

The lease at Ettrickhouse had expired and the lease at Seilebost on the Isle of Harris would commence in a few days. It was time to take possession.

Arrangements had now been made for his parents to live in a cottage on a farm in the Borders. It would be a big change: a poem, *Jamie's Farewell to Ettrick*, in *The Scots Magazine* in May, shows his sadness about a long-term departure for a remote region. But in the meantime, a visit there with friends would be fun:

> Before I can proceed I must likewise give you a sketch of the characters of each of my fellow travellers whom I shall distinguish by their christian names only. Mr William, with whom I had been intimately acquainted from his childhood, was bred to the occupation of a farmer in the country, where he likewise received his education; and had no more experimental acquaintance with nautical affairs than proceeded from having once or twice gotten a view of a harbour, and arm of the sea. He had good natural parts, which he had, by reading, improved so far, as to have acquired a partial knowledge of most of the arts and sciences. He delighted in painting, poetry, and music; was of a thoughtful disposition, absent, overbearing, and impatient of controul. Easily convinced by a single well-timed remonstrance, but immoveable by the most passionate and lengthened arguments.
>
> Mr John, on the other hand, besides a good memory and judgement, had a mind extremely sensible to all the finer feelings: a taste for the sublime and beautiful, but rather too high-flavoured, to be generally good: enthusiastically fond of poetry and music, and no mean proficient in either: paid perhaps a little more deference to the opinions and temper of others than the former, but was ten times more impatient at

being thwarted by contrary elements. From the habits of a town life, he had acquired ideas of the different degrees of mankind, and subordination of ranks, quite above what either Mr W. or I had any conception of; and thought himself justly entitled to knock down every little d-d fellow or impertinent gilpey of a girl, who did not answer a question or obey an order exactly to his mind, but withal possessed of an honest and generous heart.

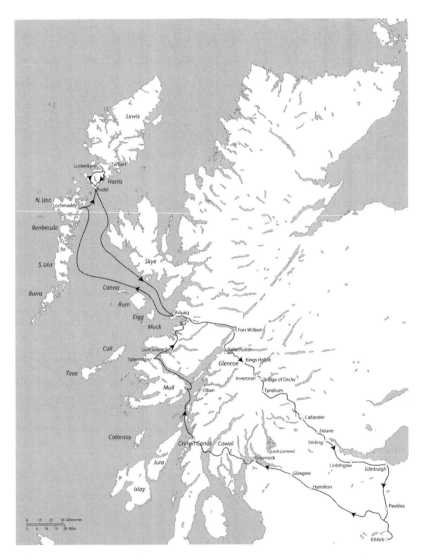

Figure 22 James Hogg's journey with William Laidlaw and John Grieve, May to June 1804. (Source: Revised from originals in de Groot, *Highland Journeys*.)

As for my own character, I leave that to be made out by you after perusing all these letters . . .[1]

I dare say never any people set out with higher expectations of a most pleasing and delightful excursion. What romantic bays, and inchanted islands, had we in fancy already visited! what verdant pastures, vernal woods, and sweet blooming blushing maids! What pretty compliments had we already etched out as best suiting the illustrious highland chieftains at whose boards we should be quaffing the delicious nectar! . . .

As we proposed walking, our travelling equipage was very simple. I had a small portmanteau, which we stuffed with each a clean shirt and change of stockings; a pocket travelling map, and a few neck-cloths. Thus nobly equipped, with each a staff in his hand, and a flashing tartan cloak over his shoulder, we proceeded on our enticing journey.

The initial stage was by foot to Glasgow, with a night on the way in Hamilton, then by 'fly boat' to Greenock.[2]

we walked out and viewed the environs of the town; and, in the evening, had a party at Park's, consisting of thirteen; where we had an elegant supper, and continued till an early hour . . . we were not a little proud at being honoured with the unexpected company of so many gentlemen of taste and learning; but we missed the ingenious Mr Galt, who was lately removed to London, and whose absence hath left an irreparable blank in the literary society of Greenock.

Cowal (May 1804):

In the openings of the glens, were some scenes of inexpressible beauty: scenes which are common enough in Cowal, and peculiar to the Highlands of Scotland. In this district, the detached and broken hills, cloathed in mourning, or otherwise, spotted and shagged like their kindred goats, are, nevertheless, skirted below with sweet-scented birches,

---

[1] Hogg's companions, thinly disguised here, were William Laidlaw and John Grieve. Laidlaw was a friend from childhood, and the son of Hogg's employer when he had worked at Blackhouse. Grieve was a cousin of Laidlaw's, also well known to Hogg. Both were younger than he was. The letters were intended for publication; presumably he did not expect that his comments about them, often critical, would stay confidential by withholding their surnames.

[2] These were 'express' passenger boats used in this area in the pre-steam era, and driven by oars and sails, and sometimes by horse in the upper reaches (details from Riddell, *Clyde Navigation*). Hogg tells us 'there was a brisk breeze from the south' and the vessel ran with 'unusual velocity', taking three hours, and was so smooth and steady that 'we were obliged to call in the aids of philosophy to convince us that we were not quite stationary'. Three hours is very fast for this journey. Henry Bell established a steamboat service here from 1812, initially in the *Comet*; in its early days, passengers would sometimes have to help to turn the fly-wheel (<http://www.dalmadan.com/?p=1090>, last accessed 8 March 2016). By 1817 there were at least a dozen steamboat services on this route, most of them operating on 'every lawful day', that is, every day but Sunday.

spreading hazels, and all the other hardy plants that have been so liberally set by the hand of nature in Scotia's glens; where they spread their simple boughs, and rear their unaffected, yet majestic tops, in defiance of the chill mountain gale, or the boisterous salt-impregnated blast from the Atlantic billows.

[We passed] rugged battlements of antient castles, fortresses of the feudal chiefs . . . scenes of blood and stratagem . . . Then the inhabitants of those regions held their properties, and even their lives, on tenures so precarious, that fear kept watch by night, and anxiety pined in listless incertitude during the day . . .

Thus the natural bias towards justice and humanity, implanted in the human breast, was gradually overturned, and every spring of moral purity in the mind tainted and sullied. What was the consequence? ravages! murders! massacres and spoils! Then the most trivial quarrels must be determined by the sword; and hundreds, nay, thousands, were doomed to atone with their blood, for the offended pride, or petty animosity of relentless chiefs; and though faithful and passive to the last degree, their all was subject to every whim and caprice of their superior. How blessed, how happy the change . . .

There, now, instead of the rapine and terror that once prevailed, love and peace, growing spontaneously up together, nourish and cherish one another . . . O my dear Sir! were you as well acquainted with the cottages and their simple inhabitants as I am, which you never will be, you would not suspect the above to be a flattering picture . . . were I to decide what class of men in the nation enjoyed the greatest share of happiness without alloy, I would, without hesitation, do it in favour of the peasantry.

. . . the cottage, Sir! the cottage is my native element! No where else is there such a free and unreserved emanation of sentiment, which, however homely and ungrammatically delivered, frequently flows from a heart fraught with manly feelings and good natural endowments . . . Believe me then, Sir, I would rather be the first man amongst the shepherds of Ettrick Forest, than the second in Edinburgh.

By foot and ferry to Crinan Loch (May 1804):

It was now growing late, while we had yet another ridge of hills to go over. We were all entire strangers to the country . . . we were soon in our usual state, drenched to the skin and mud to the knees; and had nearly precipitated ourselves over a broken bridge in the dark, which would have terminated our journey at once.

In rough weather, though, Hogg saw an opportunity with a female passenger when they were crossing Loch Fyne at Otter Ferry. He rushed on to the boat and saved a seat on the sheltered side:

desiring the prettiest of the girls to take up her birth in my bosom. – She complied without hesitation, and I screened her with my mantle. O! how my companions envied my situation: but when the sailors came, how great was my mortification, to find we had all taken up our stations in a wrong boat. We were all obliged to shift, and I being farthest in, was last in getting out, and lost not only my dearest bosom-friend, but every tolerable seat in the boat.

ROUGH RIDES TO THE HEBRIDES

After an uncomfortable walk and several days' delay due to adverse weather and the Sabbath (when no one would open the locks) they set out from Loch Crinan in a sloop, the *Johnson* – 'the most unwieldy vessel of her size that ever was made' – in fair conditions, intending to sail to Skye. There were some struggles with furious tides and an uncooperative breeze, and stops in Achnacraig in the east of Mull, then Tobermory: 'Although I did not tarry above two hours at this place last year . . . I was surprised at being told by a native who went aboard with us, that the whole village knew me.'

They set out again at about 3 p.m., 'contrary to the ardent remonstrances of an old sailor named Hugh', and:

> the sea growing prodigiously heavy, and the wind continuing to increase, the sailors were affrighted, and though ten or twelve miles advanced, turned and run again for Tobermory . . . We had got within the rocky point which bounds the north side of the harbour, and just when endeavouring to put the vessel about for the last time on that side, a tremendous gale commenced . . . She was, during the time of this short struggle, driving with great force straight upon the rocks; and the men not being able to effect any thing in the consternation they were in, a moment of awful pause ensued.
>
> Every man quitted his hold, save old Hugh at the helm . . . by a singular interposition of Providence, the ship gave a great roll backwards, and the main-sail dropped down of itself, the ropes having been previously loosened, and the vessel whirled round clear of the rocks, tho' within six, or at most, seven yards of them. Old Hugh thanked his Maker aloud for this signal deliverance.

It was too rough to weather the storm near Tobermory. The decision was made to sail into Loch Sunart, back on the mainland, despite lack of knowledge of the coastline here, shaping a course for a small island about 11 p.m.:

> The storm was all this time rather increasing, and such another night I never witnessed at that season, if ever in my life: the elements were in a tumult, and seemed to be taking flame: the pale, vivid bolts,

bursting from the rolling clouds, added horror to the scene, and to minds already nearly stupified: the sea seemed covered with sparkling fire . . .

In the midst of this confusion and anxiety, when we had past several dangerous straits, and were too far gone to retreat, judge of our consternation when we found the wind all at once turn a-head of us, with still increased violence! while we were in a strange channel which was not clear above a quarter of a mile in anyone direction, and at the dead hour of the night, when we could not see from stem to stern. Our condition may be conceived, but cannot be described.

In this situation we turmoiled, beating up until half-past one in the morning, always rather losing ground than gaining, when, at last, in spite of all our efforts, she drove so close upon a rocky isle, that we were obliged, as our last and only resource, to drop the anchors, altho' straight on the weather side of a precipitate rock . . . when we were so near the rock as to be able to touch it with a staff, the little anchor held.–The vessel struck twice; but as the shore was bold, and the anchor continued immoveable, she received little injury.

The sailors now gathered double courage, threw the trunks and valuables again out of the boat on board, and cursed, and swore again, as fast as ever. We soon hauled her a good space from the rocks, sent out another anchor by the boat, and tied the hauser to the rocky point which we first so narrowly escaped; when, thinking our danger over, we retired to the cabin, where Mr M'Alister [the ship's master] treated us with as much wine as we chose to drink . . .

But the most interesting figure of the whole group was old Hugh, who had kept by the helm from the commencement of the storm. The master, who seemed glad to resign his charge, wrought like the rest of the men in obedience to his orders.

To convey some faint idea of this picture, imagine to yourself a fair complexioned man, about sixty years of age, or upwards . . . his legs were set amazingly wide, in case *Mr Boreas* [the Greek god of the north wind], in these freaks of his, might launch him: he was all this while eating tobacco most voraciously, and not having time to spit often, the juice was obliged to find its way from each corner of his mouth in the best manner it could; yet, this was the man who alone remained firm and composed, giving orders and advice with the utmost calmness! his motto being in effect thus, *Let us do our best, and trust to God for the rest.*

They spent another boisterous night by the island in Loch Sunart, then left 'exploring our way on foot through the pathless mountains of Ardnamurchan and Moidart'. Now, a week after they first hoped to sail to the islands, after three rough nights at sea, they were back on the mainland again, battling their way north on foot to find another port to sail from. Could things get any worse?

Yes, a little: no sooner had they reached the tops than the rain started in earnest again and the wind shifted to the south, just as they'd hoped for earlier. And so they realised that if they had stayed two hours longer on the *Johnson*, they could now be sailing to Skye: 'but the whole journey was alike unfortunate'.

They set out again two days later from Arisaig in a schooner, the *Hawk of Oban*. They left around noon, with the request that the crew should take them to Harris, await their return to the boat, then bring them back to Arisaig. This time, perhaps, things would work out better:

> The fog still continued, and we saw no land until about seven o'clock A.M. had our crew steered in the direction they ought to have done, we should by this time have been in the sound of Harris; and tho' I easily perceived that they were luffing too much, I had hopes that we would land somewhere in that neighbourhood.
>
> What then was our mortification, on perceiving that we were off Boigdale-head in South Uist, a short way north of the Sound of Barra; and that after having sailed about thirty hours, to find that we were no nearer our destination than when we set out from the main land the preceding day! They could make no apology for this mistake, but only, that they foresaw a storm, and wished to reach a coast on which they could find shelter in case of necessity. They had certainly considerably mistaken their bearings; but the truth was, that they were utter strangers on the coasts of Harries . . .
>
> About mid-day we opened Loch-Madi [Lochmaddy] in North Uist, when no arguments could move them to proceed further . . . We were, however, agreeably surprised at finding a good slated inn, of two stories, where we took up our residence during the remainder of the day, and the following night. . . . the house, and every part about it, was crowded with some hundreds of Lord Macdonald's people, who were assembled to pay their rents;—what an interesting group they were, and how surprised my two friends were at seeing such numbers in a place which they had judged a savage desert, and unfit for the nourishment of intellectual life.[3]

To Harris (June 1804):

> We at length left Loch-Madi with a fair wind, and, in two hours, found ourselves in the great bason at Rowdil [Rodel] in Harries, which is one of the greatest curiosities in these countries. There are three narrow entrances into it, but the middle one is impassable, and

---

[3] Lord Macdonald (Sir Alexander Wentworth) was the sole owner of North Uist. The building in Lochmaddy that they stayed in still exists, and is nourishing intellectual life today as a museum and community centre.

very dangerous to strangers, as it is the only one which is seen; and had not the inhabitants of Rowdil observed us in a critical minute, we had infallibly been dashed to pieces, as we were entering it in full sail: but they, joining in a general shout, tossed their bonnets up into the air, and thus opened our eyes to our imminent danger; nor was it with small difficulty that we then got the vessel put safely about, on the very brink of the sunk rocks.

A pilot soon after arriving, we got safely in by the south entrance, and lodged that night at the inn in the village of Rowdil, where we got plenty of every thing, and were well refreshed. Here we all manifested considerable satisfaction at having gained in safety the place to which we were bound, after having struggled so long with conflicting elements . . . We travelled from Rowdil to Luskintyre on foot, a distance of twelve miles; there we tarried three days, which we spent in traversing the country, viewing it minutely as far as the isthmus of Tarbet.

We visited several of the cottages and shealings, contemplating their manners, and modes of tillage. We were treated in an original stile by some of the inhabitants; and, in one cottage, surprised half a score of females plying at the fulling of cloth, and braying a song with a vehemence which seemed the effect only of madness or inspiration . . .

Suffice it then to say, that after a stay of three days at Luskintyre, we travelled again to Rowdil by another way, keeping the eastern side of the island, than which a more barren and inhospitable scene is not to be met with in the highlands, being wholly covered with rocks, moss, and stagnant lakes . . .

. . . my two friends were grown quite impatient to return home; and I was obliged, reluctantly, to come away with them, without seeing either Ensay or Mr Hume; although a messenger arrived at Luskintyre with a pressing invitation for us to join them, with which, if I had been suffered to comply, a great part of my ensuing misfortunes had been prevented: so unqualified is human prudence to judge what may be the consequences of the smallest or most favourable incidents, for what I here viewed as my greatest happiness in this journey, namely their company, turned out my greatest bane.

Taking Care of Business

James, what are you doing? You have just travelled sixteen days to get here, through storms, on rough tracks and wild seas. Sometimes, lives were at risk. You're travelling with two long-time friends. They'll understand if you have business to attend to; that's what you came here for.

You have decided your future is on this farm in Harris. You signed a sub-lease last year with an agent, William Macleod, which would have

> commenced a week or two ago. You paid the first year's rent. You are entitled to take possession of this land now but have not yet done so.
> You have a pressing invitation to meet with Hume (Alexander Macleod, the owner of the Isle of Harris, including this farm) and Ensay (Hume's factor). You have not yet met either but you intend starting to farm here soon. Isn't it possible this meeting might be important?

BACK TO THE BORDERS

They departed on the *Hawk of Oban* again after five nights on Harris:

> my two friends were again seized with severe qualms, which continued during the rest of our course. Mr J., who had hitherto been quite calm and resigned, now became somewhat frenzical, and though he slept for the most part . . . As for Mr W. he always continued in a state of utter despair, from the time that the vessel began to rock, viewing our fate as certain, and our escape rather a miracle, if it should happen.

Despite the misery of Messrs J. and W. and being becalmed for a while, it was a simple trip back to the mainland:

> the breeze again set in, and bore us safely into Arisaig, where we dined, and that evening travelled to Kinloch-Enort, a stage on the road to Fort William. – When we arrived there the people were all in bed, but on rapping loudly at the door, the landlord, a big, black, terrible-looking fellow, came stark naked, and let us in: he then lighted a candle, tied on his kilt, and asked how far we had come . . .
> He then shewed us into a little damp room with an earthern floor, and set before us what cheer he had in the house for supper, which consisted of cakes, milk, and rum, for, what is very strange, he had no whisky. In this same apartment there were two heather beds without hangings, on one of which a woman and some children were lying. Mr W. was now in a terrible passion, and swore he would abandon that horrid place, and take shelter in the woods. The woman and children, however, slid away; the beds were made up with clean cloathes, and we were obliged to pass the night on them the best way we could.
> [The next day] we crossed the river at Inverlochy; and, about five o'clock, P. M. arrived at Fort William, intending to tarry there all night; but, unfortunately for us, as well as many others, no doubt, the lady of Glencoe, an amiable young woman, of the most respectable connections, had been lately carried off by an unfortunate accident, and that was her burial day . . . there was not one of the houses would admit us as lodgers: and Mr W. got into such a passion at the people's impertinence, that he

would not suffer us to take any dinner, for fear lest the abominable town should be benefited by our money . . .

We passed some scenes of incomparable beauty; cottages embosomed in wild woods, and hallows of the hills; and at a late hour arrived, weary and fatigued, at Balnachulish . . .

[C]rossing over the ferry in the morning, we bad farewell to Lochaber, and entered the famous vale of Glencoe, rendered so by the base and cowardly slaughter of the Macdonalds in 1691;[4] and also for the extraordinary ruggedness and terrific majesty of the mountains overhanging it on each side . . . Such an accumulation of the awful and sublime can hardly be conceived.

It is also supposed by some who are versed in the Gaelic etymology, that this was the birth-place of the poet Ossian . . . You will observe, my dear Sir, that I have no doubts respecting the existence of the bard; but whether his heroes had any, save in his brain, may perhaps turn out a point that will admit of discussion.[5]

Glencoe is, however, stocked with excellent sheep, that is what we are sure of; but it is hard now to discern where so many people could have resided in the glen, as seem to have lived there previous to the revolution. The day was very hot, and we arrived at the Kings' house, in the Black mount, almost parched with thirst. [Alas, despite their hopes for something stronger, they could get only tea.]

We then came over the Black mount. Rested at Inverouran; and after crossing the Orchay, and the beautiful extensive sheep farm of Auch, arrived in the evening at Tynedrum; an excellent inn in that district of Breadalbin, called Strathfillan, where the great lead mines are situated.[6]

---

[4] An infamous massacre, *Mort Ghlinne Comhann*, took place in February 1692. Clans involved in the 1689 rebellion were offered an amnesty if their chiefs would pledge loyalty to the king. An elderly chief of the MacDonalds was a few days late for the deadline, and an opportunity was seen to punish the clan. A company of soldiers, mainly from the Campbell territory of Argyll, and who had been staying as guests in MacDonald homes for twelve days, were ordered to kill their hosts at dawn – men, women and children, everyone under seventy – 'that these miscreants be cutt off root and branch'; thirty-eight were killed and another forty died in the cold, after their homes had been burned.

[5] Some forty years earlier, James Macpherson had published poetry which he claimed to have translated from ancient Gaelic, supposedly narrated by Ossian about his legendary father, Fingal. The poems were hugely popular in Britain and Europe, but were later widely considered to have been created by Macpherson himself, based on old folk tales, rather than being direct translations of ancient poetry.

[6] Lead was mined near Tyndrum over about 600 years, and particularly from the mid-1700s to 1862, but was not often profitable. Certain other metals have also been mined here, including silver for James I, and some gold to the present day. A Stirling University study, *The Lead Legacy: The Relationship between Historical Mining and Metallurgical Activity, Pollution and Health, 1730–2000*, found that this left 'a substantial legacy of physical dereliction and chemical pollution'. Effects on human health, though, were minor compared with those at mines such as Leadhills, in the Southern Uplands. Lead poisoning can cause premature death, but there must be exceptions: John Taylor, a miner, died at Leadhills in 1770, apparently aged at least 133.

> From thence we departed next morning, and in our way saw St Fillans, or the Holy Pool; and I took occasion to question a farmer, a native of that place, concerning that extraordinary superstition. But how astonished was I to hear, that even in this enlightened age, it was as firmly believed in as ever ... This pool the inhabitants believe to be supernaturally endowed with an extraordinary quality on a certain returning day each quarter of the year, and on these days, all the people, both far and near, that are in any degree deranged in their minds, are brought to it as a certain restorative.[7]
>
> ... the patients are tumbled into the pool over head and ears; then pulled out dripping wet; bound hand and foot with strong ropes, and locked up in the chapel, where they are suffered to remain until the sun rise next morning. If they are found then bound in the same manner as when left the preceding day, it is looked on as a bad omen, and they are carried home with wailings, because their offerings have not been accepted ...
>
> It is certainly not a little remarkable that this superstitious belief should prevail in an enlightened country, so late as the present day ...
>
> We arrived in Yarrow precisely in five days from the time of our leaving Harries. – Thus terminated the unfortunate journey, as it is generally called ... we never, in our way out, walked an hour without being drenched to the skin, and mudded to the knees: that we never went on the sea, though but for a few miles, without encountering storms, accidents, and dangers: nor ever, after leaving Greenock, proceeded one day by the route we intended, but either lost our way by land, or were thwarted by the winds and the sea ... we all three concluded, that an overruling Providence frowned upon our designs; and the event hath now fully justified the prediction.

Hogg resolved 'never more to take another journey, of such a nature, at my own expence' – a resolution which, of course, he was never able to keep.

The three were incompatible as travellers but the friendships survived and thrived. Mr John (Grieve) would be a huge source of support and encouragement for Hogg in the coming years. In his 'Memoir', Hogg described him as 'a friend, whose affection neither misfortune nor imprudence could once shake'.

And Mr William (Laidlaw), his childhood buddy, remained a close friend for the whole of his life. Even late in this journey Hogg would write: 'there are few of the human race whom I respect more than this gentleman'.

---

[7] Robert Heron, a writer and traveller, noted in 1792 that 'The patient is thrice immerged in the pool. He is bound hand and foot, and left for the night in a chapel. If the maniac is found loose in the morning, good hopes are conceived of his full recovery.' It is possible some of the patients in this area had suffered lead poisoning, the symptoms of which can include nerve damage, brain damage and insanity.

HARRIS IN RETROSPECT

The Harris farm venture did not proceed. Hogg had signed the sub-lease with William Macleod, an agent. Macleod's rights were challenged by Hume, the owner, who then sold some of the land. A complex train of events left Hogg with no farm, and Macleod with his £150 deposit. This was costly to Hogg. In current terms, the deposit equates to £143,000.[8]

And there was a personal cost. He'd said his farewell to Ettrick. After twenty years as a shepherd he had hoped to become a tenant-farmer, for the opportunities he saw in the Highlands. He would have to go back to being a shepherd now, wherever he could find work.

Why did he miss the meeting with Hume, the landowner, which might have been vital? Was he getting cold feet when he saw the land again, including the harsh eastern part of this, and had found how hard the sea passage could be? Was he starting to sabotage his own plans, maybe in the way that Burns had planned to move to Jamaica, then pulled out?

It seems unlikely. He purchased 'a good many sheep' and was ready to depart for Harris again a month after his return home.[9] And there was no attempt to get his deposit back until he knew the lease would not proceed.

It seems that he knew the contract was flawed, because it covered a larger area of land than Macleod was allowed to sublet. Macleod told him to lie if Hume should query it, but probably told him the risk was low. But now, surely, this must be what Hume wanted to discuss, and the deal could fall over if he had to lie about it in a meeting. So perhaps it was better to carry on, to stock the farm and assume the contract would work, and sort out the details later.

It didn't work. The real problem, though, was the flawed agreement he had signed in a burst of enthusiasm or desperation the previous year.[10]

In the long run, this was fortunate. It would have been hard to launch a literary career from the Hebrides. Had he abandoned his writing dreams then, he would have been quickly forgotten. Maybe Providence had smiled, after all.

In *Jamie's Farewell to Ettrick* there had been real sadness about leaving his homeland:

> Fareweel, my Ettrick, fare-thee-weel!
> I own I'm unco laith to leave ye;
> Nane kens the haf o' what I feel,
> Or haf the cause I hae to grieve me.

---

[8] The conversion is from the Measuring Worth website, using the 'average earnings' basis in 2014 values.
[9] Based on an article in *The Scots Magazine*, no. 67, November 1805, written by 'Z' and assumed to be by Hogg himself.
[10] Janette Currie has analysed this train of events in depth (in de Groot, *Highland Journeys*, Appendix III).

He shares his regrets for what he might have done for his beloved Ettrick:

> I had a thought, – a poor vain thought!
> That some time I might do her honour;
> But a' my hopes are come to nought,
> I'm forced to turn my back upon her.

And the vain hope of being a poet in the Outer Hebrides:

> I'll make the Harris rocks to ring
> Wi' ditties wild when nane shall hear;
> The Lewis shores shall learn to sing
> The names o' them I lo'ed sae dear.

And acceptance:

> If I should sleep nae mair to wake,
> In yon far isle beyond the tide,
> Set up a headstane for my sake,
> And prent upon its ample side;
>
> 'In memory of a shepherd boy,
> Who left us for a distant shore;
> Love was his life, and song his joy;
> But now he's dead – we add no more!'

Luckily, it didn't happen and there was more.

SIGNIFICANCE OF THE HIGHLAND JOURNEYS

The journeys would have a profound impact on Hogg. For a young man, open to new experiences but with little idea of what to expect, these landscapes would be mind-blowing. His travels through these places, with their seas and mountains bigger and wilder and more dangerous than anything he'd known, would inspire and frighten and change him forever. They would also draw him back to the Highlands.

He was thrown into social situations too, stranger and more extreme than any he would experience at home: encounters with landowners and the dispossessed, as a guest in a castle or hovel. These would challenge his principles and test his ideas to breaking point. He would learn about wealth and poverty, violence and inhumanity, which would influence his life and his writing.

And in these wild places, he was learning Highland history and culture from the source. His journeys had 'qualified the prejudices resulting from an upbringing in a district where Highlanders were feared as savage enemies of Presbyterianism and despised as ignorant and bloodthirsty savages'.[11]

---

[11] Hughes, *James Hogg*, p. 154.

They would help in his research for *The Jacobite Relics*, and inspire later poems and novels.

His travels provided sources of legends and ideas for stories, as well as the venues to set them in. Supernatural beings from Loch A'an appear in *The Queen's Wake*, some of 'Basil Lee' takes place in Lewis, and parts of *The Three Perils of Woman* are set in the Highland wilderness. They also gave him a good knowledge of farming in a range of locations, used, for example, in *The Shepherd's Guide*.

The records he left of these early visits, and especially his 1803 travels, have been used by others, and particularly as a source of information on farming, landscapes and clearances.[12]

There were many 'firsts' for Hogg from this time. When his early reports on the journeys appeared in *The Scots Magazine* in late 1802, these may have been his first prose – at least the first identifiable as his – to be published. It would be his prose, ultimately, that he would be best remembered for. This gave him a chance to write about himself, one of his very favourite subjects.

And when a letter on his 1802 journey appeared in *The Scots Magazine* in June 1803 with the signature 'The Etterick Shepherd', it was the first time this was used publicly. He'd developed it in his recent travel letters, first trying 'Shepherd' and 'A Shepherd'. The nom de plume would have its drawbacks, but it would stand the test of time. As a marketing tool it was perfect.

The journeys built new or stronger connections with friends. He met John Galt and James Park along the way, for example, and his experiences would build his links with Walter Scott; Hogg's letters and thoughts and chats with him over time would have influenced Scott's redefinition of the Highlands.

The 1803 journey provided his first real recognition outside the Borders for his writing or music. He was celebrated as a poet in Greenock and his song 'Donald Macdonald', sung often from Ardhill onwards, was an instant hit. This sort of recognition must have been a huge boost, and an incentive to do more.

Most importantly, though, the journeys brought Hogg to a crossroads. He failed in his bid to lease a farm and would soon hit a personal low, but would emerge with a clearer vision. The failure led to a crisis, a reassessment, and then to new directions. He could never let go of his farming ambitions. But writing was now a clearer focus, and would be for the rest of his life.

NOTES ON MY JOURNEYS – WESTERN HIGHLANDS AND ISLANDS

Racing with shepherds

We might assume that shepherds in Hogg's time were tough. They would travel big distances through the hills, moving or chasing sheep. Where roads existed

---

[12] For example, extracts in *Scotland's Mountains before the Mountaineers* by Ian R. Mitchell in 1998 and *The Highland Clearances* by Eric Richards in 2002.

they would often be rough, but they might be more pleasant than today when highways have often encroached on the best routes, bringing noise and risks to walkers.

I wanted to find a part of a journey that Hogg had done to see how I compared. I chose a route that followed the West Highland Way, which I guessed was a fair equivalent of those old roads, and avoided traffic most of the way. On 14 June 1804, Hogg and his mates left Ballachulish and walked to Tyndrum. On 29 July 2015, I would try the same, though in the opposite direction which suited me best at the time. I like to stay fit, but I spend a lot of time sitting. Would I make it?

I set out early from Tyndrum. It was easy going to the Bridge of Orchy (my first coffee) and on to Inveroran (a snack), arriving there late morning. And feeling great! I relished the view from the hills over Loch Tulla (picturesque). Then, a long walk over the Black Mount (lunch, sublime). I reached Kings House mid-afternoon and enjoyed some luxuries that Hogg could not: a cold beer and a change of socks.

I walk on past the Devil's Staircase (the name is worse than the reality – I'd be back to do this part in a couple of days) and on through the glen of Glencoe. We've left the West Highland Way by now, and my route is a mix of military and cycle trails where I can find them. But in some parts I take short cuts to avoid the road and I get lost or stuck in the scrub. I'm getting a bit weary now. Stunning country, though. Huge rocky landscapes with big empty spaces, and an eerie sense of a past that I know too little about.

Past Glencoe village, but no time to stop. And late in the day, fourteen hours after leaving Tyndrum, I arrive at Ballachulish Bridge, where the ferries once ran. There, I'd done it – 37 miles (60 km) over fairly rough ground, just like they did.

Purists might point out that by travelling from south to north my route was, on average, slightly downhill. It's true. But the difference was less than 800 ft (under 250 m). I'd gladly swap this advantage for the absence of traffic that Hogg and his friends enjoyed. And they were younger.

But here's the real difference. The next day I took a break (I decided to call it sightseeing). The day after Hogg et al. got to Tyndrum they carried on walking, through Glen Dochart and Callander to Doune, another 46 miles (74 km) in that day. OK, I'm convinced. They were tough.

For anyone interested, it is not too hard to find places Hogg visited on these trips. On that day in 1804, he and his companions set out by ferry from North Ballachulish. Almost certainly, they had stayed in Loch Leven Hotel, adjacent to the ferry terminal, which had operated since the mid-eighteenth century and is still in business today.

Kings House was built in the seventeenth century. It's one of Scotland's oldest licensed inns, and was used by troops after the Battle of Culloden, hence the name. Hogg passed through in June 1803 and June 1804 and was unimpressed, as was Dorothy Wordsworth in September 1803: 'Never did I see such a miserable, such a wretched place.' But there have been a few changes over the past couple of centuries.

Figure 23 North Ballachulish, probably the inn Hogg and his friends stayed in before taking the ferry over Loch Leven in 1804.

Figure 24 Kings House. Easier to get a drink now than in 1804.

Hogg stayed a night at Inveroran in 1803, and rested there in 1804. The inn here is said to date back to 1708, but it is hard to be certain that it is the same one. Dorothy Wordsworth said it was a small thatched house in 1803, and Robert Southey described it as a 'miserable hovel' in 1819. In

WESTERN HIGHLANDS AND ISLANDS (1804)

Figure 25 Inveroran Hotel, formerly a hovel. A resting place in 1803 and 1804.

1841 Charles Darwin referred to a knot of little outhouses and said that 'in one of those there were fifty highlanders all drunk'. One or more of these houses might be part of the current building, much of which dates from the mid-nineteenth century.

And they spent the night at 'an excellent inn', in Tyndrum, and I hoped to find it. I had read that S. T. Coleridge visited the Royal Hotel in Tyndrum in 1803, and assumed that Hogg and his buddies would have stayed in the same one. Alas, this was wrong; the Royal Hotel was not built until later that century, and they would probably have stayed in the Tyndrum Inn, which then occupied this site.

But that's OK. It is still impressive that, in a day's walk, it is possible to visit at least three places they spent time in, that day on 14 June 1804.

North Harris

My final visit to Harris was a quick one. I had time for a visit to the North Harris Trust, which delighted me. The land, after centuries of private ownership, had been bought by the community. The purchase, to 'throw off the shackles of feudal rule', was completed in 2013.[13] Landowners had been cooperative. Now, for just £1, a resident could buy membership in the Trust for life, and share ownership of the 64,000 acre estate. Conservation is a high priority for the Trust.

---

[13] Stephen Khan (Scotland Editor), 'Clearances in reverse bring justice to Scotland's crofters at last', *The Observer*, 16 March 2003.

It's a special area. The mountains of North Harris are built of some of the oldest rocks in the world: Lewisian gneiss, thought to be three billion years old.

I came here to see the eagles. Hogg was less enthused by these, and advocated killing them. His fear for his sheep was genuine, and possibly I would've shared it. But that was then, and this is now.

His experience would've been mainly with golden eagles, which were then down to a third of their AD 500 population, and dropping. White-tailed sea eagle populations had also been slashed over that period; they would become extinct in Scotland later, but were reintroduced from Norway last century. Despite conservation efforts, numbers are still probably lower than in 1800, about 440 pairs of golden and eighty pairs of sea eagles. Challenges remain, from habitat loss and continuing persecution.[14]

Two golden eagles soared 300 ft (90 m) above me in Meavaig, a few miles north-west of Tarbert. One might have been a chick on a practice flight with a parent. It was hard to tell at this distance. In a gusty westerly they did what was needed to stay in one place, an occasional wing-beat, nothing more. I willed them to dive lower but they kept their distance. They might have sensed my killer genes. I put my lunch money in the donation box and gave thanks to those who were battling to protect them.

Out and about in Uist

I was keen to visit North Uist. Hogg had come here, with Messrs J. and W., to escape a storm.

I sympathise with their discomfort at sea. Like them, I'm mainly a landlubber. But I love small boats, such as canoes and kayaks. You can see the whole boat at a glance, you know if it's sound, and you control your own destiny. If the weather is wild, you know you have to respect it. I feel less comfortable in a larger boat. There is so much more to go wrong, with other people to rely on, and sometimes a false sense of safety.

My time in the Solomons cemented my views. Early on, I was asked to review a shipping line. It was losing money, and maybe I could help turn it around? The directors assured me everything was fine, they just needed time. The largest of its vessels carried 800 people regularly on overnight trips. But the chief engineer showed me how these old ships were being repaired. Rusting steel hulls were patched with timber and concrete. He wrote: 'imminent danger of an all-out rupture'. They were 'risking the lives of passengers and crew on every voyage'. Life jackets had been sold or stolen during 'the conflict'. Recently a sister ship had sunk in the Philippines, with the loss of dozens of lives. Any day now the

---

[14] According to a 2012 study (Evans et al., 'The history of eagles'), populations in Britain and Ireland in 1800 (which were then, as now, mostly in Scotland) were estimated as golden eagle, 300–500 pairs; and sea eagle (white-tailed), 150 pairs. Sea eagles, the study says, tend to nest at lower altitudes than golden eagles (below 500 ft/150 m) in trees and near the water. This would suggest very low numbers of sea eagles in Ettrick Forest, which had few trees despite the name, and other inland Borders areas, although a map in that study indicates there may have been some remnant populations there.

rust holes would join up, the ship would break in half – he showed me the likely fracture line – and it would sink like a stone.

The directors dismissed his reports; this wasn't what they wanted to hear. I had recently arrived in the country and had no authority. But the night that I'd met with the engineer I had nightmares. It was a disaster, waiting for a time and place. I contacted some of the most powerful people in the country. I said that sailings should be stopped forthwith, and after some difficult meetings, they were. And within a few months, two of the three company ships had sunk at anchor, fortunately now out of service and with no loss of life. The ships had been on the brink of disaster.[15] And yet . . . the locals, in their small boats, were natural seafarers. Dugout canoes would travel long distances, out of sight of land and without a compass, in safety. As they had done for millennia.

I do not doubt that Hogg and his mates put their lives at risk several times, on the *Hawk of Oban*, with her crew with no sense of direction, and on the unwieldy *Johnson* with her crew that rejected dire weather warnings then panicked – all but one of them – when they came to pass.

Safety standards were low then. In 1801, an emigrant ship sailed to Canada with 700 people crammed in the hold, and forty-nine of them died en route; ironically, if they had been slaves fewer than 500 would have been allowed on that ship. The Passenger Vessels Act was passed in 1803 (supposedly to protect emigrants, but really designed to slow emigration). This law did not apply to coastal shipping, though, in which the risks could be high and the chances of rescue quite low.

In 1804, shortly before Hogg and his friends sailed, HMS *York* struck rocks off Arbroath and sank, killing all 491 men and boys aboard. And some years earlier, seventy ships had been lost off the east coast in a single storm.

In 2015, things looked a lot better. For reasons that made sense at the time, I took ferries from Tarbert in Harris, to Uig in Skye, then back to North Uist. The 'good slated inn' the 1804 travellers stayed in at Lochmaddy is still there, no longer an inn or filled with tenants paying their rents, but probably more attractive than ever. I camped nearby. The inn had fallen into disrepair for a while but was reopened in 1995 and now serves as a museum, café, and arts and community centre. And it serves great soup.

It was south from here that I was reminded that, even with modern transport, travel can sometimes be complicated. I'd planned to take a bus through Benbecula and catch the ferry from Lochboisdale, in South Uist, back to the mainland. That way I'd sail through the Sound of Mull, as Hogg had twice.

Simple. But a ferry breakdown led to a change of schedule. My ferry had left two hours early. No one was sure when the next one would be. I discovered this when I arrived at the terminal.

---

[15] An article on this saga, 'Lost at Sea', appears in New Zealand *Management Magazine*, March 2010, pp. 41–3. I am eternally grateful to the engineer, who risked his job to show me the hazards, and might have saved hundreds of lives in the process.

Figure 26 Taigh Chearsabhagh museum, café and community centre in Lochmaddy; still nourishing intellectual life.

'We told everyone,' they said.
'But I'm someone,' I said. 'And you didn't tell me.'
'We put it on the website this morning.'
'I wasn't looking at your website this morning. I was coming here to catch the ferry.'

I had a good point and I'm sure, deep down, they agreed. They'd contacted people with cars who had booked, but not me who didn't have to. If the ferry was two hours late that would've been fine, but two hours early was impossible. But I'd already decided I wasn't going to insist that they put on a special ferry for me. For one thing, there wasn't any.

So this meant a change of plans. And it meant the following extra forms of transport: walking, school bus, hitching, post bus, ferry to Barra, more walking, local bus, and then a ferry from Castlebay to Oban. This included travelling over two islands that I would have missed, and a stunning beach walk in Eriskay, a bit more complex but far more interesting than I'd planned. And I learnt the story of *Whisky Galore*.

The downside? Oh, yes. I still sailed through the picturesque Sound of Mull. But alas, it was in total darkness.

6 Arrivals and Departures: Life and other journeys

REPENTANCE

There were some after-shocks for a while after Hogg's journeys and the Harris debacle. He spent a summer in northern England, partly to avoid questions about his plans. He was delighted to hear his song 'Donald Macdonald' being performed – and encored three times – in an English theatre, though with no recognition for its composer.

He returned to Scotland to work as a shepherd (one offer required him to put his 'poetical talent under lock and key forever') and was making some progress with his writing. A number of his poems, songs and ballad-imitations were published, mainly in *The Scots Magazine*. He told Walter Scott: 'if ever I rise above or even to a mediocrity it is to be by my writings'. And he must have been getting a little bit famous; in 1806, Allan and James Cunningham (the former a budding poet and author) came to find him and shook hands; the latter said, 'There is not a hand in Scotland whose hand I am prouder to hold.'

In 1807 there were two significant publications: *The Shepherd's Guide*[1] and *The Mountain Bard: consisting of Ballads and Songs, founded on Facts and Legendary Tales*. These were published by Archibald Constable, after an introduction and support from Scott.

With some money in his hand, Hogg took up two Dumfriesshire farm leases, starting in 1807. And that year he was rebuked on the Stool of Repentance, following the birth of his little daughter Keatie.

Hogg and Catherine Henderson were lovers when he worked as a shepherd at Mitchelslacks, in Dumfriesshire. She named him as the father. And about three years later, Margaret Beattie would name him as the father of her child, too.

---

[1] *The Shepherd's Guide: being a Practical Treatise on the Diseases of Sheep, Their Causes, and the Best Means of Preventing Them; with observations on the most suitable farm-stocking for the various climates of this country.* This became a classic work for shepherds, store-farmers and agricultural improvers for many years.

Figure 27 James Hogg, oil painting by William Nicholson. The earliest known portrait of Hogg, in about 1815. Surprisingly, he is aged about 45 here.

James Hogg and the 'Bastard Brood'[2]

Hogg, officially at least, had two daughters while unmarried. The first was welcomed into the world in the Morton parish register records: 'Hogg & Henderson: Catharine Bastard Daughter to James Hogg and Catharine Henderson baptized at Thornhill 13th Decr 1807'. In June that year, Catherine Henderson had acknowledged herself to be 'with child in uncleanness', and Hogg acknowledged paternity. The daughter (also Catherine but known as Keatie) was apparently born in July or August.

The second daughter, born to Margaret Beattie in 1810, was greeted in parish records with: 'March 13 James Hogg and Margaret Beattie in Locherben in Fornication Elisabath'. (One can't help feeling the writers of these entries delighted in using the uppercase 'B' and 'F' beside these little girls' names.) 'Elisabath' was known as Betsy. Hogg and Margaret had been lovers and he accepted that he was the father, but said later he was never quite sure of this.

---

[2] This heading is the tongue-in-cheek title of a delightful paper by Gillian Hughes.

It was not uncommon for a child to be conceived out of wedlock then, but the kirk had tight control over what would happen next. Baptism was crucial for the salvation of the child, but was only available if the mother and father would publicly repent. The rules and norms of repentance

> involved agreeing to the support of the child for a period of several years ... Three appearances were formally required in church for 'simple fornication', six for a second offence, 26 for adultery and a year for incest. All these appearances were supposed to be made in sackcloth. A fine of £10 Scots was also levied which was waived in the case of the poor.[3]

Details of arrangements that Hogg made are unknown.

He described the experience in a letter to a friend, John Aitken, in 1817: 'I have myself stood with a red face on the Stool of Repentance.' And in 1807 he got a high compliment: 'the minister said he had that day to rebuke a man more fit to be his teacher'.

There seems to have been little pressure for Hogg to marry either woman. No doubt their families knew he'd struggle financially. (When Catherine's aunt asked why he hadn't married her, he blamed the wet weather. Catherine and her family burst out laughing and the matter was never raised again.) His 1817 letter continues: 'The mothers are both married to men much more respectable in life than ever I was ... even with their nearest relations I have never been a day out of favour.'

Gillian Hughes believes Hogg's views on sexual morality can be seen in his novel *The Three Perils of Woman*, 'both a profoundly Christian and a profoundly radical work'. She says that illegitimate children may have been the 'bastard brood' to some, but 'to James Hogg they were always primarily children'.[4]

In signing leases for two farms at once, Hogg had taken a massive risk. It didn't work. He tells us in his 'Memoir' that he had gone 'perfectly mad'.

Rent did not need to be paid until later and his funds were invested in livestock. He moved to one farm first and lost his stock in a storm. He moved to the other, and tried to make a living by grazing sheep. His debts blew out. Two years later, essentially bankrupt, he gave his creditors what he could and moved on.

DISCOVERY

Hogg returned to Ettrick, where he was now considered unemployable. But none of this, he tells us later, 'had the least effect in depressing my spirits – I was generally rather most cheerful when most unfortunate'. In 1810 though,

---

[3] Devine, *Scottish Nation*, p. 88.
[4] Hughes, 'James Hogg and the "Bastard Brood"'.

'in utter desperation, I took my plaid about my shoulders, and marched away to Edinburgh, determined, since no better could be, to push my fortune as a literary man'.

Later that year he met Margaret Phillips, a young woman who was visiting his friend – her brother-in-law – James Gray. Hogg was exploring the cultural life of the city, and was supported by his friend John Grieve, by now a well-off Edinburgh hatter. In August his song collection, *The Forest Minstrel*, was published and on 1 September the first issue of his own weekly paper, *The Spy*, appeared. This was a brave solo venture and, despite its perceived improprieties, it survived for a year.

In this period he became a member of the Forum, a public debating society, and was appointed Secretary with a salary of £20 – impressive but not always paid. Audiences often exceeded 500. Hogg always spoke, 'my confidence in myself being unbounded', and his 'Memoir' tells us he 'was in general a prodigious favourite'.

With Grieve's encouragement he took rural lodgings on the outskirts of Edinburgh, and he planned a long narrative poem based on a fictional poetic contest at the court of Mary, Queen of Scots.

In this post-journey period, Hogg displays some of his hallmarks. One is an ability to make disastrous financial decisions, combined with a tendency to repeat them, with variations, a few years later. Another is his remarkable ability to make and retain – or sometimes to make, break and regain – strong friendships. And then there is his persistence, his ability to bounce back from any knock-down. Of which, there would be many.

But much in his life was changed in 1813. *The Queen's Wake*, the poem about the poetic contest, was published by George Goldie at the end of January. He walked into downtown Edinburgh the following day, feeling 'like a man between death and life, waiting for the sentence of the jury'. It was a success – 'everything that I heard was laudatory' – and he was an instant celebrity. Suddenly there would be new friends and new opportunities.

The poem had been written, he said, 'within an incredibly short time'. This ties in with other comments he made about his work. Earlier, he said of his poetry:

> Let the piece be of what length it will, I compose and correct it wholly in my mind, or on a slate, ere ever I put pen to paper; and then I write it down as fast as the A, B, C. When once it is written, it remains in that state; it being ... with the utmost difficulty that I can be brought to alter one syllable.

In song, too: 'I had no more difficulty in composing songs then than I have at present; and I was equally well pleased with them.' Also: 'I never in my life re-wrote a page of prose.' This would account for his high level of output, and perhaps reflects a belief that the work was 'heaven sent'; critics might think it also accounts for variations in quality.[5]

---

[5] Hogg wrote about his poetry and songs in 1807 ('Memoir', p. 17) and his prose in 1832 ('Reminiscences', p. 55).

The Queen's Wake

This was a book-length poem, an imaginary story of a poetic contest between minstrels (a wake) to welcome Mary, Queen of Scots, back to Scotland after her long absence in France. It comprises a series of separate tales within a larger narrative, with the narrators of these appearing as characters. Some of these represent contemporary bards, easily recognisable by their poetry; Hogg showed that not only could he write in a range of styles, but he had the ability to write poetry as if it were written by others. The prizes in the contest were two harps, presented by the queen: one is magnificent, and is won by an aristocratic Highland poet; a simpler but possibly better one goes to the Bard of Ettrick, who represents Hogg himself, as a consolation prize. In the poem, he is poor, despised and badly dressed. In real life, a sketch of the harp would become his seal.

His poem is considered to be a landmark of British Romantic poetry. It can also be seen as a search for a Scottish identity, lost and complicated in the Union with England. One of its poems, 'Kilmeny', a tale of transportation to a fairy world, is widely seen as a masterpiece. His poem took Scotland by storm. As a poet, Hogg had arrived.

With this new success, anything seemed possible. He tried to interest Constable in a series of Scottish rural tales. He got advice from his friends on the suitability of his play, *The Hunting of Badlewe*, for the stage (this was not so favourable). And he began a poem in the Spenserian stanza (a verse form devised by Edmund Spenser for *The Faerie Queene*), eventually to become *Mador of the Moor*.

The year was going well. But it was also the year that his mother, Margaret Laidlaw, died. Hogg would miss her dearly. He said: 'I have lost the warmest, the sincerest and in a word the best friend that ever I had in this world or am ever likely to have.' He regrets that he would now have no one to be kind to (presumably his father fits into a different category). She is remembered in his poem, *A Last Adieu*: for her love, as a pupil of Nature, and for her songs of battles and fairies and ghosts.

The year 1814 was the end of an era in Scotland. There had been a threat of a French invasion for years, but the allies had entered Paris and there were hopes for an end to the wars.

Goldie published *The Hunting of Badlewe* now, and Hogg's ambitions for a stage production of this were postponed. He tells us, around this time, that he usually went on a tour in the Highlands each summer. He had of course told us, at the end of the 'unfortunate journey', that he would never do this again. Perhaps he was starting to learn to never say 'never'.

During that summer he met William Wordsworth in Edinburgh, describing him as a 'superior being', and visited him and other poets in an excursion to the Lake District.

By this time Hogg had an impressive number of literary friends. For some years he had known Scott, Galt, Gray, John Wilson, J. G. Lockhart, John M'Diarmid and Allan Cunningham. He also knew many of the city's leading literary women now: Mary Peacock (later Gray), Anne Grant, Mary Brunton, Janet Stuart and Eliza Izett.

And more recently, helped by *The Queen's Wake*, he was now in touch with R. P. Gillies, Thomas De Quincey, S. T. Coleridge and Lord Byron, as well as Wordsworth.

He met Robert Southey too, inviting him to join him at an inn in Keswick, but was shocked that Southey refused his rum punch. 'For a poet to refuse his glass was to me a phenomenon', he said. He doubted 'if perfect sobriety and transcendent poetical genius can exist together. In Scotland I am sure they cannot.' Hogg admired Southey greatly but did not meet him again.

He then proposed a half-yearly Edinburgh Poetical Repository, with contributions by leading writers, and got support and promises from some key poets. Scott, though, refused to contribute and this led to a quarrel in the autumn. George Goldie's bankruptcy then stopped sales of *The Queen's Wake*, but led Hogg to meet with the publisher William Blackwood.

He offered *Mador of the Moor* to Constable in February, and was working on *The Pilgrims of the Sun*, an adventurous poem about a young woman's out-of-body experience and tour of the cosmos, with similarities to 'Kilmeny'. (With her spirit guide she visits the warriors of Mars and the lovers of Venus, and stands at the gateway to Heaven before returning to earth again.) This was originally meant to be part of a collection, but so impressed his friend James Park that he decided to publish it separately. After delays and complications the poem was brought out by Blackwood in Edinburgh in December, and in London a little later.

In the latter part of the year, Hogg and his young friends in Edinburgh formed the Right and Wrong Club. It was a strange concept, involving meetings of heavy drinkers, all of whom had to support what any member said, whether it was right or wrong. The past few months had been awkward ones; Hogg had been waiting on unreliable publishers, and had fallen out with Scott. In this vacuum, perhaps, such a diversion appealed. The group met and drank nightly over three months – 'Sundays not excepted'. Hogg says he drank himself into an 'inflammatory fever' and ended the year confined to bed, recuperating for the next few weeks.

But 1815 brought some truly astonishing news. Hogg learned that the Duke of Buccleuch had granted him the small farm of Eltrieve Moss in the Yarrow Valley, at a nominal rent for the rest of his life. How on earth did this happen?

A couple of years earlier, he had written to the duchess enquiring about this farm, as a possible home for his parents. It had been tenanted then. But since that time, his mother, the tenant, and the duchess had all died. Harriet, the duchess, had been fond of him. She had often invited him to play cards. He had dedicated *The Forest Minstrel* to her.

When she died he published his lament for her: he could not regret her death more had she been a 'sister, lover, child' to him. The duke had then remembered her dying wish, that somehow he should help him. Hogg wrote in his 'Reminiscences' that he was subsequently a frequent guest at the duke's table, and that 'he placed me always next to him'. The rent was meant to be nominal, Hogg said, but 'it has not even been nominal, for such a thing as rent has never once been mentioned'.

The farm was about 40 acres, in a charming position. It was on a gentle slope above the Yarrow River, and overlooked the valley. The Altrive Lake stream ran by, on its way to join the Yarrow. The cottage, though, was barely habitable. It was described later as an 'auld clay biggin, which was penetrated by all the winds of heaven . . . all the plaids were hung up round the door as a screen from the cold'. His father moved in, while Hogg continued to spend most of his time in Edinburgh.

Later that year Walter Scott published a poem, *The Field of Waterloo*, to celebrate the Battle of Waterloo and the end of the Napoleonic Wars. This prompted Hogg to write a poem of the same name, but his is focused at a much more personal level, including the death-bed prayer of a Scottish soldier, far from home. And later he also wrote *To the Ancient Banner of Buccleuch*, for a massive football game, with teams of hundreds led by him and by Scott.

In 1816 he contributed songs to John Clarke-Whitfeld's *Twelve Vocal Melodies*, and planned a collected edition of his own poetry. *Mador of the Moor* was published in April. He gave up on his poetical repository after problems with contributors, and turned it into a collection of his own parodies instead, published as *The Poetic Mirror* in October. The volume was successful, and a second edition was published in December.

The next year William Blackwood began the *Edinburgh Monthly Magazine* with Hogg's support, which they hoped would rival Constable's *Scots Magazine*. Blackwood had recently signalled his aim to become a leading publisher. But he quickly fell out with his editors, who left to work with Constable on a rebranded *Edinburgh Magazine*. Hogg stuck with Blackwood, helping to launch a revamped *Blackwood's Edinburgh Magazine*, and getting it off to a controversial start with his 'Translation of an Ancient Chaldee Manuscript'. This was a description of the rivalry between the two magazines and their unnamed but recognisable supporters, written in pseudo-biblical language.

William Blackwood was a force to be reckoned with. He had started out as a vendor of old and rare books. He branched into publishing, and his firm would become the most successful Scottish publisher in the early nineteenth century. His magazine was seen as an organ of the Scottish Tory party. It would carry scurrilous attacks on other writers, and would be considered by many to be immoral, too personal, too partisan and lacking in gentility.

A Glasgow newspaper editor, insulted in its pages, tried to have Blackwood horse-whipped. Blackwood, 'armed with a bludgeon, and apparently somewhat intoxicated', fought back. Hogg, seen as a Blackwood supporter, was then challenged to a duel. The stakes were getting high now, and Hogg took time out in the Borders. It was a sensible retreat. This was not play-fighting: a few years later the editor of *London Magazine* was shot and killed in a duel with a Blackwood agent, following an exchange of literary criticisms.

An 1818 review called the magazine 'the vilest publication that ever . . . soiled the annals of literature'. It sold well. Writers publishing through Blackwood's firm included Scott, De Quincey, Galt and Coleridge. Later writers would include George Eliot, Anthony Trollope, Joseph Conrad, E. M. Forster and John Buchan.[6]

Hogg's *Dramatic Tales*, four plays in two volumes, were published in 1817. And he spent much of the summer at his farm in the Yarrow, writing songs for *Hebrew Melodies*, a Byron-inspired collection proposed by the composer W. E. Heather.

In 1818 *The Brownie of Bodsbeck; and Other Tales* was published by Blackwood, Hogg's first novel. This was a change for Hogg; poetry, not prose, had long been the pre-eminent literary art form and had always been his main priority. And by this time he was working hard on *The Jacobite Relics of Scotland*, his major role for the year. The proposal for a collection of Jacobite songs had come from the Highland Society of London to George Thomson, and he had passed this on. Hogg had previously provided songs for Thomson's *A Select Collection of Original Scottish Airs*. In the course of the *Jacobite Relics* project he developed a working relationship with his nephew, Robert. (Some years later, Blackwood asked Robert to edit one of Hogg's manuscripts, to remove any 'objectionable or superfluous' material.)

And around this time he built an 'elegant stone cottage' on his little farm, and called it Altrive.[7] He hoped to cover the cost in part by a new one guinea subscription edition of *The Queen's Wake*.

The next couple of years brought changes on a number of fronts. He met Margaret Phillips again. Their relationship had been on and off for nearly a decade. This time it was real. In 1820 they married and moved into the little cottage in Altrive.

Margaret Phillips and James Hogg

When James Hogg and Margaret Phillips first met in 1810 he told his friend, 'Margaret's the lass for me.' But from here, progress was slow and sporadic.

Margaret was fresh from finishing school then, good-looking with dark hair and eyes, and 'a well-developed figure'. She had a sense of humour, and came from a conservative, prosperous farming background. She was the third significant Margaret in his life, after his mother and Margaret Beattie, his recent lover.

Hogg was openly flirtatious with many women, particularly those who were intellectual and unconventional. Would this new relationship, with

---

[6] Blackwood family members continued to run the firm for more than a century, and led its expansion into London. Its decline began at the height of the Battle of Britain. Douglas Blackwood, its manager and a fighter pilot, looked down from 25,000 ft to see the firm's office and millions of books ablaze. *Blackwood's Magazine* battled on until 1980.

[7] This is now called Eldinhope, and a larger farm up the valley is called Altrive. The elegant stone cottage still stands, but has been changed and enlarged.

a woman from a more conventional background, last? There were some affectionate letters. A few years later though, in a time of depression after falling out with Scott, Hogg described her as cold, and said he had never loved her.

Things warmed up a bit when they met again in 1819. He proposed quite quickly and Margaret accepted, provided her parents approved. Some months went by. And nothing happened. Then he confessed that he had 'an aversion to the married state'. He told her about his illegitimate daughters. She asked him if telling her this was due to honesty or a wish to break off the intended marriage.

Then finally, in March 1820, some real heat and tenderness. A date was agreed. A letter he sent her ends with 'Farewell my dearest Maggy till I see you . . . the braes of Yarrow will soon be wildly bonny.' They were married in April. James was 49. Margaret was 30.

Once married, the doubts seem to dissipate. He wrote to Robert Southey a few years later: 'I am now myself a husband to a wife whom I love from my soul.'

Happily ever after? It's hard to be certain, but from a distance the marriage seems to have been loving, supportive and respectful. James continued to enjoy the company of lively women, but there is no evidence of an affair. In discussions with a friend at one stage he suggested a degree of boredom, but perhaps it was just with domesticity. He told Margaret later, though in a different context, 'there is a principle in my constitution that requires constant excitement'.

They would have five children: James (born in 1821), Janet (aka Jessie, 1823), Margaret (1825), Harriet (1827) and Mary (1831). In his poem to the infant Harriet he would say:

> And thy sweet mother, too, the nearest
> To thee and me, the kindest, dearest.

There is a portrait of Margaret in her later years, in the Dunedin Public Art Gallery on the other side of the world. She looks rather sad. There is one of Hogg half a mile away, in the Hocken Gallery. He looks a bit grumpy. I've suggested to the directors that, occasionally at least, they should be brought together.

Some significant works were published around this time: *A Border Garland*, a song collection, including 'Bonnie Prince Charlie'; *Winter Evening Tales*, Hogg's second work of fiction; and a revised edition of *The Mountain Bard*; and he was working on a long Border Romance. *The Jacobite Relics* were published in two volumes, in 1819 and 1821. Music was included for most of the songs in these, but the collection received some criticism; in some cases he may have included the version of a song that he liked best, rather than the most authentic.

Hogg's father Robert, who had been at Altrive for five years with a housekeeper, and with Hogg from time to time, died there at the age of ninety-two. The old Duke of Buccleuch, his friend and patron, died and was succeeded by his son, a boy in his early teens at school in Eton. James and Margaret's first child was born, then baptised on their wedding anniversary in 1821. And just after that, Hogg turned down Scott's suggestion that he attend King George IV's coronation in London; the event clashed inconveniently with a more important occasion, the annual St Boswell's Fair.[8]

TURBULENT TIMES

About this time, just when things are looking good, the problems start. Hogg's often turbulent relationships with friends and other writers, it seems, were often matched by his arrangements with his publishers.

An updated 'Memoir of the author's life', included in the revised *Mountain Bard* in early 1821, causes an outcry as people named in it take offence. George Goldie, his previous publisher whom he accused of commercial malpractice, is rather unhappy. A savage, anonymous review of the memoir appears in *Blackwood's Edinburgh Magazine*. Blackwood had promised Hogg that nothing would be published 'but what you yourself shall previously see', but this had not been done.

Hogg is furious. He asks Scott about Blackwood: 'Shall I answer him in print? pursue him at law . . .? or knock out his brains?' Scott said no to the last; he would only give his support if Hogg could knock any brains *into* a bookseller. Making matters worse, it turns out later that the review, insulting and complete with pig puns, had come from his friend John Wilson. Hogg had not previously detected 'any malice or evil intent' in Wilson. He announced: 'I never will forgive him, especially for not once acknowledging it to me.'

There were savage reviews and distortions and insults among writers in these times. Hogg would be called a liar. But was he? There were errors of forgetfulness, of convenience, of not taking the time to check. The description of his discovery of Burns, of his own birth date, and his writing of 'Donald Macdonald', for example, are contradictory. There are minor errors in the reports from his journeys (and no doubt in mine).

There would be real lies too, but not his alone. Lies and creativity were closely aligned. A current writer explains that era:

> In Edinburgh taverns, around the university and in magazines such as Blackwoods, it was acceptable to take one stance early in the day and

---

[8] In *A Search for Scotland* (p. 110), R. F. Mackenzie described this decision and said, 'Belatedly we are discovering that Hogg chose the better part. If Scotland is to become healthy, to become whole, we should listen to him rather than Scott, because he got his priorities right.'

an opposite one by dinner time. Contradiction was as much a sign of mental nimbleness as it was of a 'divided nature'.[9]

Hogg was a master of contradiction. He lived comfortably with his divided self. He was shepherd and poet, rude and sophisticated; peasant and literary professional, humble and egotistical. His work was written and oral, fiction and non-fiction, in English and in Scots. He was a Jacobite, happy to see the end of old enmities; he sided with the landowner and the dispossessed. Even in a magazine he could see two versions of himself. His friends were radical and conservative, rich and poor, and he spoke to all of them exactly the same.

On his 1803 journey he concluded that 'truth tells aye best'. But when he spoke at the Forum he learnt 'the pulse of the public, and precisely what they would swallow, and what they would not'. And sometimes, for sure, he would get it wrong.

In 1821 he completed his Border Romance too, but fell out with his recently favourite publishers, Oliver & Boyd; they had impressed him with their work on *Winter Evening Tales*, but now refused to publish this one, partly due to the battle over his memoir.

And there was much worse on the horizon, though perhaps it wasn't obvious yet. That same year, Hogg signed up to a nine-year lease of the large farm at Mount Benger, a part of the Duke of Buccleuch's estates. It was a venture for which he was hopelessly under-capitalised. Two well-qualified farmers, he tells us, had already been ruined here in the past six years. He took this on 'in opposition to my own judgement'. James, one has to ask: 'Why?'

And another complexity: later that year, Hogg was ill with measles, a dangerous disease at the time. At his age, he thought, to get this was 'quite ridiculous'. His wife and little son stayed away.

Meanwhile, disaster was striking Margaret's family. In 1821 her sister Jessie died of consumption (tuberculosis) at Altrive. The next year her brother Peter died. Then her brother Walter was bankrupted and her parents lost most of their money as a result. And the following year her brother John died overseas. (That same year, happily, Margaret gave birth to a second child.)

When they had been wealthy, Margaret's parents had promised funds to help with the farms. Now, everything had changed. As well as the stone cottage at Altrive, there was an old cottage at Mount Benger, small, thatched and low-roofed. It made sense (didn't it?) for James and Margaret and their two little children to move to Mount Benger, and for Margaret's elderly, now impoverished parents to move to Altrive. So in 1823, at Hogg's suggestion, everyone moved.

Through the chaos, his writing continued. As Burns had before and Scott would do later, Hogg was inspired by growing financial pressures to lift his output. There were regular poems, articles and songs in magazines and annuals, many of them now in Archibald Constable's less lively *Edinburgh Magazine* and

---

[9] Brian Morton, reviewer of Karl Miller's *Electric Shepherd*, in *The Observer*, 17 August 2003.

his revamped *Scots Magazine*, since the break with Blackwood. A four-volume collection, *The Poetical Works of James Hogg*, was published by Constable, earning Hogg an impressive £200.[10]

Hogg was involved with Scott in the new King George IV's visit to Edinburgh in 1822, and wrote *The Royal Jubilee*. The king sent thanks for the 'gratifying proof of his genius and loyalty'. And his Border Romance, now called *The Three Perils of Man*, was published by Longman of London that year, a firm that Hogg had approached to do this a few years before.

The Three Perils of Man: War, Women and Witchcraft is an epic tale of Michael Scott, the Wizard of Aikwood, and of war between the English and Scots for possession of Roxburgh Castle. It combines humour, history, high-speed action and fantasy in an extraordinary series of overlapping plots and sub-plots. It was criticised by Walter Scott for its 'extravagance in demonology' but impressed others with its energy and innovation.[11]

It must have impressed the publisher, who accepted a companion novel the following year. *The Three Perils of Woman: Love, Leasing and Jealousy* combines two stories that echo each other hauntingly. One is set in Edinburgh and the Scottish Borders in the early 1820s, the other in the Highlands around the time of the Battle of Culloden. It challenges many of the attitudes and assumptions of the established elite of Hogg's day. For example, it refuses to gloss over the atrocities committed by the victors after Culloden, and it questions social attitudes to prostitution and other matters in his own times. It is radical and unsettling and did not sell very well.

Hogg received £150 for each of the *Three Perils* works. But despite his high level of output, he was going backwards quickly; he had to borrow to pay his first year's rent at Mount Benger.

Tibbie Shiel and James Hogg

Tibbie (Isabella) Shiel was born in Ettrick in 1783, about a mile from where Hogg was born and thirteen years later. She worked for his parents before she was married. Then, after her husband died, she ran an inn still known as Tibbie Shiels, on the strip of land between St Mary's Loch and Loch of the Lowes. Hogg was a frequent visitor there, and his monument, with its dreamy eyes, looks over this. And more than forty years after Hogg died, she was buried in Ettrick kirkyard a few yards from him.

---

[10] *The Scots Magazine* itself has had a remarkable life. It began in 1739. Hogg was first published in this in 1794. Constable bought it in 1801. It has continued, with some gaps, until the present day – the oldest magazine in the world still in publication. Constable's business failed in 1826, but he started up again, then died in the following year. The firm itself still operates, with changes, as Constable & Robinson – probably the oldest independent publisher in the English-speaking world still operating under its founder's name.

[11] Hogg was quite critical of this book later ('a mass of diablerie'), but most current critics are far more positive.

There is more to the story, but how much more? Had there been romance and was there ever 'an affair'? I'd heard a few rumours.

There might have been romance. Years later, Tibbie told a visiting fisherman: 'Yon Hogg, the Shepherd, ye ken, was an awfu' fine man. He should hae ta'en me, for he cam coortin' for years, but he just gaed away and took anither.'[12]

Tibbie got married in 1806 when she was twenty-three. Hogg was not married to Margaret Phillips then – that would be still fourteen years in the future. But his significant other might have been Catherine Henderson, who had his baby the following year.

Tibbie's husband Robert died in 1824, when she was about forty-one. But by that time, Hogg had been married for about four years. So if he had come courting, it was most likely before 1806, before Tibbie was twenty-three. But was this really courting, or was it Jamie the poeter, then in his mid-thirties, flirting with a much younger woman? It's hard to be sure.

Robert, a mole-catcher and dry-stane dyker, was a little younger than Tibbie was.[13] Tibbie might have met him about the time that Hogg had 'gaed away'. And when Robert died, she started the inn to support herself and her six children.

It was a respectable business. She did not sell whisky, visitors brought their own, but she provided everything else. She did not tolerate swearing. She had thirteen beds but there was also the floor, and she would accommodate up to thirty-five. She would take in gentlemen only; women were too fussy. In the early years of the inn, Hogg was perhaps her best customer. He brought the literary set, and they all brought visiting sportsmen.

Tibbie slept in a box bed off the lounge. Hogg often slept a few yards away, behind a settee, with a hinged section that could be used to roll him straight into bed at the end of a big night. There seems to be no suggestion of infidelity, and Margaret did not seem to be worried by the overnight stays.

Their lives continued to be interlinked, and there were signs of Hogg acting in loco parentis after Robert's death. When the girlfriend of her son Thomas was pregnant, and Thomas seemed likely to escape to America, Hogg urged that he should marry her, and he finally did. Hogg offered the advice 'as if I were advising my own son'.

The writers would come: Scott, Robert Chambers, Grieve, Wilson, Cunningham, Wordsworth, De Quincey, Lockhart, J. S. Blackie, Glassford Bell, William Aytoun and Scott Riddell. R. L. Stevenson came later.

---

[12] Quoted in Stoddart, *Angling Songs*, p. 42.
[13] Moles dug holes, an inconvenience to sheep. Dry-stane dykers built mortarless walls with interlocking stone; many walls built on farms in Scotland at that time are still rock solid today. I am indebted to Tibbie's descendant Peter Richardson for much of the information in this section.

And there was fun. Blackie wrote in a poem, 'A Lay of St Mary's Loch': 'He who knows not Tibbie, knows not Scotland in her happiest mood.' And at the wedding of her son in May 1832, as reported later in *The New York Times*, Hogg:

> appeared, rod in hand, and with a fiddle bestowed in the folds of his inseparable plaid; and how the instrument in question, in the hands of the bard, inspired that night as much hilarity as ever sprang from contact of horse-hair and catgut.[14]

(Hogg, then in his sixties, played until 4 a.m. and rolled into bed.)

The *New York Times* article said: 'A genuine friendship would seem to have subsisted between the strangely-assorted pair.' Certainly, if there had been romance, it was never allowed to spoil a special friendship.

At about age eighty, Tibbie thought she was ready to die and gave away her clothes. Then she lived another fourteen years, dying at ninety-four. She ran the inn for more than fifty years, until the day she died.

In 1824 there were two significant publications. There was a dark and daring novel: *The Private Memoirs and Confessions of a Justified Sinner*. And *Queen Hynde*: an epic poem in six volumes, a tale of romance and adventure set in the times of the Viking raids. Hogg and many others believed it was the equal of *The Queen's Wake*. In the market, though, it was a failure. From these extraordinary works, Hogg would earn nothing.

Meanwhile, although he had developed links with other publishers, and maybe just because he missed dealing with his former firm, Hogg wrote to William Blackwood again, saying, 'should I never see your face again I shall always wish you well'. Blackwood responded in like manner, the dispute was ended as quickly as it had started, and the working relationship grew.

There were two new and different links with *Blackwood's Edinburgh Magazine* (known informally as *Maga*). *The Shepherd's Calendar* appeared in this, a regular series of stories by Hogg begun in 1819 and revived in 1823. (This has no similarity to *The Shepherd's Guide*, his handbook for shepherds and sheep farmers.) It was welcomed by Blackwood, both for its quality and as a way of reducing Hogg's debt to the firm; half his fee was paid in cash, the other half offset against his account. The series was published in book form later, but from this, too, Hogg would earn nothing.

The other link had begun in his absence. A regular series, *Noctes Ambrosianae*, appeared in *Maga*, with contributions from a range of writers and notably

---

[14] *The New York Times*, 12 August 1878, following Tibbie's death in July; the article was reprinted from *The Scotsman*, 29 July 1878.

Figure 28 The Ettrick Shepherd and Tibbie Shiels Inn. Happy memories.

Wilson. The series portrayed fictional or exaggerated gatherings in a local tavern, usually attended by 'The Shepherd' who had an unmistakable likeness to Hogg. The character was mocked, sentimentalised, or treated as a 'boozing buffoon', though was sometimes a source of profound rural wisdom. *Maga* was widely distributed in Britain and the British Empire, and for a time this unflattering caricature was better known than Hogg himself. For many readers, it was hard to separate the two. However embarrassing, Hogg usually accepted this alter ego and sometimes decided that any publicity was good. Margaret hated it.

> ### Confessions of a Justified Sinner
>
> *The Private Memoirs and Confessions of a Justified Sinner: Written by Himself: With a detail of curious traditionary facts and other evidence by the editor* was published, unsigned, in 1824. It received a hostile reception. The *Westminster Review* lamented 'that the author did not employ himself better than in uselessly and disgustingly abusing his imagination'. Hogg, who admitted later to being the author, said it 'did not sell very well – so at least I believe, for I do not remember ever receiving any thing for it'.
>
> It comprises two incongruent narratives, the views of the same events of the 'editor' and the 'sinner'. The 'editor's' version is presented as rational and objective, but he exposes himself as narrow-minded and unreliable. Robert Wringhim (the 'justified sinner') has been brought up to believe that he is predestined to eternal salvation. He becomes in thrall to an enigmatic companion who is able to direct Robert's beliefs to evil purposes, convincing him that it is his mission to 'cut sinners off with the sword', and that murder can be the correct course of action. But is the companion the devil, a figment of Robert's imagination, or perhaps just an aspect of his own personality? Robert descends into despair, madness and finally suicide. The novel concludes with a return to the 'editor's narrative' which explains how the sinner's memoir was discovered in his grave. Hogg makes a brief appearance as himself in this section, unhelpful and expressing scorn at the plan to open the grave.
>
> The novel can be viewed in many ways: as a satire on totalitarian thought, a psychological study of a religious fanatic, a supernatural parable, or an early example of crime fiction. Vitally, it provides no answers. It succeeds, partly due to its ambiguities.
>
> Like many at the time, Hogg himself may have under-rated its qualities: 'it being a story replete with horrors, after I had written it I durst not venture to put my name to it'.
>
> It is now recognised as a major text in European Romanticism and was described by writer Iain Crichton Smith as 'a towering Scottish novel, one of the very greatest of all Scottish books'. Walter Allen, writer of *The English Novel: A Short Critical History*, called it 'the most convincing representation of the power of evil in our literature'.[15]

Meanwhile, back on the farm . . . Hogg continued writing, he said, 'as if in desperation'. There was the farm itself, but this was handled largely by workers with little supervision. A farm hand said that Hogg would usually write until two or three in the morning. Numerous visitors came, expecting food and

---

[15] Iain Crichton Smith, quoted in Hogg, *Justified Sinner*, p. xii; Walter Allen, quoted in <https://en.wikipedia.org/wiki/The_Private_Memoirs_and_Confessions_of_a_Justified_Sinner> (last accessed 7 March 2016).

lodging and entertainment. Perhaps to divert some of these, he founded the modest Gordon Arms inn at Mount Benger.[16] Meanwhile, the rent is overdue and debts are spiralling out of control.

Another daughter is born in 1825. The next year he fears he is 'liable to arrestment' for his debts. His father-in-law, whom Hogg has described as 'an excellent old man, reduced from great affluence to a total dependence on me', dies in 1827. Margaret's mother moves into Mount Benger but dies the following year. A third daughter, their fourth child, is born in 1827. In that year, Hogg and others establish the St Ronan's Border Games – to encourage greater cheerfulness. And then he starts a school in an old shed in Mount Benger, across the road from the Gordon Arms, and invites the teacher to stay with them; the school would operate until 1962.[17]

Hospitality

We hear, at various times in Hogg's life, of an endless stream of visitors. He would describe the household as being 'like a swarm of bees at the casting and can scarcely all get within the door of our cell', and later, 'My house has never emptied this summer . . . like an over-crowded small inn – A great number of most respectable and beloved visitors and about as many very queer chaps.' It must have been challenging at times.

But if it was a problem, it was partly his fault. He was widely believed to be quite well off, and he did not often refute this. In 1828, in the depths of his financial crises, he sent some friends a high-energy welcome:

> they must come and stay with the old shepherd for two or three days & nights . . . they shall have a bedroom to themselves & as good a bed as Ettrick Forest can boast & they shall have oceans of curds & cream, cheese, whey kern milk & brose & butter.

And that's before we start on the whisky.

Charlotte Scott, wife of Walter, described Hogg's home (in her French accent) as 'de hotel widout de pay'. It was open to all comers. But it can be a tough tap to turn off, as he must've found when he was struggling with deadlines.

He wrote to Margaret, regretting 'the total loss of time of ten times more value to me at this period than all the beef and whisky that we consume'. There was an attempt, probably futile, to discourage casual visitors:

---

[16] Hughes, *James Hogg*, p. 199.
[17] The school was established in 1828. Hogg was determined his children should not suffer the disadvantages that he had. With additions and rebuilding, it continued in use for more than 130 years until 1962 when, with the help of a school bus, the children of the valley would move to Yarrow Primary School (Parr, *James Hogg at Home*, p. 60; see also Miller, *Electric Shepherd*, p. 262).

smoke from the fireplace in his study was diverted to the kitchen chimney, so passers-by would not know if he was home. But could he, or would he, really change anything? He wrote in 1830: 'Sociality is so completely interwoven in my nature that I have no power to resist indulging in it.'

When I lived in Uganda there was not much accommodation around, and travellers who had heard of us came from every direction. We were obliged to tip our housekeeper when we had guests, so she would welcome everyone in. We would often arrive home to a full house and have to introduce ourselves. At that time – these being the Idi Amin years – supplies were scarce and tricky to get.

Two friends arrived from Ethiopia. One had hepatitis and went to see our doctor. Then an American couple came whom we didn't know, each of them with hepatitis. They'd been camping in town in the rainy season and went to our doctor, who told them they should get out of the rain and stay with us, because we already had a guest with hepatitis. We divided our food, utensils and bedding, half for the hepatitis people, half for the others. It worked. Two weeks later everyone got better. But we were ready for a break.

In the Solomon Islands, hospitality is obligatory. I helped to set up a public library in Malaita, and employed a local man to run it. He slept in the library to save long walks from his village. His wife moved in too, and their baby was born there. Then their extended family arrived, then more ... And a short time later, I heard reports that sleeping bodies were blocking the aisles. 'Too many,' I told him. 'Unprofessional,' he agreed. We decided I should put up a sign: 'The Librarian will lose his job if anyone other than his wife and children sleep here.' He was delighted. I could restrict his visitors but, in his culture, he could not. The problem was solved.

I have a theory that hospitality is never lost, it just gets passed on. A young woman I had met briefly, a Hogg enthusiast, invited me to stay when I came to Scotland. 'I'll sleep on the floor,' I told her. 'No you won't,' she said. 'Hogg had so many visitors. I have a spare room and I couldn't let his descendant sleep on the floor.' James, it might take a couple of centuries, but favours do come back. This one's for you.

And a postscript: the Solomon Islands library baby was named after me. His parents gave him my middle name, 'James', a name that had come from my Scottish ancestor. (For reasons that are hard to explain, 'Brus' is a rude word in the Solomons.) So somewhere in those islands there's a young boy, born between the library shelves, who is named after the Ettrick Shepherd. And probably has no idea why.

Hogg did not – and anyway, could not – renew the lease on Mount Benger when it expired in 1830. It would not help that he'd been accused of poaching on his landlord's land. Nor did it help his own position that he had built additions and a barn at Mount Benger, at his own cost. The family returned to Altrive.

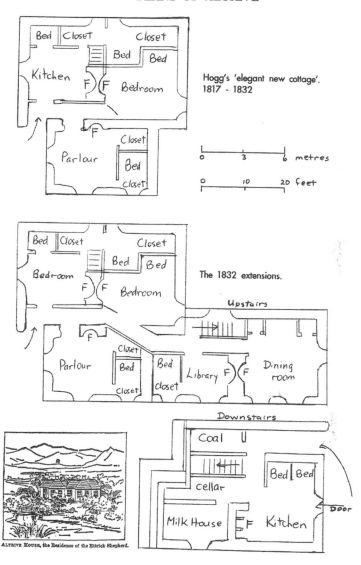

Figure 29 Floor plans of James Hogg's single storey 'elegant stone cottage' at Altrive, and his later additions to make it 'a very fine place'.

Hogg's excess livestock had dropped to half its value: 'the speculation left me once more without a sixpence in the world – and at the age of sixty it is fully late enough to begin it anew'. He wrote: 'Everything is to be taken from me even to my books'; the books and a few other items, though, seem to have survived. He looked at his young family – four children, roughly the ages that he and his brothers had been when his father was bankrupted – and saw that history was repeating itself.

His output throughout this time had been astounding. For much of this period there had been at least one major work in each year. There had been other works too, some linked to his love of music: *Select and Rare Scotish Melodies* in 1829; an extended version of *The Border Garland* in 1830; and *Songs by the Ettrick Shepherd* in 1831. There had been items for periodicals and numerous lesser pieces. But the income had not matched the costs.

In this turmoil, how was he feeling? Again, he surprises:

> One may think, on reading over this Memoir, that I must have worn out a life of misery and wretchedness; but the case has been quite the reverse. I never knew either man or woman who has been so uniformly happy as I have been; which has been partly owing to a good constitution, and partly from the conviction that a heavenly gift, conferring the powers of immortal song, was inherent in my soul. Indeed so smooth and happy has my married life been, that on a retrospect I cannot distinguish one part from another, save by some remarkably good days of fishing, shooting, and curling on the ice.[18]

Sports, Lust and Happiness

From his childhood days of competing against himself, Hogg's passion for sports never left him. At one stage, in the depths of his financial and farming woes, he thought he might have to give up sports. But he quickly thought better: 'I do not expect that I can live long without them.'

There was a range of outdoor activities and some of them would end at Tibbie Shiels Inn. Friends would recall later 'how Hogg would electrify the company with picturesque descriptions of fishing adventures, winding up, it might be, with the triumphant production of a large bull trout'.[19]

There was the big game of 'football' in 1815 (it was based on an old game, and perhaps more like 'handba' or the later game of rugby). This was at Carterhaugh, near the meeting of the Ettrick and Yarrow waters, using the rivers, almost a mile apart, as goals. Scott led Selkirk and other townsmen, and Hogg led Ettrick and Yarrow. Several hundred people played on each side, with 6,000 watching and cheering.[20] After five hours, when dusk intervened, the game was drawn at 1–1 but the result was fiercely disputed. A rematch was planned, but never happened. (Scott said a couple of years later, 'it was not always safe to have even the game of football between villages; the old clannish spirit was too apt to break out'.)

---

[18] Hogg, 'Reminiscences', p. 55.
[19] Quoted in Garden, *Memorials*, pp. 184–5.
[20] Groves, *St Ronan's Border Club*, p. 7.

Figure 30 *The Celebration of the Birthday of James Hogg, 1770–1835* by Sir William Allan, 1823 or 1825. Hogg is at the left, Sir Walter Scott beside him, and John Wilson proposes a toast. (Source: Reproduced with permission of the Scottish National Portrait Gallery. Purchased with the aid of the Art Fund 1998.)

Hogg made another, more important contribution though. Alistair Moffat wrote:

> In 1827 the St Ronan's Games were launched at Innerleithen at Hogg's instigation . . . [He] was an all-rounder, good at foot-racing, wrestling, fishing, curling and archery, but his motivation went far beyond to what he detected as contemporary social problems. In the wake of the agricultural revolution many people were leaving the land to find employment in the textile mills of the growing towns. Hogg worried about the effects of social dislocation as the old life on the land changed abruptly and sometimes bafflingly . . . Hogg sympathised and, engagingly, he also wanted people to have more fun.[21]

Hogg presided over and competed in the Games for a number of years. Lockhart said that Hogg, even up to his sixties, 'exerted himself lustily in the field, and seldom failed to carry off some of the prizes, to the astonishment of his vanquished juniors'.[22] A newspaper report said: 'the competitors seemed to think his presence far more inspiring than the prize they contended for'. He won archery events though he 'never drew a bow until after he was sixty'. The gatherings preceded the revival of the Highland Games, which had been outlawed in the previous century. They were described in London as the Scottish Olympics; more than 3,000 people attended in 1832.[23]

Hogg wrote: 'With regard to all the manly exercises, had it not been for my own single exertions I think they would have been totally extinct in the Border districts . . . exercises, such as appears not to have existed for a century and more.' He often paid for the prizes himself (what with? one might ask). The *Edinburgh Weekly Journal* wrote in 1828, about these and other events: 'These are the original border games of the south, and have been kept alive by Mr Hogg's exertions alone, in Ettrick and Yarrow for a space of nearly forty years.'[24]

Even if Hogg had achieved nothing else in his life, these would have been an impressive gift to the region. The St Ronan's Border Games are still running today. They are no longer just 'manly exercises' though; males and females compete as equals.

The value of such activities in difficult times can be immense. After five years of conflict in the Solomon Islands, many young people in Malaita were suffering from drug, alcohol and violence issues. These were greatly

---

[21] Moffat, *The Borders*, pp. 444–5.
[22] Lockhart, *Life of Sir Walter Scott*, p. 317.
[23] Groves, *St Ronan's Border Club*, pp. 13, 26.
[24] Quoted in Groves, *St Ronan's Border Club*, pp. 5, 24.

> reduced when multi-sport contests between neighbouring villages were introduced, and fitness became a top priority. In Nelson, New Zealand, I helped set up a trust providing outdoor adventures for 'youth at risk' and have seen the benefits over many decades.
>
> I inherited my ancestor's sporting enthusiasm but alas, not his ability. A career highlight was playing international rugby, but this was for Uganda, not a leading rugby nation. And I've played tennis for more years than Andy Murray and Federer combined, without discernible improvement.

With the termination of the Mount Benger lease, maybe things were turning a corner. Hogg had made a good beginning with the newly arrived young duke. At a social gathering, he says: 'he conversed while there more with me than any other'. (He tells his wife, wide-eyed, that he was 'literally covered with gold over the whole body with epaulettes and star'.) The new duke subsequently 'acted nobly . . . he sent orders to his factor to drop all claims whatever on the heavy arrears'. But Hogg's finances were complicated by the fact that he was not formally bankrupted; whenever he earned some money, a creditor would find another old bill to be paid.

For now, at least, he was getting a relatively good income from a range of magazines and periodicals. There were more of them now. London magazines such as *Fraser's* were relatively free from sexual prudery, and would sometimes publish work that Blackwood rejected. Payments were not large, but were certain and prompt. Literary merit was often less important than avoiding offence to readers' sensitivities. At one stage Hogg was reprimanded for sending a ghost story to a publication for young women.

He was not the only one with financial problems around this time. Walter Scott, then Britain's best-known and most successful author, faced financial ruin in 1826 when the publisher Constable and then the intertwined Ballantyne printing business failed, leaving Scott, a partner in the latter, owing around £120,000. His wife died the same year. Rather than bankruptcy, he chose to try to pay off his debt by increasing his literary output, a phenomenal effort that occupied the rest of his life, and probably shortened it. He died in 1832, and his debts were finally discharged a short time later.

> ### Walter Scott, Part 2
>
> Scott (Sir Walter since 1820) had had a turbulent couple of decades. His writing career had taken him from Border ballads to poetry to the historical novel, which he is considered to have invented, as well as to some plays, biographies and other non-fiction. He rediscovered the long-lost Scottish crown and sceptre in the depths of Edinburgh Castle,

and stage-managed the visit of King George IV to Scotland in 1822. In the process he invented clan tartans, and redefined the Highlands and Scotland itself.

To southerners, the Highlands had long been seen as barbaric, a place of violent conflict, religious fanaticism and bloodshed. Scott's gift to the country was to assign that to the past, to accentuate the positives, to popularise Highland culture and tourism, and to imagine a positive, peaceful future, 'blending the bravery and romance of the Highlander with the good sense and loyalty of the Lowlander'.[25] It was a fine blend.

Over this time he was also an advocate, judge, prominent Tory and Highland Society member, and long-term President of the Royal Society of Edinburgh. His legacy is huge, including saving the Scottish pound note; his portrait appears on Bank of Scotland notes, in gratitude.

He was a frequent source of advice and support to Hogg, and occasionally of funds as well. They held each other in high regard over three decades. Usually, at least. They had the falling out in 1814, when Scott would not support the planned poetic repository. This prompted Hogg to think of other times when Scott might have undervalued him, and to write him an angry letter [James, please don't send it!] effectively ending their friendship.

But after 'time out', and hearing that Scott was enquiring after him daily, Hogg wrote to him: 'I answered yours intemperately and in a mortal rage . . . I find there are many things which I yearn to communicate to you and the tears always rush to my eyes when I consider that I may not.' Scott immediately invited him to breakfast, and they picked up their friendship where they had left off.

They last met at the Gordon Arms in autumn 1830. They walked a short distance together and Scott supported himself on Hogg's shoulder, saying he had never leaned on one firmer or surer. His health was failing. He had the first of several strokes a few months later, then had a long trip to Europe. When he was sick, Hogg said, 'there is nothing in nature so painful to contemplate'. Scott died shortly after his return, and Hogg wrote that he had 'lost the best and most steady friend that I have ever had in the world'.

As Hogg's family grew – their fifth child arrived in 1831 – and visitors came, the three-room Altrive house would have felt quite small. Despite their precarious financial state, he decided the time was right for expansion. For reasons that are far from clear, he would tell Blackwood (with whom he'd now been in and out and back in favour) in 1831: 'I am building an addition but have thought it prudent to do it in your name', adding later that receipts for this were to be 'made out in your name as if you had built the house for me'. Around the same time (in a letter which started 'I have a queer story to tell you') Hogg would ask him for cash when his horse died; Blackwood paid.

---

[25] Lamont, *When Scotland Ruled the World*, p. 118.

But then: a second falling out with Blackwood, apparently unrelated to the house additions. A number of irritations, over items published or not published, had come to a head. Hogg wrote to Blackwood: 'Save with regard to *publishing* in which I never will submit to be treated with such absolute contempt again I beg that we may be the same as we have ever been. You have starved me fairly out of my house and country.' And: 'I'm very glad your contempt has driven me to this.' His suggestion that, apart from publishing, their relationship could be unchanged was wishful thinking. This time there could be no going back.

Hogg may have had a back-up plan. He had new connections in London, including James Cochrane, a new publisher, who would publish his *Altrive Tales*. At short notice he sailed in *The Edinburgh Castle*, a wooden paddle steamer, arriving in London on the last day of 1831. It would be a life-changing visit.

LIONISED IN LONDON

Edinburgh had become stifling, with infighting and criticism from the literary elite, of which Hogg, with his rural manners and little education, could never be a part. He was welcomed in London with open arms. Reports of this period say he was *lionised*: 'given a lot of public attention and approval, treated as a celebrity'.

In large part, his reputation here was due to his alter ego, his fictional character in *Noctes Ambrosianae*, without whose fame he might have slipped into the city unnoticed. People were surprised he was so presentable. From the moment he stepped off the boat he said he was 'eaten up with kindness'.

Less than two weeks later he wrote to Margaret:

Notwithstanding of all the caressing I have met with, which is perfectly ridiculous, I hate London, and I do not think that either flattery or profit can ever make me love it . . . I never get home before three in the morning . . . it is almost a miracle that I keep my health so well . . . I have received in the last three days three hundred invitations to dinner.

There may be some Hogg hyperbole there, but it's an indication of how he felt.

On occasions, he was invited to speak to hundreds of gentlemen at a dinner. The *Atlas*, a London weekly paper, described his manner of public speaking: 'The mixture of shrewdness and fun in his manner, his looks, and his words, must be seen to be understood.'

Respectable ladies were not usually present at a public dinner. Hogg found it curious that they were not permitted to eat or drink. He described being taken upstairs later to meet them 'and shown like any other wild beast all the ladies courtesying and flattering and begging for one shake of my hand such flummery I never saw in this world'.

Aside from such engagements, he stayed with James Cochrane, his new publisher, wrote some pieces for him, worked on the first volume of *Altrive Tales*, and published a devotional manual for children, *A Father's New Year's*

Gift. And Hogg – he who should know about such things – became concerned about Cochrane's financial stability.

In the course of the visit, there were suggestions he would be offered a knighthood. Hogg wrote to Margaret: would she like this? (It would cost £300 initially, and where on earth would this come from? He seemed keen enough to be talked out of it.) She replied:

> From my heart I can say I like no such titles . . . I think a title to a poor man is a load scarcely bearable . . . did I possess five thousand a year I should wish to be unencumbered with a title I want no more than to be the wife of plain James Hogg.

He was approached by a group of literary friends about this time, with concern for Margaret. Would he have any objection to them buying a small annuity for her? Hogg was almost twenty years older than she was, and there was a risk she could be left with a destitute family. He replied: 'I did not come to London to beg but to try my fortune as an author.' Margaret was told later and appreciated their kindness, but totally agreed with his response.

This would have been a tough time for her, with five children to care for, the youngest just a few months old. The house alterations, of course, were incomplete and unpaid for. There was the small farm, and the inevitable messy business dealings to attend to. How long could she do this alone?

Figure 31 James Hogg's house at Altrive (now Eldinhope). The top floor was added later.

ALTRIVE, AT LAST

Hogg's heart was never far from home. When he heard in March that his son had been unwell, he wrote to Margaret: 'Your last has fairly upset my resolution of remaining here my dear boy's health being far dearer to me than either honour or riches . . . I am positively worried with kindness . . . I positively will not come to London again without you.'

He returned home three months after he had left. Blackwood, no doubt aware of Hogg's metropolitan celebrity, finally published *A Queer Book* in April 1832 (this was a volume of ballads, about which Hogg said, 'It will be a grand book for thae Englishers for they winna understand a word of it').

A connection that Hogg shared with Blackwood, as well as with Scott, was their Tory sentiments. Hogg was a natural conservative, with a love of traditional values. He had strong links with Sir Robert Peel, who would be prime minister for a short time in Hogg's lifetime. He also had strong feelings for the disadvantaged, though, and had many radical friends. And a number of close non-literary friends as well, such as artists William Nicholson and John Martin, and scientist Sir David Brewster (among other things, the inventor of the kaleidoscope).

Late in life he began to query his own politics: 'People's principles seem to be born with them, for, God knows, I never had any interest in being a Tory.'[26] He was angered by the growing gap between rich and poor. The traditional values were being lost regardless, and both Whig and Tory policies were destroying the community spirit he'd grown up with, by making 'the distance between master and servant wider and wider'; farm workers were reduced to 'a state of absolute slavery'.

The first volume of *Altrive Tales* was published after his return home, but Cochrane's financial failure stopped the sale and production of this soon afterwards. Hogg was supportive of Cochrane: 'it is for you and your lovely family that I grieve far more than for myself'. A Glasgow publisher then offered Hogg a substantial fee for producing a new edition of the works of Robert Burns, with a memoir of the poet.

And later that year, after Walter Scott's death, he was considering a Scott biography. It was something he said in *Altrive Tales* he would do if he outlived him: 'a mental portrait, the likeness of which to the original shall not be disputed'.

The additions to the Altrive cottage were built without intruding on the family; when they were finished, the wall between the two parts was broken through, and suddenly the house had doubled in size. Hogg was able to announce later: 'I have made this cottage a very fine place now. A house of ten rooms kitchen dairy; and five cellars!!'

The next year, 1833, started badly. On a visit to Edinburgh he fell through the ice when curling and for a time he was seriously ill.

---

[26] Quoted in Hughes, *James Hogg*, p. 228.

He sent a collection of anecdotes about his thirty-year friendship with Scott for publication in London but withdrew it in deference to Lockhart, Scott's son-in-law and official biographer. But these were highly marketable. He told Lockhart that he wanted to see them published sometime, but Lockhart would not accept the idea.

Hogg was now quite well known in America, and some of his works had been reprinted there. Several of his nephews had emigrated there now. A wealthy American landowner, Dr Rose, had met one of these, also named James Hogg. He discovered this young James's family link, and told him: 'that is the name best known to us here of all the names in the world . . . you and I shall never part as long as we live'. Amazingly, he immediately offered him a farm, stocked with 1,000 sheep. About this time, Hogg wrote of his American market: 'I am, however, happy to hear from every corner of the great community of the west that I am more read here, and oftener reprinted, than any other living author.'

A number of agents were visiting Hogg in pursuit of material, and he received an offer for the anecdotes. In the end, it was probably not about the money; he was not usually guided by this. But he'd written a story about someone he knew and loved, and he wouldn't want to waste it. He sent a revised version to America in June for publication there, possibly believing this would not be known in Britain. [James, is this realistic?]

The *Familiar Anecdotes of Sir Walter Scott* was published in New York in April 1834. A pirated version, *The Domestic Manners and Private Life of Sir Walter Scott*, appeared in Glasgow in June. Lockhart was furious. Hogg's friendship with him did not, could not, survive.

Hogg's account of Scott, it seems, was honest enough, but tactless. He said, for example, that Scott had 'a too high obsession with titled rank'. Many would agree with this but Lockhart, who shared this obsession, could not. Hogg was entitled to do what he did, but should always have known it would come back to bite him.

Cochrane was now back in business as a publisher, and Hogg offered him what would be *Tales of the Wars of Montrose*. Cochrane's wife had run off with his business partner and Hogg's loyalty to Cochrane was partly driven by sympathy. By this time he had also reached an agreement with Blackie and Son for the publication of *Tales and Sketches by the Ettrick Shepherd* (eventually published in six volumes in 1836–7).

Importantly, the young Duke of Buccleuch granted Hogg a ninety-nine-year lease for the house and a sliver of land at Altrive, which would provide some security for Margaret and the children; now she could retain the property after his death, or receive a small payment in lieu. Hogg was ecstatic. Finally, he would have something he could leave his family. He wrote in 1835: 'not a day passes over my head on which I do not feel grateful for it'.

But it was a time of sad departures. Both his younger brothers left for America with their large families; Robert, his youngest brother, died in transit and was buried at sea. (Hogg might even have considered emigration himself but had been 'so long identified with Scotland and Ettrick Forest, that I cannot leave them'.) His life-long friend William Laidlaw – his 1804 travel buddy – left for a job in the Highlands. The loss of his company would be 'a blank to me which cannot be filled up again'. And early in 1834 Robert, his favourite nephew, who had worked as his literary assistant, died of tuberculosis, aged just thirty-one.

Hogg, as we've seen, handled break-ups badly but was surprisingly good at make-ups. The breach with William Blackwood was mended, once again, in May 1834. By this time, though, Blackwood was terminally ill with cancer and died a few months later. The firm and *Maga* continued, but Hogg's links with them were weakened. He had some happy times with John Wilson, his old adversary and friend, whom Hogg had once called 'an ideot and a driveller'. Perhaps he believed his falling out with Lockhart might also be resolved.

Hogg's output, by anyone's standards, was still impressive. He revised his work on the edition of Burns, now with William Motherwell as co-editor, and parts of this were published. His *Lay Sermons* was published in 1834, and *Tales of the Wars of Montrose* in early 1835. Magazine contributions continued. But there are hints, and some of them from Hogg himself – 'the fire of genius is beginning to flag' – that his best writing might be behind him.

He had, too, recently discovered he was older than he had thought. He assumed he was born on 25 January 1772. How surprising it would be, then, to discover he was baptised fourteen months before that.

He seems healthy enough in mid-1835, when Margaret leaves him to take Harriet to Edinburgh for a few weeks, for help with the little girl's twisted foot. He finds time for some fishing and curling and drinking, and to entertain with his fiddle. He is back at the St Ronan's Border Games that summer, involved in judging and organising and curling and archery. In August he is well enough to go out shooting as usual (for which he has ordered two gallons of whisky) and to take what would be a final look at Blackhouse and other scenes of his youth.

He had always had a robust constitution. He'd been hit by all the usual ailments – accidents, measles, fever from heavy drinking, and the near-death experience that coincided with Burns's date of death – but he would bounce back quickly. (He'd been unwell earlier with 'water on the chest'; impossible, he told his doctor, because he never drank water.) He seemed to have a high tolerance to stress, and often seemed to enjoy it. He had loving and supportive family and friends.

Not only that, but he still looked youthful. He had a young wife and family, as well as his love for sport, and people often assumed he was a decade younger than he was. In 1828 he told a friend he had known for decades: 'If you saw me you would think me younger like by a good deal than when you first saw me.' And he was described in the *Edinburgh Literary Journal* (6 August 1831), in a visit to the St Ronan's Games:

> The first face that greeted us on landing at Innerleithen was that of the Ettrick Shepherd, who seems to have renewed his youth. Hogg's form and face show less of the inroads of time than those of any man we know – he must have a frame of iron.

And he had good genes for longevity. His father had died at ninety-two, his mother at eighty-four. At sixty-four, he might have assumed he was good for another couple of decades. His daughter, Mary, would write later that he 'knew nothing of the ailments of sedentary or dyspeptic authors, [and] had an unfailing flow of animal spirits'.

He had, though, 'never acquired the self-preservation that generally grows with age and was inclined to be reckless both with his money and his health'. Both were running out. He had grown up on defeats and got through life, whether in his writing or sport or as the life and soul of the party, by pouring everything into the moment.[27] The drive that took him from illiteracy to fame would also drive him to other excesses.

Life changed in October 1835. He was confined to bed. He had tremors that brandy couldn't fix. He was suffering from liver failure.[28] He and others around him knew the end was near.

Margaret and the children were there. Alexander Laidlaw came to visit every day, and later never left the room. Tibbie Shiel was there to the end, helping over a period of four weeks; he gave her his beloved silver pocket-watch. On 21 November 1835 Hogg died in his bed in Altrive. He was probably – depending on his actual birthdate – just nearly sixty-five. William Laidlaw said he departed calmly and 'with as little pain, as if he had fallen asleep'. He was buried among his close relations at Ettrick, on a dismal winter's day, just a hop, step and a jump from where he had first arrived.

---

[27] Hughes, *James Hogg*, p. 303.
[28] Was this caused by alcohol? It's possible. Liver failure can be caused by long-term alcohol consumption, but also by cirrhosis, hepatitis and inherited disorders. Based on his own descriptions of abuse in the latter half of his life, though, the first must be a strong contender.

Figure 32 Ettrick kirkyard gravestones. James Hogg (right), Will o'Phaup and close relations.

7 Life after Death: A never-ending journey

BEYOND THE GRAVE

James Hogg, the husband and father, was gone. What now? Margaret and the children, ranging in age now from four to fourteen, were devastated. They would struggle financially. Margaret wrote a month after her husband had died: 'All that remains of what was once Mr. Hogg's belongs to his creditors, and it is my desire that they should understand that I so consider it.' She said that he would have felt the same. She was regarded as destitute then, though it turned out a little better than that.

Hogg, the writer and character, lingered a while. Lockhart, still quite grumpy about the *Familiar Anecdotes of Sir Walter Scott*, wrote about him in his own biography of Scott: 'it had been better for his fame had his end been of an earlier date, for he did not follow his best benefactor until he had insulted his dust'. (To be fair, Lockhart praised him there too, including 'the most remarkable man that ever wore the *maud* of a shepherd'.)

William Wordsworth was more generous, writing in *Extempore Effusion upon the Death of James Hogg*:

> When first, descending from the moorlands,
> I saw the Stream of Yarrow glide
> Along a bare and open valley,
> The Ettrick Shepherd was my guide . . .
>
> The mighty Minstrel breathes no longer,
> Mid mouldering ruins low he lies;
> And death upon the braes of Yarrow,
> Has closed the Shepherd-poet's eyes . . .

In his latter years Hogg had been widely admired as a writer, but much of this had been due to his success in overcoming the disadvantages of his peasant birth and lack of education, and the tone was often condescending. In time, this admiration would fade.

Editions of his works continued to be published but in a badly bowdlerised form. *Bowdlerised* . . . 'having material removed that is considered improper or offensive from a text or account, especially with the result that the text becomes weaker or less effective'. Some of his most interesting pieces – those that dealt with the most challenging issues – were omitted entirely from these republished works.

This was intended to avoid offending the increasing delicacy of the age. It resulted in watered-down versions that were respectable but lacking the life force that made them unique. It was well intentioned, but it was a death by a thousand cuts. Interest in his works waned in the century after his death.

Hogg the man was remembered. John Wilson had predicted that fifty years after his death, a statue of Hogg would look out over St Mary's Loch and Tibbie Shiels Inn. In fact, it took half that time. There is a fine stone statue of the shepherd, with plaid and stick and his favourite collie at his feet. He sits comfortably on a pedestal, as he never would in life. In his left hand is a scroll showing the last line of *The Queen's Wake*, 'taught the wandering winds to sing'. The sculptor, Andrew Currie, was born in Ettrick Forest and had known Hogg. The community raised the funds. The monument was unveiled on 28 June 1860 in front of a crowd of 2,000 people. It was an assemblage, *The Southern Reporter* said, 'such as we have no record of in the past'.

Figure 33 James Hogg looks down over St Mary's Loch and Tibbie Shiels Inn. Hector, the sheepdog he wrote a loving poem to, looks up at him.

In 1898, a monument was erected at his birthplace, the cottage there having long been removed. And his sandstone face had appeared, with Burns and Byron and other writers, on an aspect of the Edinburgh Scott Monument.

His influence would be seen on some other nineteenth-century writers and novels. Parts of Emily Brontë's *Wuthering Heights* and R. L. Stevenson's *The Strange Case of Dr Jekyll and Mr Hyde* and *The Master of Ballantrae* show clear reflections of *Justified Sinner*, particularly in their treatment of evil strangers and influences.

His life story, of humble beginnings and self-improvement, and the democratic and humanitarian themes in his work, appealed in North America. Suzanne Gilbert writes: 'Hogg's American popularity meant that writers such as Irving, Cooper, Poe, Emerson, Hawthorne, Melville, Thoreau and Longfellow were familiar with him, as they acknowledged in their own published work and correspondence.'[1]

And later, some unexpurgated versions of his works would appear. But it was almost too late. Those who had known Hogg's name had moved on, and it would be hard to win a new audience in the tumultuous twentieth century.

Almost too late. But not. A turning point came in 1947, when a new edition of *Justified Sinner* was published with an introduction by French author André Gide. He writes that he read it 'with a stupefaction and admiration that increased at every page'. He hoped it would 're-emerge from the shades' to the 'belated glory to which I believe it has a right'. His view was influential. The same year, Gide won the Nobel Prize in Literature 'for his comprehensive and artistically significant writings, in which human problems and conditions have been presented with a fearless love of truth and keen psychological insight'.

This paved the way for critical reassessment of Hogg and his works, especially from the 1960s. A new audience was not so offended by indelicacy, felt comfortable with his darkness and daring and humour, and was attracted by the breadth of his writing, his originality and power.

New editions continued to appear. Significantly, from the mid-1990s, a new scholarly edition, the Stirling/South Carolina Edition of the Collected Works of James Hogg (published by Edinburgh University Press), was begun. The passion of the late Professor Douglas Mack was pivotal in getting this off the ground. When complete, this will run to thirty-nine volumes. For the first time, some of these have been published as Hogg originally wrote them.

His impact is seen on current writers. Novelists such as Irvine Welsh of *Trainspotting* fame, Ian Rankin, best known for his Inspector Rebus novels, and James Robertson, whose books include *The Fanatic* and *The Testament of Gideon Mack*, cite Hogg as a major influence. And, in Canada, there is a curious link with Nobel Prize-winning author Alice Munro.

---

[1] Gilbert, 'Hogg's reception and reputation', p. 45.

It has been a remarkable resurrection, with a multitude of afterlives. It could be a major study in itself.

This chapter, though, will consider just a few snippets . . .

WEE HARRIET AND OTHER STORIES

Margaret was married to Hogg for just fifteen years. Then she was a widow for almost thirty-five years. She and the family moved to Edinburgh in 1838. She had a small annuity from the Duke of Buccleuch in exchange for the use of Altrive, and had some income from publications. Friends would help: a 'goodly sum of £1500' was raised from the community and put into trust. From this, the children received the education their parents had hoped for. There was a small government grant, and much later – after eighteen years of widowhood and much campaigning by Hogg's friends – a Royal Warrant for £50 a year. Margaret died in Linlithgow in 1870 and was buried in Edinburgh, too far from Ettrick for a final trip there. Her husband's grave and hers are cross-referenced though, lest there be any doubt.

Of the couple's family, only Harriet would have any children. I'm pleased she did, of course. She is my great-grandmother.[2]

Harriet Sidney Hogg had been born in December 1827, and was named after Hogg's late friend and patron the Duchess of Buccleuch. Hogg wrote *A Bard's Address to his Youngest Daughter* the following year (though later she would become his second-youngest), a warm, welcoming poem which began:

> Come to my arms my wee wee pet
> My mild my blithesome Harriet
> The sweetest babe thou art to me
> That ever sat on parent's knee . . .

Harriet had a twisted foot, apparently a result of being dropped by a servant when she was a baby. This caused a lameness which required special care and footwear. Hogg wrote: 'I can hardly think of my darling being put into steel boots like ancient covenanters.' When she was four and a half years old he said she was 'her father's darling'; he seems to have spent more time with her than with the other children in her early years. Walter Scott took a special interest in the little girl with the lame foot, having suffered a similar disability himself. But this must have improved; she and her siblings sometimes crossed the Yarrow River on their way to school on stilts.

---

[2] It might seem surprising that my link to Hogg involves so few generations. We are a family of slow breeders. I am writing about my great-great-grandfather 246 years after he was born, the relevant birth dates being James 1770, Harriet 1827, Bob 1862, Scott 1912 and Bruce 1949. And while some young people today might, if they are lucky, meet their own great-great-grandparent, for me there was little chance: mine reached adulthood not last century, nor the one before that, but in the one before that one.

Harriet was nearly eight when her father died. She went to school in Edinburgh but little is known of this period. She was twenty-seven when she married Robert Gilkison in 1855. They had eleven children, two of whom died in infancy, with the last being born in 1869. Robert was quite wealthy. He owned two cotton mills, and the family lived in a big house in Glasgow.

But things changed. One mill burnt down, apparently under-insured. Then the City of Glasgow Bank collapsed in 1878 due to fraud and mismanagement, taking the last of their savings with it. It was time to start again, but where?

In 1879 the couple and their nine children sailed in the *Forfarshire*, a three-masted sailing ship, to Dunedin, New Zealand, arriving 106 days later. There is no record of their motivation. Family lore suggests it was 'pride', but they had some friends there too. A wealthy cousin in Scotland had paid the fares in exchange for the family silver.

And now, when things might've got better, they didn't. Just ten weeks after their arrival – in less time than it took to sail there – Robert died suddenly from a stroke.

Poor wee Harriet. She had just left Scotland and was now in the furthest place from it on earth. She must have known she could never go home, would never see her family there again. She was a widow with nine children. She turned fifty-two a few days after Robert died. She must have been feeling utterly bewildered.

Four of her nine children were still of school age. She was not quite destitute, not quite in such dire straits as her father had been when she was born, or her grandparents had been earlier, but she was left with minimal assets. There were few income opportunities in Dunedin at the time, particularly respectable work for ladies.

She started a small private school with her adult daughters. Subjects included singing and dancing, reading and writing. She also trained country girls to be maids. Just a few years earlier she'd been raising her own children in Glasgow with the help of live-in nurses and maids.

It was a tough start in a new country. She left few clues as to how she was feeling. People in Dunedin said she was brave. A letter she sent to her brother, a couple of years after their arrival, is filled with facts, not feelings, and with touches of humour: 'we are not all quite Heathen yet, how long this may be said I cannot say'. She looks stoic in a photo about this time. She was described later as having 'an intense love of nature and of poetry'. Bob, her elder son, said, 'How we came through I don't know. People were exceedingly kind and helpful.'

And then in 1884, four years after her husband, Harriet died as suddenly as he had.[3]

---

[3] For much of this information I am indebted to Liz Milne, another New Zealand Hogg descendant, and her private publication of *Harriet: Moments in the Life of a Victorian Lady* (2000) and a series of twelve newsletters, *Descendants of James Hogg* (2000–3).

Figure 34 Harriet Gilkison (née Hogg), aged about 42; 'her father's darling'.

This is not the place for a family history. I want to mention Bob, Hogg's grandson and my grandfather though, for his Scottish and his Hogg connections.

Bob was born long after Hogg died, and was sixteen when they left Scotland. He had pleaded to be left behind, where he was sure he could study and support himself. But he adjusted quickly to his new home, studied law, and was soon supporting other family members. Later he wrote two books on local history, one on goldmining, and numerous articles on topics as diverse as natural history and Mary, Queen of Scots. He campaigned for prison and law reform, and was a driving force for the founding of a free public library in Dunedin. He was a keen sportsman and mountaineer.

Bob made three trips back to Scotland. In 1911, he and his wife travelled in Europe by bike and on foot, and were in Britain when Mary, the last of Hogg's children, died. He arranged for the remainder of Hogg's possessions to be donated or shipped to New Zealand.[4]

---

[4] Some items were given back to Scotland: to the University of Stirling and to the James Hogg Exhibition. Others are in New Zealand collections: in the University of Otago Special Collections, the Hocken Collections, the Otago Museum, Otago Settlers Museum and the Alexander Turnbull Library. Some remain in family ownership.

Figure 35 Gilkison Falls, draining a glacier on Mount Earnslaw/Pikirakatahi. There is a strong link here to Hogg and his love of the hills.

In 1918 he worked in volunteer roles, close to enemy lines in France. He was fifty-six. In his spare time he gave talks to soldiers on New Zealand history, helping to take their minds, even briefly, off the horrors of the trenches. He visited Scotland before returning home.

His final trip was in 1935 for the centenary celebrations of Hogg's death. He had named his younger sons James Hogg Gilkison (my uncle) and Walter Scott Gilkison (my father). Bob is remembered for his love of the mountains and of history and literature, for his empathy for the disadvantaged, and for his storytelling.

And just briefly, one more generation, the one before mine: there's a wild and wonderful waterfall in southern New Zealand called Gilkison Falls. It was named after my father, for his exploration and books about mountains and his efforts in forming a National Park there. But the love of the hills that led to this began generations before, on the other side of the world. James, part of this is for you.

THE BURNS CONNECTION

There is something else about Harriet. When she married, she created a link to Robert Burns. Her husband's grandfather was Captain Richard Brown.

Burns and Brown met in Irvine in 1781. Burns was twenty-two and impressionable; Brown was a few years older and, well, impressive. Burns wrote later:

> This gentleman's mind was fraught with courage, independence, magnanimity, and every noble manly virtue. I loved him, I admired him to a degree of enthusiasm; and I strove to imitate him . . . His knowledge of the world was vastly superiour to mine, and I was all attention to learn.

There was a downside though: 'He was the only man I ever saw who was a greater fool than myself when woman was the presiding star . . . Here his friendship did me a mischief.' (Brown's response was that Burns 'had nothing to learn' when they first met; later, Burns would have at least twelve children by four women.)

The poetic influence is more important here, though. Burns was learning flax dressing at the time, but they discussed some verses he had written. Brown suggested sending some to a magazine. Burns wrote to him later: "twas actually this that gave me an idea of my own pieces which encouraged me to endeavour at the character of a Poet'.[5]

---

[5] Details from the Irvine Burns Club, at <http://www.irvineburnsclub.org/captrichardbrown.php>, and the Burns Encyclopedia, at <http://www.robertburns.org/encyclopedia/BrownRichard175315 11833.124.shtml> (both last accessed 24 November 2015). The seven known letters from Burns to Brown were in Harriet's possession at the time of her death but were sold or donated later.

Since Brown inspired Burns, and Burns inspired Hogg, is this where the Hogg story should start? For me this link means that my great-great-great-grandfather (on one side) encouraged Burns to be a poet, and Burns inspired my great-great-grandfather (on another side) to do the same. And until I started writing this, I had no idea of the connection.

Figure 36 *Robert Burns Listens to the Stories of Captain Richard Brown, in 1781*, by T. & E. Odling, 1965. (Source: Reproduced with permission of Irvine Burns Club.)

TRACKING THE BROOD

Much family history has been written by Hogg descendants, but all of it is incomplete. What became of his other daughters, born before his marriage, and any of their descendants?

We hear of these daughters occasionally, in letters, during his lifetime. He seems to have been in contact with them and their families, at least from time to time. He describes them in loving terms to his friend, John Aitken, when they were eleven and eight. In 1833, when Hogg was sick in Edinburgh, Betsy (the younger, then about twenty-two) looked after him. There is a record in a letter about this time of a young son of Keatie's who had died.

Since then, I don't know. Some of Betsy's descendants were located in Manchester some years ago, but contact has been lost. Then, when I was travelling in Scotland, I met with someone who may be descended from Keatie. Keatie might have had the surname Hogg at one time, but her mother Catherine was a Henderson, who later married Hogg's cousin, David Laidlaw. These are all common names; it's not clear which of these Keatie would have used, and it's been hard to track her and any family she had. It was a lovely meeting and I hope we are related, but some of the dates and names didn't line up. Some years ago, when a family tree was grown in New Zealand, we were certain that we knew all of Hogg's descendants. Now I am just as certain that we don't. Somewhere, someone will know more. I look forward to joining some dots.

JUSTIFIED SINNER: BACK FROM THE DEAD

The Private Memoirs and Confessions of a Justified Sinner, unpopular in his own time, seemed certain to die with Hogg. But this was republished several times after his death, in the nineteenth and early twentieth centuries, in various forms. Eventually, the book revived the author. For an old book, it seems to have struck a chord with modern readers and writers.

Karl Miller, in the *Times Literary Supplement*, called it 'A work so moving, so funny, so impassioned, so exact and so mysterious that its long history of neglect came as a surprise which has yet to lose its resonance.'

Irvine Welsh described it as 'one of the best, most brilliant books ever written'.[6] The authors of *David Steel's Border Country* called it 'the most profound, penetrating and mystical novel ever to come out of Scotland'.[7] Ian Rankin, in his preface to *Justified Sinner*, says the book has 'not only continuing but urgent relevance'.[8]

Sir Sean Connery – the real James Bond, to some of us – wrote:

> But no tales of the divided self, of internal battles between good and evil, of doubles or doppelgängers, have ever been better explored than in James Hogg's portrayal of the power of evil in his masterpiece *The Private Memoirs and Confessions of a Justified Sinner*.[9]

And Michael Fry stated, 'many think it is the finest of all the nation's novels in the miraculous subtlety of its construction', adding:

> Now all appreciate its Gothic horror, its dissection of bigotry, its relentless satire of religious hypocrisy, its honest realism about criminals and prostitutes, its acute analysis of mental breakdown and schizophrenia. It is rich not only in content but also in form.[10]

---

[6] Kelly, *Irvine Welsh*, p. 11.
[7] Steel et al., *David Steel's Border Country*, p. 24.
[8] Rankin, 'Preface', p. xii.
[9] Connery and Grigor, *Being a Scot*, pp. 121–2.
[10] Fry, *New Race of Men*, p. 363.

It has inspired numerous writers, and variations on its themes. Rankin says 'without it there'd be no Dr Jekyll or Miss Jean Brodie. It has provided the central trope in Scottish literature, yet seems as fresh as the day it was written – and more relevant than ever.'[11] Sometimes there is a deliberate and open reference to the book. James Robertson's *The Testament of Gideon Mack* starts and ends with an editorial, and opens the latter with a question, just as Hogg did: 'What can this work be?' His Gideon Mack encounters the devil, but in a modern context. Emma Tennant's *The Bad Sister* shows us an ominous 'Gil-Martin', the same name as Hogg's evil influence. Gillian Hughes describes other connections.[12]

There have been several stage versions of the story performed, and one as an opera. But will *Justified Sinner* be a movie? It has already been done in Poland in 1985, but not yet in English. Film director Douglas Gordon said it is 'just begging to be made into a movie'. There have now been several screenplays written in English. Connery describes one which 'might well have turned out to be that elusive first masterpiece of the Scottish cinema'; he recalls the unfulfilled ambition of John Grierson, the documentary maker who coined the term 'documentary', for this.

The project is listed under 'Current Productions' on the Rob Roy Films website but is not yet over the line.[13] It will be a challenging film production – is Gil-Martin, the novel's evil influence, real or is he just a figment of Wringhim's imagination? Sometime, though, this movie will happen.

HOGG AND HIS WORLD

It's sub-zero in Toronto. Down jackets are tossed on a table by the door. Fifty people, warm and enthused, are discussing Hogg, his friends and detractors, aspects of his works and his world, over three days in late winter, 2015. They've come from the UK, USA, Canada, Norway, Finland, Switzerland and New Zealand.

Papers are presented with titillating titles: 'Deceit and Duality', 'A Peculiarly Scottish Obsession with Confession'; 'When Fire is Set to the Mountain'; 'Tibby Hyslop's Respectable Spinsterhood'. Most people here know things about Hogg that he didn't know himself. Could he have guessed that 180 years after his death, this meeting would be happening?

The average age here seems quite young. I do a quick calculation. It comes to just 39.5 years. It's a healthy sign for the future. These conferences take place somewhere in the world every two years, and plans are under way for the next, in Stirling in 2017.

There is a banquet on the final night. The main speaker is a direct descendant of Tibbie Shiel, who was once wooed by Hogg. We clink glasses and try to work out what, exactly, wooing meant.

---

[11] Rankin, 'Preface', p. viii.
[12] Hughes, '*The Private Memoirs*'.
[13] <http://www.robroyfilms.co.uk/current-productions/> (last accessed 3 December 2015).

Conferences are run by the James Hogg Society, which also publishes *Studies in Hogg and his World* annually, and other works occasionally, and hosts a James Hogg Blog.

The Society was founded in 1981 to encourage the study of Hogg's life and writings, and to bring interested parties together. In Scotland and much further afield, it's doing exactly that.[14]

ALICE MUNRO AND JAMES HOGG

In April 2015, I almost met Alice Munro. She's perhaps the most interesting person I ever almost met.

She is one of the world's great storytellers, and has been winning awards since the 1960s. *The Atlantic Monthly* called her 'the living writer most likely to be read in a hundred years' time'. In 2009 she won the Man Booker International Prize, an award given every two years to a living author of any nationality for a body of work in English. And then, in 2013, she received the Nobel Prize in Literature for her work as 'master of the contemporary short story'.

I had loved Munro's writing for years. More recently, I discovered we had something in common. We are both descendants of the far-fam'd and larger-than-life Will o'Phaup and his wife Bessie Scott, James Hogg's maternal grandparents. (These were her great-great-great-great-great-grandparents; for me there is one less 'great'.) So we had a connection, and this was my chance. I would be travelling to Canada for the 'Hogg and his World' conference – could we meet?

'Yes,' I was told in March, but a few days later, sadly, 'no'. She'd had a health setback. I sent my best wishes. She thanked me and sent her 'good luck' for the conference; a short time earlier, she had hoped to be at this.

Munro (née Laidlaw) describes her links to her ancestors and Ettrick in *The View from Castle Rock*. Her ancestor, Hogg's first cousin James Laidlaw, left Scotland for North America, and later his son William and his family did too. (This James was not a writer, and thought that 'Hogg, poor man' wasted his time making up lies.)

Intriguingly, critics are noticing storytelling similarities between Hogg and Munro that are even more important than their genes. The two share a skill in revealing, not telling. Their stories move backwards and forwards in time. They use unreliable narrators. They relish ambiguity.

A researcher, Adrian Hunter, makes comparisons between Munro's 'A Wilderness Station', a short story in *Open Secrets*, and Hogg's *Justified Sinner*. Each author represents the stories' subjects but 'without taking possession of' them. They work 'backward from assumed knowledge toward

---

[14] The Society website is hosted by the Division of Literature and Languages, University of Stirling, at <https://www.stir.ac.uk/arts-humanities/research/areas/thejameshoggsociety/>; the blog is at <http://jameshoggblog.blogspot.com/> and is based in North America (both last accessed 9 February 2016).

contradiction and uncertainty'. They show us characters so sure of what is right that they forget to question the facts. The stories lack 'reliable witness accounts', and their writers give us no easy answers.[15]

Magdalene Redekop, a Canadian researcher, wrote: 'It would be difficult to exaggerate the influence of Hogg on the writing of Munro.'[16] She says that Munro had told her that Hogg interested her very much, 'which for Alice, probably means that she read everything he wrote ... she called him a liar, but she called herself that too'. Lynne Truss, a reviewer of Munro's *Friend of my Youth*, said 'the presence of James Hogg signalling wildly from the past is impossible to overlook'.

Both set out to destabilise their readers, and they refuse to provide a tidy conclusion. And they seem to share a common fascination: with confessions and with sinners.

Figure 37 Alice Munro, Nobel Prize winner and James Hogg relative.

---

[15] Hunter, 'Taking possession', pp. 118, 116.
[16] Redekop, 'Alice Munro'. The comment that 'Hogg interested her very much' is from Redekop's presentation at the 2015 'Hogg and his World' conference.

HOGG AND GENDER ISSUES

In his stories, Hogg introduces us to some lively, assertive and unforgettable women.

In *Tibby Hyslop's Dream*, the central character risks her job and her future when she rejects amorous requests, first from her employer, then from a neighbour. But she goes on to live a full life as a happy, respectable spinster.

In *Maria's Tale*, Hogg's heroine is a servant who loses her chastity, and hence her employment, when she is seduced and made pregnant, then abandoned by her master's son. Forced to leave her own parish with no reference, Maria would face a tough future with a young child and little chance of a respectable source of income.

In *Justified Sinner*, Bell is a prostitute whose beautiful spoken English suggests a fall from her social origins. But in times when prostitutes were considered to be consistent liars, her word would prove more reliable than evidence from more 'respectable' sources. Her fall highlights the risk to other women who might meet adverse circumstances.

And in *Mador of the Moor*, we meet two women who react quite differently to their illegitimate pregnancies. Ila, from a peasant background, faces public scorn but is determined to keep her baby, while Matilda, a lady from the gentry, kills her baby rather than risk the family name and the economic value of her supposed chastity.

These stories were unpopular. They clashed with gender stereotypes in literature at the time, were unsettling to genteel readers, and were considered subversive. Writers were expected to endorse the values of the privileged and powerful, and avoid topics that challenged these. Critics focused on Hogg's indelicacy and lack of formal education.

A researcher at Stirling, Barbara Leonardi, has analysed a range of Hogg's stories through a current lens.[17] She concludes that he gave a voice to women from a wider social scale than was usual in literature. They include some very memorable, proactive characters from the margins of society. They are often unconventionally independent, and usually with high moral values. Some are beautiful, while sometimes there is no physical description; in either case their appearance is not their main attribute.

The stories address some major social issues and double standards. Prostitution was usually off-limits in literature, but was clearly a fact of life; Hogg empathised with women who were forced to resort to this. Chastity was highly valued in women, both in the upper classes, to ensure that property was not transferred to an illegitimate child, and for servants, to whom it was vital for finding and keeping a job. But the rules were different for men.

His characters challenge the morality of the Scottish kirk, which would not christen children of unwed mothers unless both parents agreed to repent.

---

[17] Leonardi, 'Exploration of gender stereotypes', pp. 270–81.

This was a problem if the father could not be found, and the kirk's strict rules could then put mothers and infants at risk. Hogg's women did not all strive for marriage and, if they did, it was usually to be a partner not an appendage. They are often his protagonists, and they will not be treated lightly.

Other stories focus on men and their stereotypes. In 'Basil Lee' a soldier in a Highland regiment is scared to death in the imperial wars in Quebec, and is treated as a hero but was not. In *The Three Perils of Woman* a husband resists but finally comes to accept his wife's son, though conceived with her previous lover. In *Mador of the Moor* a father provides support to an erring child in a way that would be commendable today, but might have been considered too weak at the time. The men, when challenged in these stories, become more human and slightly less rigid.

Maria's Tale was fiercely criticised yet Hogg published it twice more, without any significant change. It seems it was more important to him to expose the perils of sexual exploitation of servants by their masters, than to accommodate bourgeois readers' sense of literary decorum.

Leonardi concludes that in a time when standards of politeness and delicacy were moving towards their later Victorian prudery, it was often hard for Hogg to please his critics. Rather than try to, he decided that first he should write to please himself. In the process he produced work that was pleasing to later critics, and characters that were attractive to twenty-first-century readers.

It is perhaps not surprising that Hogg's stories would be populated by real flesh-and-blood women, not with the pure but improbable ones so favoured in literature at the time. The first woman he knew was his mother, a strong personality who would never let herself be stereotyped.

And beauty, he'd learnt, was more than skin deep. Even 'Muckle-mou'd Meg', whom we met in Chapter 1, had other qualities. She may have been the ugliest woman in the Scottish Borders but, Hogg wrote in 'The Fray of Elibank', 'her nature was generous, gentle an' free'.

ST RONAN'S BORDER GAMES

'You can stand up there a bit,' suggested the handicapper for the 'Race roond the Toon'. He'd asked politely how fast I was and I told him 'not very'. He had possibly formed this impression already. So I stood where he said, and I ran around the central blocks of Innerleithen, and I came in fifth. And this part might not be in the record books, but if they had an 'over 60s' section, I think I probably won it.

It was the first event on the final day of Games Week, in the annual St Ronan's Border Games. The contest was started by Hogg and others in 1827. They've been held every year since then, apart from some years of the World Wars. They're now believed to be the oldest organised sports meeting in Scotland.

It's a big week, partly because it's usually ten days long. The games are combined with the Cleikum Ceremonies, the celebration of St Ronan, an itinerant monk, banishing the Devil from town. Once again, the Devil is incinerated on a

Figure 38 Race roond the Toon, St Ronan's Border Games, Innerleithen, with the author not winning. (Source: Helen Barrington Photography.)

hilltop on the final night. But there's more: bagpipes and flowers and fancy dress parades. Some young people parade with costumes and a sign: 'Innerleithen dresses better than Peebles'. Suck on that, Peebles.

The Games founders are not forgotten. Their praises are sung in the anthem 'On, St Ronan's!' and their names – Scott, Hogg, Bell – appear on the banner. Hogg had worried that people were becoming 'decidedly less cheerful' than in his youth. He wanted people to have fun.

They do: 188 years later people are dressing up, getting fit, competing and playing music. I am asked to give a short speech; I say that I can't take credit for anything an ancestor did, but we can all be inspired by someone who couldn't even write but decided to be a great writer anyway. A newspaper report said my speech produced 'peals of laughter'; I suspect they were mainly to do with my funny accent.[18]

I am delighted to be asked to present the final athletics award, too. And, after my fifth placing in the 'Race roond the Toon', I am feeling unmistakably cheerful.

MEN, BALLS AND BORDERS

A 'football' game took place at Carterhaugh on 4 December 2015, the 200-year anniversary of the 1815 game that Hogg and Scott had played. This was just after the Rugby World Cup and the four-yearly battle for the William Webb Ellis Cup.

Why William Webb Ellis? He is supposed to have invented the game when he was playing football and 'first took the ball and ran with it', at Rugby School (of course) in England in 1823. Though, it turns out, the rumour that he had invented it did not emerge until over fifty years later, some years after his death, and is based on some pretty dodgy evidence.

There's another theory. The game might have started with the game in the Borders on 4 December 1815. Not only did they kick and pass and run with the ball, but they included scrums and tackling and various other rugby-like activities. Maybe this was rugby's genesis, in Carterhaugh, eight years earlier than the event that might (or might not) have happened at Rugby School, and it was led by Scott and Hogg.

Ian Landles, a Borders historian, talks about that first game: 'It was a massive game of rugby, they reckon 1,000 people took part . . . we look on that as being the start of rugby union football rather than the William Webb Ellis theory.'

Scotland and New Zealand played a big part in the 2015 Rugby World Cup. New Zealand won, beating Australia in the final. But maybe Scotland – complete with a Hogg and a Laidlaw – should have been there in Australia's place. Only an error by the referee in the final minutes of their quarter-final, acknowledged later, let Australia edge out Scotland. And if Scotland had met New Zealand in the final, what a game that would have been.

---

[18] 'Special guest celebrates Games history', *Peeblesshire News*, 25 July 2015.

The tenth Duke of Buccleuch tossed the ball up into the air to start the 2015 game – a contest akin to a rugby lineout – just as his ancestor had in 1815. He said: 'The possibility that the first great sporting event in rugby took place in the Borders is something we definitely need to celebrate.'

And the winner? After a major battle the local team came out on top, 1–0. Until the next time . . .

NOTES ON SOME RANDOM VISITS – EDINBURGH AND THE BORDERS AGAIN

I was on my way south after a month in the Highlands. I left the tranquil eastern banks of Loch Lomond at dawn. I got a ride to Glasgow, caught a train, and suddenly I'm back in Edinburgh. It's mid-festival season and the culture shock is profound. Crowds and chaos, and music pumping on every corner. I talk to a woman who has the world record for body piercings: 9,500. I find I've just missed 'Paul Bright's Confessions of a Justified Sinner'. There's so much going on it's hard to keep track. I love this place. I miss the Highlands. I check into a hostel in the Cowgate. A sign outside says: 'Not all those who wander are lost.'

The Book Festival is in full swing. I meet with James Robertson in the authors' yurt. We chat, among other things, about Hogg and Independence – would he have been a 'yes' or a 'no'? In the nineteenth century, we know, he was a Scottish patriot, but was committed to a united Britain. A lot has changed since then, with social upheavals that no one could have predicted. Robertson reminds me that Hogg was 'a bit of a Jacobite'.

I meet with Ian Rankin in his favourite pub, just around the corner. We discuss *Justified Sinner* as a movie. He has written a screenplay but says he is not sure if it could, or *should*, be made. But with the right director, and a few other things . . . I am convinced it will be. I'm sure he is too. He talks about Hogg's novel, years ahead of its time and relevant today. It's about religious fanaticism, and the sense that even murder can be carried out to achieve its goals. He ponders this. 'Good we've got all that stuff sorted out now,' he says.

Robertson and Rankin have busy lives, and the Edinburgh International Book Festival must be peak season for them. Each has connected with Hogg and been inspired in some way. For this reason, they've made the time to meet with me. I feel privileged.

There was a survey under way to find the 'Greatest Scottish Novel'. *Justified Sinner*, I find out later, is ranked in third place, behind only the trilogy *A Scots Quair* and *Kidnapped*.[19]

---

[19] Reported in *The Independent*, 5 October 2015. Votes were cast during the summer of 2015 at all Scottish branches of Waterstones bookshop and via postal and telephone voting through a newspaper. *Trainspotting*, the most-read Scottish novel, came further down the list, as did works by Alasdair Gray, Muriel Spark, John Buchan, Walter Scott and Iain Banks. In the top ten, *Justified Sinner* is the earliest novel by almost sixty years.

I catch a bus back to the Borders, two weeks too early to take the new train. There are some things I need to catch up with.

It is late summer. It's energising and it feels like spring is starting all over again. I catch up on some local news. Rab Wilson, the first James Hogg writer-in-residence, has launched his book *Hairst* earlier in the year. It contains a poem, 'The Hogg Monument', in Scots. At the launch, the Duke of Buccleuch quoted the final line of that poem, the line that was borrowed from the statue, and that the statue in turn had borrowed from *The Queen's Wake*: 'He taught the wandering winds to sing.'

I meet with Judy Steel, who ran a Hogg museum for many years, and published a book and directed a couple of plays of his works. She tells me, 'I've had a lot of fun with him over the years.'

The Gordon Arms, where Scott and Hogg last met, was damaged by fire in May 2015. The sign recalling that meeting has survived. The owners are planning a rebuild.

I cycle to Altrive. It's called Eldinhope now, and the Altrive/Altrieve name has migrated further up the valley. I am excited to see the house that Hogg built. He built it in two stages, and a top storey was added later. It is empty now, with only a few rabbits to welcome me. It is built in solid stone and it certainly looks as if it's good for another century or two. But I am wondering if it is weatherproof and if it might deteriorate while it's empty. The location is as charming as ever, and it is easy to imagine a fitting future for this house. A writers' retreat maybe? There is some local enthusiasm for this. I'll maintain a close interest from afar.

I ride to the top of the Ettrick Valley road. I want to go further, but I'm running out of time and rain is threatening. I'll have to leave. I tell myself it doesn't matter. But it *does*.

The place I didn't get to is Over Phawhope, possibly best known as a bothy on the Southern Upland Way. But it's more significant than that: this was the home of wild Will o'Phaup, the place where he and Bessie Scott would raise six children, including Hogg's mother. And it must have been here that Hogg's young literary friends met in January 1794 – at that time it was empty – and were blamed for causing a violent storm. (Hogg was absent that time but they were thought to have 'met that night at the herd's house o'Everhaup, an' had raised the deil'.)

Hogg said:

Old Upper Phaup, was one of the most lonely and dismal situations that ever was the dwelling of human creatures . . . the last retreat of the spirits of the glen – before taking their final leave of the land of their love, in which the light of the gospel then grew too bright for their tiny moonlight forms.[20]

I read about it later. Douglas Gibson, Alice Munro's editor, had been there. He wrote:

---

[20] Hogg, *Shepherd's Calendar*, p. 107.

It was supposedly the highest farm in Scotland . . . The old farm buildings were a surprise and a delight. Usually a visit to a 300-year-old farm site will produce either a heap of rubble showing only bare outlines or, perhaps worse, a working farm where literary intruders are not routinely welcomed, by man or dog.

Miraculously, Far Hope is preserved in something close to its original state, and is unoccupied yet at the same time open to all comers as a 'bothy' . . . Inside, a literary tourist can pace the rough stone floor, seeing the original kitchen layout around the fireplace, and easily imagine the old family's straw bedding in place. A stroll around the silent outbuildings reveals where the horse was stabled, along with the milk-providing cow. Sheep pens, the farm's raison d'être, are prominent, and the Ettrick provides running water at the door.[21]

I missed it, because I didn't know all of this until I was home in New Zealand. Bad traveller, bad research! I self-flagellate for an hour or so. But luckily, I'll be back for a book launch. This time I'll sleep in the bothy.

Figure 39 Over Phawhope, the eighteenth-century home of Will o'Phaup (and occasional haunt of fairies and den of shepherd poets). (Source: Reproduced with permission of Andrew Lawson, www.mountainsofscotland.co.uk.)

---

[21] Gibson, *Stories about Storytellers*, p. 348. The spelling of this place varies, as Gaelic names have been anglicised. A 2005 leaflet *The Southern Upland Way: Place Names* shows 'Phawhope: the valley of different colours.'

Finally I'm back in Edinburgh and it's Departure Day. I leap up at dawn, to the extent those words can apply to me at that hour. I'm working on a hunch. The past few mornings have started out misty. I would climb up early to Arthur's Seat, and perhaps I would see the 'halo of glory' that George Colwan had seen in *Justified Sinner*. This is the phenomenon that Hogg's editor described, the 'little wee ghost of the rainbow' that his shepherd boys knew, and the apparition Hogg would have known from years in the Ettrick Forest hilltops. It would be striking, romantic, and the perfect ending to my story.

I'd seen it before in antipodean mountains. There is a rainbow in the mist, fully circular apart from a wee gap at the bottom where it's shaded by the top of the hill. And there in the centre of this vivid halo – a revelation, no matter how many times you've seen it before – is your own shadow, maybe magnified many times your size.

George was entranced by 'its most vivid hues . . . all the colours of the heavenly bow . . . and inhaled its salubrious breeze'. It's real. The circular rainbow is a 'solar glory'. And the observer's giant shadow in the centre is the 'Brocken spectre'. I checked Wikipedia: it is caused by the sun, shining from behind you, interacting with tiny water droplets in the mist in front. Your shadow in the middle can move and change size by itself, due to the flow of the cloud. It is also sometimes seen from aircraft, in which case the halo is a full circle.[22]

But more from Wikipedia:

> This atmospheric effect also makes at least one appearance in Gothic fiction. In James Hogg's *The Private Memoirs and Confessions of a Justified Sinner*, George Colwan walks to the top of Arthur's Seat on a foggy day, while his half-brother Robert Wringhim secretly follows him with murderous intent. George sees shimmering colored light in front of him. Then he sees the shadow of an enormous dark figure advancing toward him threateningly—the Brocken spectre created by the shadow of Robert sneaking up behind him. In other words, the 'good' George is surrounded by a glory, while the 'evil' Robert appears as a dark spectre.[23]

I pass a dog-walker and some random insomniacs. The path winds round the hillside, getting steeper near the end. Heavy breathing now, but my legs don't want to stop. I scramble over rocks on the final stretch, then step onto the top and . . . nothing. Not the fairy-tale ending I'd hoped for. The view is stunning but the mist has gone. Shades of green and grey and blue fade away, in every direction, beyond the horizon. From the city, there's the sound of traffic like someone vacuuming downstairs. I suck in fresh air, knowing that I'll be breathing recycled stuff soon.

---

[22] Less romantically, it can also sometimes be seen from the top of a building.
[23] 'Glory (optical phenomenon)', Wikipedia, <https://en.wikipedia.org/wiki/Glory_(optical_phenomenon) (last accessed 6 September 2015).

And then, a day-and-a-bit later, flying into Auckland, out my starboard window, there is the glory: a full rainbow halo with the shadow of a Boeing 777 in the middle. Wikipedia tells me: 'The scientific explanation is still the subject of debates and research.' Hogg tells me in *Justified Sinner*: 'the better all the works of nature are understood, the more they will be ever admired'. Happily, both of these are true.

THE EDITOR'S NARRATIVE

What can these journeys be?

Each of them – Hogg's 1802, 1803 and 1804 journeys, his own life and his afterlife – took on a life of its own, and went to places quite unexpected at the start. Mine did too.

I will not attempt a tidy summing-up. That would be un-Hogg-like, and it would not do. But I can try to say what I learnt.

I had followed my ancestor through Scotland. I stumbled on some of the same rocks. I was in some of the same houses and met descendants of people he knew. I had been smitten by those sublime Highland landscapes, and been bitten by descendants of some of the same midges.

I had known a bit about his writing. I learnt a bit more. He might (or might not) have been a genius. Some of his works, at least, are considered pure genius but the quality can be uneven. That's perhaps inevitable if he thought his inspiration came straight from Heaven; how would he know which bits to reject or change? There was more humour in his stories, and he was far more prolific than I'd realised. His range and imagination are astounding.

I was increasingly intrigued by his character. There is much here that is lovable: the generosity, his incurable tenacity, the courage and loyalty, his bounce and his sense of fun. But it was his flaws and eccentricities I'd grown to love: the passion and bluntness that he could not tame, the quirkiness, the indelicacy, the contradictions, and the ability, just when things seemed to be going well, to somehow make sure that they didn't. There was more of *everything* than I had imagined, and certainly more sport and music and chaos. Above all, it was his ability to surprise, to inspire and sometimes frustrate, that continued to attract me. Even after I learnt more about him, whenever I predicted what he would do next I got it wrong at least half the time.

On the trail, I knew that if we had walked together we would've had a wonderful few days. For a while I would hang on his every word. He would be in charge, of course, he would just assume that. Then we would have a major bust-up about something. No doubt we'd stomp off in our different directions. But we'd connect again and it would work, it'd be amazing again. For a while, at least.

So I had learnt about his writing, and I learnt more about Hogg the man. There was a third strand though, another dimension, with more components than I had ever anticipated: it was 'Hogg's world'. And everywhere I looked it became more fascinating and profound and would lead somewhere else, so there was always something more to explore. There was Scotland itself, its mountains and landscapes and people and culture, today and 200 years ago. There were witches and castles and magic and humour. There were his kith and kin and contemporaries: bards and backstabbers, family and female companions, Romantics and role models, lively characters I hadn't expected to meet. There were his connections in the twenty-first century: the writers and scholars and storytellers and enthusiasts. There was a world I'd been plunged into that I'd known nothing about. I loved it and got lost in it.

It was a moving target. The more I learnt, the more fascinating it was, and the more I needed to know. It will continue beyond this book.

And my final discovery was this: as I learnt about my ancestor, I became more interested in everyone else's ancestors too.

LAST WORD

> Greater ease of spirit, a sweeter, richer, more animated and easy flow . . . more vivid and awful sublimity, can hardly be found.
> Capel Lofft, *Monthly Magazine* reviewer, 1813

> He is the poet laureate of the Court of Faery.
> John Wilson, professor and author, 1819

> [S]uch an air of simplicity and rusticity that you believe him sincere in every thing . . . he is in truth spiriting away your own judgement.
> The *Atlas*, London weekly paper, 1832

> His vanity seems to be immense, but also his good nature . . . he *is* a real product of nature, and able to speak naturally, which not one in a thousand is.
> Thomas Carlyle, writer and philosopher, 1832

> [A] true son of nature and genius, hardly conscious of his own powers . . . a depth and a brightness that filled [Walter Scott] with wonder . . . a thousand little touches of absurdity, which afforded him more entertainment, as I have often heard him say, than the best comedy.
> J. G. Lockhart, writer, editor and biographer, 1837

> He was undoubtedly a man of original genius, but of coarse manners.
> William Wordsworth, poet, 1843

> It is long since I can remember being so taken hold of, so voluptuously tormented.
> André Gide, author and Nobel Prize winner, 1947

[C]lear eyes that could look beyond the explainable and the rational.

Judy Steel, playwright and poet, 1985

[T]he unlikely man who helped give the word 'personality' its modern meaning.

Karl Miller, biographer, 2003

[T]he split-personification of the age, a man of many parts, a part of many men.

Andrew O'Hagen, reviewer, 2003

[A]n authentic and vibrant voice, more a successor to Robert Burns than a protégé of Walter Scott.

Alistair Moffat, historian, 2007

In his own lifetime Hogg was best known as a heaven-inspired and naïve Scottish rustic ... disliked rather than praised for disturbing conventional readerly preconceptions.

Gillian Hughes, biographer, 2007

I like to write about myself: in fact, there are few things which I like better.

James Hogg, author and poet

Aye, Hogg was a gey sensible man for a' the nonsense he wrat.

Tibbie Shiel, innkeeper

Naturae Donum – Nature's Gift (James Hogg's seal)

Appendix A. Walks with James Hogg: Some possibilities

The following is based mainly on my own jaunts, and can be seen as a source of ideas but should not be used as a guide. Some of these trips will require suitable fitness, maps, equipment, clothing, food, drinks and weather.

1 THE BORDERS

There is so much to choose from here:

- The James Hogg Exhibition is housed in the (now mothballed) school in the Ettrick Valley, off the B709, and close to his birthplace. It is open on certain days of the week, May to September; check for current information at <http://www.jameshoggexhibition.com>. A visit here should also include Hogg's grave and that of his grandfather Will o'Phaup (and other relatives as well as Tibbie Shiel) at the kirk nearby.
- 'Going the Whole Hogg in Ettrick', a walk in some of Hogg's footsteps on the AA website, at <http://www.theaa.com/walks/going-the-whole-hogg-in-ettrick-420373#directions>. It starts and ends at the village hall in Ettrick, across from the Exhibition. The guide says the walk is 'hard' but it isn't really.
- The James Hogg monument and Tibbie Shiels Inn at St Mary's Loch, on the A708. Handbooks such as *Walks in the Ettrick & Yarrow Valleys* and *25 Walks: The Scottish Borders* would help if you want a longer walk, to link this area with the Ettrick Valley (above).
- The Gordon Arms (junction of A708 and B709; at the time of writing, this was in the process of reopening after a major fire; check <http://www.thegordonarms.com/> for updates). Walk, ride or drive past the nearby Mount Benger farm, and Eldinhope, earlier known as Altrive (on B709, about half a mile south-west of that junction). This is the house that Hogg built and lived in with his family (apart from the top level).

- Visit the St Ronan's Border Games, Innerleithen (events take place over about ten days in July) and the St Ronan's Wells Visitor Centre and Museum (seasonal, April to October; check before visiting).
- Over Phawhope Bothy, the one-time home of Will o'Phaup and family, is easily accessible from the Potburn road end at the head of the Ettrick Valley. This bothy is on the Southern Upland Way, 'Beattock to St Mary's Loch' section, and is open to the public. Part way down the valley is Nether Phawhope and 'Will o'Phaup's Leap', where he leapt over the flooded river.
- The Southern Upland Way, starting east of St Mary's Loch and heading north, also passes Blackhouse Farm where Hogg worked as a shepherd for ten years.
- Information on the Southern Upland Way and other walks can be found at <http://www.walkhighlands.co.uk/southern-upland-way.shtml>, <http://www.southernuplandway.gov.uk/> and <http://www.ettrickandyarrow.co.uk/>.
- Other worthwhile visits include the old St Mary's kirkyard (2.5 miles/4 km north of the Hogg monument on the A708, signposted from the side of the road, or this can be included in the new 'Ring of the Loch' walk) and Grey Mare's Tail (5.5 miles/9 km south from the monument on the A708); both are mentioned in Hogg poems. Also the former home of Sir Walter Scott at Abbotsford (near Melrose), the Duke of Buccleuch's Bowhill House (3.5 miles/6 km west of Selkirk) and Sir Walter Scott's Courtroom in Selkirk.

James Hogg Trail

A James Hogg Trail, together with notes for guidance, existed in the Borders for some years. Given the number of outstanding locations in a very small area, I think consideration should be given to the further development of this. This could combine his grandparents' house, his birthplace and early workplaces, the inns where he ate, drank and played, a farm he rented and went broke in, places that inspired him, the sports event he started, the lochs he fished, the house he lived and died in, his grave, the Exhibition and the monument. And no doubt more that I missed. From some initial enquiries there was considerable enthusiasm for this, and further developments are likely.

2 TAKE A WALK IN THE FOOTSTEPS OF THE JUSTIFIED SINNER

An excellent online guide to many of the locations used by Hogg in *Justified Sinner*, developed by Alasdair and Peter Thanisch, together with maps and photographs, is at <https://www.stir.ac.uk/media/schools/artsandhumanities/english/ThanischandThanischWalkintheFootsteps-CR.pdf>.

3 LOCH A'AN/LOCH AVON

There are various ways to get to this loch. One is to walk in from Tomintoul, up the River Avon/Glen Avon. It's a long way and initially a bit dull, but it keeps getting better and better, and is well worth the trip. Watch for supernatural beings. Hogg returned down the valley, but it is more interesting to traverse a small saddle to the north of Loch A'an and walk out to Glenmore. Strenuous. Parts of this trip are described on the Walk Highlands website, at <http://www.walkhighlands.co.uk/cairngorms/creag-mhor.shtml>.

4 INVERARAY CASTLE AND GARDENS

Worth a visit. Imagine how challenging this must have been for a shepherd who had just walked in from the wilds of Ettrick Forest.

5 BEN ALDER

It's a long way in, and not a route that Hogg actually followed, but a walk in this area provides some insight into the loss of the eternal snows that he described in 1802. Take a map (OS 42) and a route guide such as the Walk Highlands website, at <http://www.walkhighlands.co.uk/cairngorms/ben-alder.shtml>, or the *Central Highlands* guidebook by Nick Williams.

6 WEST HIGHLAND WAY

You could, of course, do all 96 miles (154 km) of this track. Otherwise, if you want to follow some of Hogg's routes you could do the section from Tyndrum to Fort William. This will include places he visited, such as Kings House and Inveroran, and travelled over, such as the Black Mount and Devil's Staircase. Tyndrum to Fort William is 43 miles (69 km); allow three days. (In 1803 he came from Inveraray, joined this track at Bridge of Orchy, and travelled north; in 1804 he and friends joined this trail near the southern end of the Devil's Staircase, and travelled south.) Ben Nevis, near the north end of this trail, would also show the loss of 'huge masses of eternal snow' described by Hogg in 1803. See <http://www.walkhighlands.co.uk/west-highland-way.shtml>.

7 CRAIG TO KINLOCHEWE

The Walk Highlands website tells us: 'This is the Old Pony Track, an old drove road used by poet and novelist James Hogg, the Ettrick Shepherd, in 1803', which is a good enough reason to walk it. (If you are coming to Craig by road from the south, check the road sign about Hogg and the ferry at the south end of Loch Carron on your way.) This track is 10 miles (16.5 km), goes over the Coulin Pass, is part of the much longer Cape Wrath trail, and is not difficult. See <http://www.walkhighlands.co.uk/torridon/craig-kinlochewe.shtml>.

8 POOLEWE TO LITTLE LOCH BROOM

This trip through 'The Great Wilderness' could be started from Letterewe, as Hogg did, but Poolewe gives easier access. There are two useful bothies, at Carnmore, near the south end of Fionn Loch, and Shenavall, to the south-east of Loch na Sealga. Take a good map (OS 19) and allow two or three days. *Wainwright in Scotland* (p. 55) says cheerfully, 'It is an expedition only for the very fit: weaklings and novices must expect to perish.'

9 HIKES IN THE HEBRIDES

- A circuit of Harris should include visits to the arid east, the ancient church at Rodel, the Seallam! Visitor Centre, and Seilebost (where Hogg hoped to lease a very large area of land, from the stunning north-west of the Harris peninsula right over to the east coast).
- They are missing from his travel reports but Hogg must have visited the striking Callanish Standing Stones in Lewis in 1803, which appear in his story 'Basil Lee'.
- In 1803 Hogg spent time around Loch Bracadale in the west of Skye. He climbed one of the two Macleod's Table hills, probably Healabhal Mhor, which has easier access and great views.
- In North Uist, he and his friends stayed in the building that is now Taigh Chearsabhagh museum, arts centre and café.

10 EDINBURGH

They are not marked as such, but there are many significant sites in Edinburgh:

- The Justified Sinner website (see point 2 above) covers many of them, including Arthur's Seat.
- Certain parts of the city played an important role in Hogg's life, including the Grassmarket, where he came to sell his sheep and where his *Scottish Pastorals* of 1801 was printed, and Candlemaker Row, the site of his old hostelry (first used by him as a shepherd and later in his glory days, apparently from habit and affection).
- There are some specific buildings, still standing but now put to different uses: Tweeddale House, the premises of the old Oliver & Boyd printing works (in Tweeddale Court, opposite the Scottish Storytelling Centre on the High Street); 45 George Street, the grand new location of Blackwood from 1830 (Hogg comments on this in letters and wrote a song about it); 20 George Square, home of Hogg's friend and fellow fiddle-player Robert Sym; 4 Buccleuch Place, home of James Gray where Hogg met Margaret his future wife in 1810; and 39 North Castle Street, Walter Scott's Edinburgh residence.
- A number of libraries and other institutions such as the National Archives of Scotland hold documents, manuscripts and paintings. Portraits of Hogg

are held at the Edinburgh Central Library (Edinburgh Room and Fine Art Department) and at the Scottish National Portrait Gallery (not all displays are permanent and it is best to contact National Galleries of Scotland if wanting to see any particular works). Great rainy day refuges.

This list is far from complete. It would be good to expand on this over time, and it might be possible for more of these sites to be formally recognised in future.

Appendix B. Walking the Highlands: Gear carried

JAMES HOGG

1803
'I again dressed myself in black; put one shirt and two neck-cloths in my pocket; took a staff in my hand, and a shepherds plaid about me: and left Ettrick on foot.'

1804
'As we proposed walking, our travelling equipage was very simple. I had a small portmanteau, which we stuffed with each a clean shirt and change of stockings; a pocket travelling map, and a few neck-cloths. Thus nobly equipped, with each a staff in his hand, and a flashing tartan cloak over his shoulder, we proceeded on our enticing journey.'

Elsewhere Hogg mentions his journal, cash, books, letters, knife and a watch.

Hogg's gear therefore comprised:
Own clothing
Portmanteau (travel bag)
Spare shirt
Spare stockings
Neck-cloths
Staff
Plaid/Tartan cloak
Map
Cash
Journal
Books
Letters of introduction
Knife
Pocket watch

Total items carried = approx. 18

AUTHOR

2014/15
Backpack
Light daypack
Sleeping sheet (or ultra-light sleeping bag in 2015)
Down jacket (to supplement sheet or sleeping bag when camping)
Tent, poles and pegs (single, lightweight)
Sleeping pad (self-inflating)
Knife (Swiss Army)
Passport
Credit cards and cash
Driver's licence and other documents
Maps and compass
Books (including *Highland Journeys*)
SYHA Hostel Guide and *SIH Hostel Guide*
Diary and notebooks
Cell phone and charger
Camera and charger
Plastic mug and spoon
Poncho (doubles as a groundsheet)
Survival blanket (ultra-light)
Running shoes or boots
Light sandals
Socks (x 4)
Underwear (x 4)
Long johns
Trousers (with lots of pockets)
Shorts
Bum bag
Light sweater
T-shirts (2 polypropylene, up to 6 in total)
Insect repellent
Hat and midge net
Personal items: toothbrush, toothpaste, razor, shampoo and first aid (about 20 items, all tiny)
Mountain towel
Water bottle
Food
Head lamp
Glasses and sunglasses
Gloves

Total items carried = approx. 80

N.B. I was equipped for camping which Hogg was not; this accounted for about ten of my items. I sent some of this equipment by bus on the Tyndrum–Ballachulish section, on the day that I competed with Hogg's trip. A GPS or similar might have been useful on my travels. But I needed to get lost occasionally.

Select Bibliography

There are more detailed bibliographies on the James Hogg Society website, in the various Stirling/South Carolina Research Edition of the Collected Works of James Hogg (S/SC) publications and in books such as Gillian Hughes's *James Hogg: A Life*.

Where appropriate, the date of first publication is shown in square brackets.

SOURCES

My most-used sources were *Highland Journeys*, *James Hogg: A Life*, *Electric Shepherd*, and Hogg's 'Memoir' and 'Reminiscences', all shown below.

Allan, David, *Making British Culture: English Readers and the Scottish Enlightenment, 1740–1830* (Abingdon: Routledge, 2008).
Buchanan, Rev. John Lane, *Travels in the Western Hebrides from 1782 to 1790* (London: G. G. J. and J. Robinson and J. Debrett, 1793).
Connery, Sean and Murray Grigor, *Being a Scot* (London: Weidenfeld & Nicolson, 2008).
de Groot, Hans (ed.), *Highland Journeys*, S/SC (Edinburgh: Edinburgh University Press, 2010).
Devine, T. M., *The Scottish Nation, 1700–2000* (London: Penguin Books, 2000).
Evans, Richard J., Lorcán O'Toole and D. Philip Whitfield, 'The history of eagles in Britain and Ireland: an ecological review of placename and documentary evidence from the last 1500 years', *Bird Study*, 59:3 (2012), pp. 335–49.
Finlayson, Iain, *The Scots* (London: Constable, 1987).
Fry, Michael, *A New Race of Men: Scotland 1815–1914* (Edinburgh: Birlinn, 2013).
Garden, M., *Memorials of James Hogg, the Ettrick Shepherd*, 2nd edn (Paisley and London: Alexander Gardner, 1887).
Gibson, Douglas, *Stories about Storytellers* (Toronto: ECW Press, 2011).
Gilbert, Suzanne, 'Hogg's reception and reputation', in Ian Duncan and Douglas S. Mack (eds), *The Edinburgh Companion to James Hogg* (Edinburgh: Edinburgh University Press, 2012), pp. 37–45.

Graham, Henry G., *The Social Life of Scotland in the Eighteenth Century*, 2nd edn (London: Adam & Charles Black, 1901).
Greenwood, Susan, *The Illustrated History of Magic & Witchcraft* (London: Anness Publishing, 2011).
Gros, Frédéric, *A Philosophy of Walking* (London: Verso, 2015).
Groves, David, *James Hogg: The Growth of a Writer* (Edinburgh: Scottish Academic Press, 1988).
Groves, David, *James Hogg and the St Ronan's Border Club* (Dollar: Douglas S. Mack, 1987).
Harrison, S. John, Sandy Winterbottom and Richard G. Johnson, *Climate Change and Changing Patterns of Snowfall in Scotland* (Edinburgh: Scottish Executive Central Research Unit, 2001).
Hogg, James, 'Memoir of the author's life', in *Altrive Tales*, [1832] ed. Gillian Hughes, S/SC paperback edn (Edinburgh: Edinburgh University Press, 2005), pp. 11–52.
Hogg, James, *The Private Memoirs and Confessions of a Justified Sinner: Written by Himself: With a detail of curious traditionary facts and other evidence by the editor*, [1824] ed. P. D. Garside, S/SC paperback edn (Edinburgh: Edinburgh University Press, 2002).
Hogg, James, *The Queen's Wake: A Legendary Tale*, [1813] ed. Douglas S. Mack with Meiko O'Halloran and Janette Currie, S/SC paperback edn (Edinburgh: Edinburgh University Press, 2005).
Hogg, James, 'Reminiscences of former days', in *Altrive Tales*, [1832] ed. Gillian Hughes, S/SC paperback edn (Edinburgh: Edinburgh University Press, 2005), pp. 53–78.
Hogg, James, *The Shepherd's Calendar*, [1829] ed. Douglas S. Mack, S/SC paperback edn (Edinburgh: Edinburgh University Press, 2002).
Hughes, Gillian, 'James Hogg and the "Bastard Brood"', in Gillian Hughes (ed.), *Studies in Hogg and his World*, 11 (Stirling: The James Hogg Society, 2000), pp. 56–68.
Hughes, Gillian, *James Hogg: A Life* (Edinburgh: Edinburgh University Press, 2007).
Hughes, Gillian, '*The Private Memoirs and Confessions of a Justified Sinner*: afterlives', in Ian Duncan and Douglas S. Mack (eds), *The Edinburgh Companion to James Hogg* (Edinburgh: Edinburgh University Press, 2012), pp. 140–6.
Hunter, Adrian, 'Taking possession: Alice Munro's "A Wilderness Station" and James Hogg's *Justified Sinner*', *Studies in Canadian Literature*, 35:2 (2010), pp. 114–28.
Johnson, Samuel and James Boswell, *A Journey to the Western Islands of Scotland* and *The Journal of a Tour to the Hebrides* (London: Penguin Books, 1984).
Keightley, Thomas, *The Fairy Mythology, Illustrative of the Romance and Superstition of various Countries – Scotland* (London: George Bell and Sons, 1892).
Kelly, Aaron, *Irvine Welsh* (Manchester: Manchester University Press, 2005).
Lamont, Stewart, *When Scotland Ruled the World* (London: HarperCollins, 2002).
Land Use Consultants, *An Assessment of the Impacts of Climate Change on Scottish Landscapes and their Contribution to Quality of Life*, Scottish Natural Heritage Commissioned Report 488 (Inverness: Scottish Natural Heritage, 2011).
Leonardi, Barbara, 'An exploration of gender stereotypes in the work of James Hogg' (PhD thesis, University of Stirling, 2013).
Leyden, John, *Journal of a Tour in the Highlands and Western Islands of Scotland in 1800* (Edinburgh and London: William Blackwood and Sons, 1903).
Lockhart, J. G., *Life of Sir Walter Scott*, vol. 5 (Edinburgh: Robert Cadell, 1827).
Macculloch, John, *The Highlands and Western Isles of Scotland* (London: Longman, Hurst, Rees, Orme, Brown, and Green, 1824).

MacKenzie, Osgood Hanbury, *A Hundred Years in the Highlands* (London: Edwin Arnold, 1921).
Mackenzie, R. F., *A Search for Scotland* (London: Fontana Paperbacks, 1991).
Miller, Karl, *Electric Shepherd: A Likeness of James Hogg* (London: Faber and Faber, 2005).
Moffat, Alistair, *The Borders: A History of the Borders from Earliest Times* (Edinburgh: Birlinn, 2007).
Moffat, Alistair, *The Sea Kingdoms – The History of Celtic Britain and Ireland* (London: Harper Collins, 2001).
Munro, Alice, *The View from Castle Rock* (London: Vintage, 2007).
Oliver, Neil, *A History of Scotland* (London: Phoenix, 2010).
Parr, Norah, *James Hogg at Home: Being the Domestic Life and Letters of the Electric Shepherd* (Dollar: Douglas S. Mack, 1980).
Rankin, Ian, 'Preface', in James Hogg, *The Private Memoirs and Confessions of a Justified Sinner* (Edinburgh: Canongate Books, 2008), pp. vii–xiii.
Redekop, Magdalene, 'Alice Munro and the Scottish nostalgic grotesque', in Robert Thacker (ed.), *The Rest of the Story: Critical Essays on Alice Munro* (Toronto: ECW Press, 1999), pp. 21–43.
Richards, Eric, *The Highland Clearances* (Edinburgh: Birlinn, 2002).
Riddell, John F., *Clyde Navigation: A History of the Development and Deepening of the River Clyde* (Edinburgh: John Donald, 1979).
Smout, T. C., *A History of the Scottish People 1560–1830* (London: Fontana Press, [1969] 1985).
Steel, David, Judy Steel and Charlie Wait, *David Steel's Border Country* (London: Weidenfeld and Nicolson, 1985).
Stoddart, Thomas Tod, *Angling Songs* (Edinburgh and London: William Blackwood and Sons, 1889).
Thomson, Rev. Thomas (ed.), *The Works of the Ettrick Shepherd* (London: Blackie & Son, 1874).
Wainwright, Alfred, *Wainwright in Scotland* (London: Michael Joseph and BBC Books, 1988).
Watson, Adam and Iain Cameron, *Cool Britannia: Snowier Times in 1580–1930 than Since* (Rothersthorpe: Paragon Publishing, 2010).

KEY WORKS BY HOGG

The Stirling/South Carolina Edition of James Hogg

Published by Edinburgh University Press, in order of publication:

1. *The Shepherd's Calendar*, [1829] ed. Douglas S. Mack (1995).
2. *The Three Perils of Woman*, [1823] ed. David Groves, Antony Hasler and Douglas S. Mack (1995).
3. *Tales of the Wars of Montrose*, [1835] ed. Gillian Hughes (1996).
4. *A Series of Lay Sermons*, [1834] ed. Gillian Hughes and Douglas S. Mack (1997).
5. *Queen Hynde*, [1824] ed. Suzanne Gilbert and Douglas S. Mack (1998).
6. *Anecdotes of Scott*, [1834] ed. Jill Rubenstein with Douglas S. Mack (1999).
7. *The Spy*, [1810] ed. Gillian Hughes (2000).
8. *The Private Memoirs and Confessions of a Justified Sinner*, [1824] ed. P. D. Garside with an Afterword by Ian Campbell (2001).

9. *The Jacobite Relics of Scotland [First Series]*, [1819] ed. Murray G. H. Pittock (2002).
10. *Winter Evening Tales*, [1820] ed. Ian Duncan (2002).
11. *The Jacobite Relics of Scotland [Second Series]*, [1821] ed. Murray G. H. Pittock (2003).
12. *Altrive Tales*, [1832] ed. Gillian Hughes (2003).
13. *The Queen's Wake*, [1813] ed. Douglas S. Mack with Meiko O'Halloran and Janette Currie (2005).
14. *The Collected Letters of James Hogg: Volume 1 1800–1819*, ed. Gillian Hughes with Douglas S. Mack, Robin MacLachlan and Elaine Petrie (2005).
15. *Mador of the Moor*, [1816] ed. James Barcus with Janette Currie and Suzanne Gilbert (2005).
16. *Contributions to Annuals and Gift-Books*, ed. Janette Currie and Gillian Hughes (2006).
17. *The Collected Letters of James Hogg: Volume 2 1820–1831*, ed. Gillian Hughes with Douglas S. Mack, Robin MacLachlan and Elaine Petrie (2006).
18. *The Forest Minstrel*, [1810] ed. Peter Horsfall, Peter Garside and Richard D. Jackson (2006).
19. *A Queer Book*, [1832] ed. P. D. Garside (2007).
20. *The Mountain Bard*, [1807] ed. Suzanne Gilbert (2007).
21. *The Collected Letters of James Hogg: Volume 3 1832–1835*, ed. Gillian Hughes (2008).
22. *The Bush aboon Traquair and The Royal Jubilee*, ed. Douglas S. Mack (2008).
23. *Contributions to Blackwood's Edinburgh Magazine: Volume 1 1817–1828*, ed. Thomas C. Richardson (2008).
24. *Midsummer Night Dreams and Related Poems*, ed. the late Jill Rubenstein and completed by Gillian Hughes with Meiko O'Halloran (2008).
25. *Highland Journeys*, ed. H. B. de Groot (2010).
26. *Contributions to Blackwood's Edinburgh Magazine: Volume 2 1829–1835*, ed. Thomas C. Richardson (2012).
27. *The Three Perils of Man*, [1822] ed. Judy King and Graham Tulloch (2012).
28. *Songs by the Ettrick Shepherd 1831*, ed. Kirsteen McCue (2014).
29. *Contributions to Musical Collections*, ed. Kirsteen McCue (2015).

Forthcoming S/SC titles

Scottish Pastorals, together with other Early Poems and 'Letters on Poetry', ed. Suzanne Gilbert.
Memoir of Burns, [1836] ed. Patrick Scott.
Contributions to International Periodicals, ed. Adrian Hunter.
The Brownie of Bodsbeck, ed. Valentina Bold.

OTHER SOURCES

Published works

Batho, Edith C., *The Ettrick Shepherd* (London: Cambridge University Press, 1927).
Duncan, Ian and Douglas S. Mack (eds), *The Edinburgh Companion to James Hogg* (Edinburgh: Edinburgh University Press, 2012).

Hogg, James, *Altrive Tales*, [1832] ed. Gillian Hughes, S/SC paperback edn (Edinburgh: Edinburgh University Press, 2005).

Hogg, James, *The Pilgrims of the Sun; A Poem* (Edinburgh: Blackwood, 1815).

Hogg, James, *The Poetical Works of James Hogg*, 4 vols (Edinburgh: Constable, 1822).

Hogg, James, *The Private Memoirs and Confessions of a Justified Sinner*, with an introduction by André Gide (London: The Cresset Press, 1947).

Hogg, James, *Songs by the Ettrick Shepherd* (Edinburgh: Blackwood, and London: Cadell, 1831).

Hogg, James, *A Tour in the Highlands in 1803* (London: Alexander Gardner, 1888), published after discovery of records by Mary Garden, Hogg's youngest daughter.

Hughes, Gillian, *Hogg's Verse and Drama: A Chronological Listing* (Stirling: The James Hogg Society, 1990).

I'll Sing Ye a Wee Bit Song: Selected Songs of James Hogg, CD, performed by Sheena Wellington, Kirsteen McCue and David Hamilton, published by The James Hogg Research Project, 2007. CD can be downloaded free from <http://www.jameshogg.stir.ac.uk/cd.php>.

Mack, Douglas S., *Hogg's Prose: An Annotated Listing* (Stirling: The James Hogg Society, 1985).

Steel, Judy (ed.), *A Shepherd's Delight: A James Hogg Anthology* (Edinburgh: Canongate Books, 1985).

Websites

The James Hogg Blog: <http://jameshoggblog.blogspot.com/>

The James Hogg: Research website: <http://www.jameshogg.stir.ac.uk/>

The James Hogg Society: <https://www.stir.ac.uk/artshumanities/research/areas/thejameshoggsociety/>

And finally, a site for dog-lovers (includes 'The Author's Address to his Auld Dog Hector'): <http://www.bordercolliemuseum.org/Hogg/hogg1.html>

Glossary

This is a rough guide to some Scots and other words that baffled me, and that others also might not know. These have been taken mainly from glossaries in Stirling/South Carolina Research Edition of the Collected Works of James Hogg publications.

First, some approximate conversion rates:

1 yard = 0.9 metres (m)
1 foot = 30 centimetres (cm)
1 mile = 1.6 kilometres (km)

A Scottish mile was slightly longer than the English mile (approximately the length of Edinburgh's Royal Mile, but length could vary) until it was abandoned in the nineteenth century

£1.00 = $1.45 (US dollars, approx. as at January 2016)

a'	all
aboon	above
ahint	behind, at the back of
amaist	almost
ane	one
anither	another
a'thegither	altogether
aught	anything
auld	old
bairn	child; baby
baith	both
banes	bones
beag/bheag	small (Gaelic)
beinn/ben	mountain peak (Gaelic/Scots)

beuk	book
biggin	building, especially a house or cottage
bogle	ghost
bonnie	pretty, attractive
bothy	rough hut, accommodation for workers or travellers
brae	hillside; slope
braw	fine, handsome, splendid
burn	watercourse (ranging in size from a large stream to a small river)
ca'	call, summon
callant	lad, youth
cannie	cautious, prudent, astute; lucky
certes	assuredly
chiel	man, fellow
cot	cottage
croft	small agricultural landholding, usually with a dwelling
crofter	one who has tenure and use of a croft, usually as a tenant farmer
deil	devil
deil a	not a, never a
dens	narrow valleys, especially ones with trees
dinna	do not, does not
durst	dared
durst not	did not dare to
dyke	stone or turf wall
ee; een	eye; eyes
ern	eagle
factor	person who manages an estate
fell	steep hill; high land
gae/gang; gaed	go; went
gar	to cause or make someone do something
gate	way, fashion
gay/gey	very, great
gayan	very
gie/gi'e	give
gillies	giddy young women
gilpey/gilpy	a mischievous, frolicsome boy or girl
gin	if, whether
gleann/glen	deep valley in the Highlands, narrower than a strath (Gaelic/Scots)
goodman	male head of a household
goodwife	female head of a household
haggis	savoury pudding made from sheep's offal and oatmeal
hairst	harvest
hale	whole

hauch	low, level ground by stream
haud	hold
head	highest part of a valley; hill summit
hog/hogg	young sheep yet to be shorn; domesticated pig
holm	small island; low-lying land by a river
hope	secluded valley
ilk/ilka	each, every
joost	just
kelpie	a water demon, typically taking the form of a horse
ken; kend	know; knew
kine/kye	cows
kirk	church
laird	owner of an estate
laith	to hate, loathe
lang; langer	long; longer
langsyne	long ago, long since
law	hill
lees; leeing	lies; lying, telling lies
linn	a deep, narrow gorge; waterfall
loch	lake; part of the sea almost surrounded by land (latter sometimes called a sea loch)
mae	more
mark	sum of money amounting to two-thirds of a pound, either in Scots or English
marrow	partner, equal, match
maud	grey-striped plaid cloak or wrap
maun	must
meat	food in general
mhor/mor	big, large (Gaelic)
mire	boggy place, wet or swampy ground
mony	many
muckle	much in quantity or degree, a great deal of
neist	next
ony	any
ower	over
park	enclosed piece of land
pen	hill
pike-staff	long walking-stick with a spike on the bottom
plaid	long rectangle of twilled woollen cloth worn as an outer garment
ploy	venture or undertaking; a piece of fun, a trick or joke
puir	poor
queer	amusing, entertaining
reave	steal, plunder
reiver	raider, mainly in the Scottish–English Borders

sair	sore
shieling	small house or hovel; a shepherd's hut
Shirra	Sheriff, chief legal officer responsible for the peace and order of a county
sic/siccan	such
staff	walking stick, probably with a spike on the bottom
steading	the buildings on a farm, sometimes including the farmhouse itself
store-farming	sheep farming
strang	strong
strath	large valley, typically wide and shallow (usually wider than a glen)
tacksman	leaseholder who sublets; may retain some land for own use; often related to the landowner
tither	the other, the second of two
torr	hill, rock (Gaelic)
unco	remarkable, extraordinary; great
wae	sad
war/waur; warst	worse; worst
wat	know, knew
wedder	wether, male sheep, usually gelded
wee	little, tiny, small
winna	will not
woo	wool
wrat	wrote
yon	that, those

INDEX

There are frequent references to James Hogg in this book, with most not included in this index. References to his works are listed here under his name. There are frequent references to the Scottish Borders and Highlands in the text but these are not indexed under those headings. Some individuals are referred to according to their link to Hogg, e.g. 'friend', 'daughter'. References to illustrations are shown in *italics*.

Africa (analogies), 18, 30, 44, 62, 120, 125
Aitken, John (friend), 105, 142
Allan, David (historian), 46
Allan, William (artist), 123
Altrive (originally Eltrieve Moss, later Eldinhope), 108–9, 110, 110n, 113, 121, 126, 128, 129, 130, 132, 137, 152, 158
America, popularity in, 130, 136
ancestry, vii–ix, 1, 1–4, 60–1, 120, 125, 137n, 145, 155–6
Argyll, John Campbell, 5th Duke of, 47–9, 47n, 60
Argyll, Torquhil Ian Campbell, 13th Duke of, 59–61
Athol, 4th Duke of, 27
Aviemore, 39, 41

Ballachulish, 97, 98
Ballantyne (printers), 12, 125
Beattie, Betsy (daughter, but usual surname uncertain), 103–4, 142
Beattie, Margaret (lover), 103–4, 110
Bell, Glassford, 115, 150
Ben Alder, 30–2, 57–8, 58, 160
Ben Nevis, 50, 59, 160
Blackhouse (farm), 6, 8, 8, 11, 131, 159
Blackie, J. S., 115–16
Blackie and Son (publisher), 130

Blackwood, William (publisher), 108, 109–10, 110n, 112, 114, 116, 125, 126–7, 129, 131
Blackwood's Edinburgh Magazine ('Maga'), 109–10, 112, 116–17, 131, 168
Boswell, James, 44–6
Brewster, Sir David (scientist, friend), 129
Brocken Spectre, 154–5
Brontë, Emily, 136
Brown, Captain Richard, 141–2, 142
Brownies, 2, 4, 15–16
Brunton, Mary, 108
Buccleuch, Charles Scott, 4th Duke of, 13, 108–9, 112
Buccleuch, Harriet, Duchess of, 108, 137
Buccleuch, Richard, 10th Duke of, 151, 152, 159
Buccleuch, Walter Scott, 5th Duke of, 112, 113, 125, 130, 137
Burns, Robert, 6–7, 10, 12, 14, 48, 94, 112, 113, 129, 131, 136, 141–2, 142
Byron, Lord, 108, 110, 136

Cairngorms, Cairngorms National Park, 24, 31–2, 35, 39–42
Campbell, Colonel John, 47–8
Campbell, Lady Charlotte, 47, 60
Canna, Isle of, 74

Carlyle, Thomas, 156
Clearances, 35-7, 55-7, 70, 80, 96
Cochrane, James (publisher), 127-8, 129, 130
Coleridge, S. T., 45, 99, 108, 110
Connery, Sir Sean, 143-4
Constable, Archibald (publisher), 103, 107, 108, 109, 113, 114, 125
Coulin Pass, 64, 64, 160
Cunningham, Allan, 103, 108, 115

Dalwhinnie, 57-8
de Groot, Hans, xi, xiii
De Quincey, Thomas, 22, 108, 110, 115
Defoe, Daniel, 44
devil, 6, 17-20, 118, 144, 148, 152
Devil's Staircase, 50, 97, 160
Dumfriesshire, 19, 103, 105

Edinburgh, viii, 9, 11, 12, 24-6, 81, 106, 107, 108, 109, 112-13, 114, 127, 129, 131, 137, 138, 142, 151, 154, 161-2
Edinburgh Magazine (Constable), 109, 113
education, 4, 7, 12, 52, 83, 119, 119n, 127, 134, 137, 138, 147
emigration, 36-7, 55-7, 70, 101, 130-1
Ensay, Isle of, 73
Ettrick, 21, 23, 81, 114, 137, 158
Ettrick Forest, 1, 6, 13-15, 17, 19-20, 20-3, 86, 94-5, 100, 105, 107, 119, 122, 124, 131, 135, 145, 154, 158
Ettrick Kirk, 4, 21, 114, 132, 133, 137, 158
Ettrick River/Valley, 4, 13-15, 19-20, 122, 152-3, 159
Ettrickhall (birthplace), 4, 5
Ettrickhouse, 4, 11, 24, 37, 43, 76, 83

fairies, 2, 3, 15-16, 21, 32-3, 39, 59, 107, 152, 153, 156
farming, 1, 4, 7, 8, 9, 11, 13, 24, 27, 36, 37, 43, 52, 55-7, 67, 68-9, 70, 76, 80, 94, 96, 113, 118, 124, 129, 153
Fionn Loch, 53, 54, 65-6, 161
fishing, 14, 73, 74, 122, 124, 131
football (a precursor to rugby), 109, 122, 150-1
forests, 14, 29, 56, 78, 100
Fort William, 43, 49, 50, 91, 160

Forum (Debating Society), 106
Fraser's Magazine, 125
French Wars, 8, 9, 52, 70, 75, 107, 109
Fry, Michael (historian), 143

Galt, John, 76, 76n, 85, 96, 108, 110
gender issues, 147-8; *see also* women
George IV (King), 112, 114, 126
ghosts, 2, 17, 59, 107
Gibson, Douglas (editor, publisher, writer), 152-3
Gide, André (author), 136, 156
Gilbert, Suzanne, xiii, 136
Gilkison Falls (New Zealand), *140*, 141
Gilkison, Bob (son of Robert and Harriet), 38, 139, 141
Gilkison, Harriet (Hogg's daughter), 138, *139*, 141; *see also* Harriet Hogg
Gilkison, Robert (Harriet's husband), 138
Gillies, R. P., 108
Glasgow, viii, 9, 85, 130, 138
Glen A'an/Avon, 32-5, 39-42, 160
Glencoe, 31, 92, 92n, 97
Glenshee, 28, 35-6
Goldie, George (publisher), 106, 107, 108, 112
Gordon Arms Hotel, 119, 126, 152, 158
Graham, H. G., 44
Grampians (mountain range), 8, 24, 29-32, 50, 59
Grant, Anne, 108
Gray, James (friend, Margaret Hogg's brother-in-law), 106, 108
Gray, Mary (née Peacock), 108
Greenock, 76, 85, 96
Grieve, John, 83-5, 85n, 91, 93, 106, 115

Harris, Isle of, 52, 67-72, 70, 73, 76, 78-81, 80, 83, 89, 90-1, 94-5, 99, 161
Harris, North, 99-100
Hebrides, 43, 52, 55-7, 67-75, 76-82, 87-91, 94-5, 99-102, 161
Henderson, Catherine (lover), 103-5, 115, 143
Henderson, Keatie (daughter, but usual surname uncertain), 103-5, 142-3

Hogg, Catherine (daughter) *see* Keatie Henderson
Hogg, Elizabeth (daughter) *see* Betsy Beattie
Hogg, Harriet (daughter), 111, 131, 137–8, 139; *see also* Harriet Gilkison
Hogg, James, 104, 123
  attitude (outlook), 28, 105–6, 113, 122, 155
  birth, 4, 7, 131
  children, 103–5, 111, 112, 113, 119, 126, 129, 134, 137–9, 142–3
  death, 23, 132, 133, 134–5
  drinking, 14, 26, 31, 31n, 52, 73, 88, 108, 115, 131, 132
  finances, 54, 94, 105, 113, 114, 119, 121–2, 125, 126, 134, 137
  health, 7, 108, 127, 129, 131–2
  Highland Journeys, significance, x–xi, 95–6
  marriage, 110–11
  music *see separate listing*
  parents, 4, 11, 24, 43, 76, 83, 108; *see also* Robert Hogg *and* Margaret Laidlaw
  politics, 20, 50–1, 51n, 53, 57n, 95, 113, 129
  religion *see separate listing*
  sports *see separate listing*
  statue, 20, 50, 86–7, 114, 117, 135, 135, 152, 158–9
  women, 6, 10–11, 108, 110–11, 115
  SELECTED WORKS
  Altrive Tales, 127, 129
  'Bard's Address to his Youngest Daughter, A', 111, 137
  Border Garland, A, 111, 122
  Brownie of Bodsbeck, The; and Other Tales, 110
  'Communications on the Diseases of Sheep', 11
  'Donald Macdonald', 8, 52, 96, 103, 112
  Dramatic Tales, 110
  Familiar Anecdotes of Sir Walter Scott, 130, 134
  Father's New Year Gift, A, 127
  'Field of Waterloo, The', 109
  Forest Minstrel, The, 106, 108
  Hunting of Badlewe, The, 107
  Jacobite Relics of Scotland, The, 96, 110, 111
  'Jamie's Farewell to Ettrick', 83, 94–5
  'Kilmeny', 107, 108
  Lay Sermons, 131
  'Love Adventures of Mr George Cochrane', 10
  Mador of the Moor, 107, 108, 109, 147, 148
  'Memoir of the Author's Life', 106n, 112, 113, 122, 142
  'Mistakes of the Night, The', 6
  Mountain Bard, The, 77, 103, 111, 112
  Pilgrims of the Sun, The, 108
  Poetic Mirror, The, 109
  Poetical Works of James Hogg, The, 114
  Private Memoirs and Confessions of a Justified Sinner, The, 21, 116, 118, 143–4, 151, 151n, 154–5, 159
  Queen Hynde, 116
  Queen's Wake, The, 96, 106, 107, 108, 110, 116, 135, 152
  Queer Book, A, 129
  'Reminiscences of Former Days', 106n, 109
  Scottish Pastorals, 11, 161
  Select and Rare Scotish Melodies, 122
  Shepherd's Calendar, The, 116
  Shepherd's Guide, The, 96, 103, 116
  Songs by the Ettrick Shepherd, 8, 122
  Spy, The, 106
  Tales and Sketches by the Ettrick Shepherd, 130
  Tales of the Wars of Montrose, 130, 131
  Three Perils of Man, The, 111, 113 ('Border Romance'), 114
  Three Perils of Woman, The, 51n, 57n, 96, 105, 114, 148
  To the Ancient Banner of Buccleuch, 109
  Winter Evening Tales, 10, 77, 111, 113
  Works of Robert Burns, The, 129, 131
Hogg, Lucky, 1–2
Hogg, Margaret (wife), 110–11, 113, 115, 117, 119, 122, 127, 128, 129, 130, 131, 132, 134, 137, 161; *see also* Margaret Phillips

Hogg, Robert (father), 1, 2, 4, 5, 11, 109, 112
Hughes, Gillian, xi, xiii, 104–5, 157
Hume *see* Alexander Macleod

Innerleithen, 22, 124, 132, 148, *149*, 159
Inveraray Castle, 47–9, 47n, 59–61, *60*, *61*, 160
Inveroran, 49, 97, 98–9, *99*
Izett, Eliza, 108

Jacobites, 3, 9, 50–1, 51n, 96, 110, 111, 113, 114, 151
'James Hogg and his World' conference, 144–5
James Hogg Exhibition, 21–3, *23*, 139, 158
James Hogg Society, 43, 145, 169
Johnson, Samuel, 44–6, 51

Kelp, 69–70, 81
Kelpie *see* Water Horse
Kings House, 49, *50*, 92, 97, 98, 160

Laidlaw, Alexander (friend), 6, 132
Laidlaw, James (employer at Blackhouse), 6
Laidlaw, Margaret (mother), 2, 6, 11–12, 107, 108, 110, 132, 148, 152
Laidlaw, William (friend), 6, 10, 11, 83–5, 85n, 91, 93, 131, 132
Laidlaw, William (Will o'Phaup, maternal grandfather), 3–4, 16, 21, *133*, 145, 152–3, *153*, 158
Leith, 26
Letterewe, 52–3, 65, 161
Lewis, Isle of, 52, 67, 69, 71, 76–8, *77*, 161
Leyden, John, 34, 72
Little Loch Broom, 53, 54, 65–6, *66*, 67, 161
Loch A'an/Avon, 32–5, *33*, 38, 39–42, *42*, 96, 160
Loch Carron, 52, 63–5, *63*
Loch Ericht, 30, 57
Loch Maree, 52–3, *54*, 64–5
Loch Sunart, 87–8
Lochmaddy (North Uist), 89, 101, *102*
Lockhart, John Gibson, 108, 115, 124, 130, 131, 134, 156

London, 110, 112, 125, 127–9
Longmans (publisher), 114
Luskentyre (Isle of Harris), 68, 80, *80*, 90; *see also* Seilebost

M'Diarmid, John, 108
Mackenzie, George (Dundonnell), 66
Mackintosh, Robert (of Ashintully), 35–6
Macleod, Alexander ('Hume', Harris landowner), 90–1, 94
Macleod, William (tacksman, Luskentyre), 90, 94
magazines (and periodicals), 109, 112, 113, 114, 122, 125, 131, 141
Martin, John (artist, friend), 129
Mary, Queen of Scots, 106–7, 139
Miller, Karl, 3, 143, 157
Moffat, Alistair (historian), 12, 124, 157
Mount Benger (farm), 113, 113–14, 119, 120, 125, 158
mountains, 19, 24, 28–35, 35n, 38, 43, 46, 50, 50n, 53, 57–8, 58–9, 65, 73, 75, 88, 92, 95, 100, 141, 156
movie, *Justified Sinner*, 144, 151
Mull, Isle of, 75
Mull, Sound of, 75, 76, 87, 101–2
Munro, Alice, 15, 136, 145–6, *146*
Murray, Margaret ('Muckle-mou'd Meg'), 1, 148
music, 6, 8–9, 11, 12, 14, 22, 24, 52, 71, 71n, 73, 83, 96, 111, 116, 122, 131, 150, 151, 155, 161

New York Times, 116
New Zealand, viii, 16, 35, 38, 58–9, 66, 78, 79, 82, 125, 138–9, 141, 143, 150
Nicholson, William (artist, friend), 104, 129
Noctes Ambrosianae, 116–17, 127

Oliver & Boyd (publisher), 113, 161
Ossian, 10, 92
Over Phawhope (bothy), 152–3, *153*, 159

Park, James (friend), 76, 96, 108
Peacock, Mary, 108
Peel, Sir Robert, 129
Pennant, Thomas, 44–6, 65, 71

Perth, 24, 27
Phillips, Janet (mother-in-law), 113, 119
Phillips, Margaret, 106, 110–11, 115; see also Margaret Hogg
Phillips, Margaret's siblings, 113
Phillips, Peter (father-in law), 113, 119
poverty, 7, 18, 24, 26, 19–20, 51, 53–5, 57, 69–70, 71, 95, 113, 129
Press Gangs, 75–6
prostitution, 26, 114, 143, 147–8

Rankin, Ian, 136, 143–4, 151
religion, 9, 15, 17–18, 28, 28n, 36, 54, 55, 71, 71n, 74, 95, 147–8
Right and Wrong Club, 108
robbery, 51, 51n, 61–3
Robertson, James, 136, 144, 151
Rodel, 72, 72, 79, 89–90, 161
Romanticism, 10, 30, 107, 118
Rum, Isle of, 74–5

St Fillan's Holy Pool, 93
St Mary's Loch, 20, 34, 114, 135, *135*, 158–9
St Ronan's Border Games, 22, 119, 124, 131, 132, 148–50, *149*, 159
Sanday, Isle of, 74
Scotland, viii, 9, 17, 21, 44–6, 49, 54–5, 55–7, 59, 68–9, 78, 79, 82, 112n, 126, 156
Scots Magazine, The, 6, 37, 83, 96, 103, 109, 114, 114n
Scott, Charlotte (wife of Walter, née Charpentier), 12, 119, 125
Scott, Michael (wizard), 1–2, 114
Scott, Sir Walter, 11–12, 13, 22, 28, 30, 47, 96, 103, 108, 109, 110, 111, 112, 113, 114, 115, 122, 123, 125–6, 129, 130, 134, 137, 150, 152, 156, 157, 159, 161
sea voyages, 67, 87–8, 89–90, 91, 100–2
Seallam! Visitor Centre (Isle of Harris), 79, 161
Seilebost (Isle of Harris), 80, *80*, 83, 161; see also Luskentyre
sheep farming, x, 1, 4, 9, 14, 24, 36–7, 43, 55–7, 68–9, 70, 80, 92, 94–5, 96, 103, 105, 113, 118, 153
shepherds, 1, 4, 6, 7, 14, 31, 67, 86, 94, 96, 103, 113, 116, 134, 154
Shiel Bridge, 51

Shiel, Isabella (Tibbie), 22, 114–16, 132, 144, 157, 158
Skye, Isle of, 43, 73–4, 74, 78, 81–2, *82*, 161
snow, 15, 28, 30–1, 31–2, 50, 58
Solomon Islands (analogies), viii–ix, 16, 18, 81, 100, 120, 124
Southern Upland Way, 22, 152, 159
Southey, Robert, 98, 108, 111
sports, 3–4, 10, 14, 82, 122, 124–5, 131–2, 148–50, 150–1
Stevenson, R. L., 115, 136, 144
Stirling, 43, 139, 144
Stornoway, 67
Stuart, Janet, 108
supernatural, the, 32–3, 33n, 34–5, 39, 77, 93, 108, 152, 156; see also brownies; fairies; ghosts; water horse; witches

Tarbert (Isle of Harris), 67, 78, 81, 100
Tibbie Shiels Inn, 20, 22, 114–16, *117*, 122, 135, *135*, 158
Tobermory, Isle of Mull, 87
Tomintoul, 8, 24, 39, 41, 160
Trossachs, The, 43–4
Tyndrum, 92, 97, 99, 160

visitors, 118–20, 126

walking, ix, 79, 80–1, 97–9
water horse, 33–5, 77
Welsh, Irvine, 136, 143
West Highland Way, 97, 160
wilderness, 29–33, 50, 53–4, *54*, 65, 92, 95–6, 161
wildlife, 40–2, 43–4, 44n, 73, 73n, 100, 100n
Wilson, John, 7, 108, 112, 115, 116–17, *123*, 131, 135, 156
witches, 1–2, 17–18, 20, 156
women (roles and stereotypes), 1n, 9, 11–12, 17–18, 26, 26n, 47, 52n, 53, 56, 56n, 57n, 71–2, 72n, 108, 114, 115, 127, 138, 147–8
Wordsworth, Dorothy, 45, 97, 98
Wordsworth, William, 22, 45, 107–8, 115, 134, 156

Yarrow River/Valley, 13–15, 108–9, 111, 122, 134, 137, 158–9